Irish Encounters:
Poetry, Politics and Prose since 1880

Irish Encounters:

Poetry, Politics and Prose

since 1880

Edited by
Alan Marshall
and
Neil Sammells

SULIS PRESS

First published in 1998 by

SULIS PRESS
Newton Park
Bath BA2 9BN, UK

Printed by Antony Rowe Ltd.,
Chippenham, Wilts.

Cover design by Malcolm Herrstein Design

ISBN
0 9526856 3 9
0 9526856 4 7 (pbk)

British Library Cataloguing in Publication Data

· A catalogue record of this book
is available from the British Library

Contents

CONTENTS

Acknowledgements

We would like to thank Blackstaff Press for permission to use the poetry of Padraic Fiacc and John Hewitt, and the University of Ulster Library for the use of the correspondence in their John Hewitt Collections. Parts of Gerry Smyth's essay in this book appeared in his *The Novel and the Nation: Studies in the New Irish Fiction*, published by Pluto in 1997. We are very grateful to colleagues in the Faculty of Humanities at Bath Spa University College for their support and advice in preparing this volume - in particular Tracey Hill, and Margaret Tremeer and Julie Ann Rowell who both did sterling work on an unwieldy manuscript. Our greatest debt, of course, is to our contributors.

1

Introduction

Neil Sammells

In *The Colonial Encounter* (1977), Molly Mahood focuses on six novels (by Conrad, Achebe, Forster, Narayan, Greene and Naipaul) 'all concerned with the experience of colonial rule and its aftermath' and in so doing announces her intention to 'find ways in which historical thinking on imperialism and on the relinquishing of empire, as distinct from the mere chronicling of imperialist rule, might shed light on the traditional and central concern of literary criticism: the work of art as the figment of a particular sensibility.'[1] Central to this project, of course, is the encounter she engineers between black and white writers, placing 'novels from new literatures alongside some of the best English novels of the twentieth century and by close and appreciative readings to establish their parity.' She goes on:

> I should be very happy if my juxtapositions did something to persuade the guardians of the pure English tradition of fiction that we do not need to change our criteria in approaching Third World novels. So I have put my six novelists together as if they were all writing in the great circular room envisaged by E.M. Forster. After all, the resemblance to the Reading Room of the British Library becomes the closer if some of those 'approximated by the act of creation' are from tropical lands.[2]

Mahood's ambivalence towards the 'pure English tradition' is revealing: although she deploys the idea of purity ironically, her own analysis is predicated on assimilating 'new literatures' to that tradition. In her colonial encounter, black writing proves itself , in some cases, to be whiter than white. This is not the place to dwell on the ideological underpinnings of Mahood's liberal humanism - though it is hard not to note that the black and white writers she issues with a reader's pass are all male.

A number of the essays in this collection describe encounters between Irishness and Englishness far removed from the simple assimilative model Mahood employs to restate the power-relationship between colonised and coloniser. William Hughes, for instance, unpicks the tangled relationship between Englishness and Irishness in Bram Stoker and Colin Graham describes a cultural encounter between Ireland and England at the apparently arcane level of poetic form, and explores the notion of 'transculturation', which declares the boundaries between coloniser and colonised to be unstable - tracing the way cultural forms migrate and mutate across apparently rigid demarcations of identity. For Graham, then, the colonial encounter takes place - in postmodernist terms - in a liminal space: the colonised is not assimilated by the coloniser, the encounter changes both. In his account of Field Day, Tom Herron is similarly concerned with liminality in the notion of the 'Fifth Province' - the cultural space in which old hatreds might be transformed and transcended; and Willy Maley's discussion of Joyce asks if it is possible to construct a notion of national identity that is inclusive rather than exclusive. Perhaps the essays by Graham, Herron and Maley (and, indeed Gerry Smyth's on the border dialogues between sanity and insanity in the contemporary Irish novel) might more accurately - if awkwardly - be described as post-postcolonial criticism. Kevin Barry has claimed that the principal object of postcolonial criticism is the recuperation of a native, colonised culture: 'to discover what has been repressed' in order 'to find out how it might have spoken, how it can be represented.'[3] This involves, inevitably, the reconstruction of an authentic native voice and modes of representation: as in David Lloyd's claims for the radical implications of allegory.[4] Postmodernism, of course, challenges notions of authenticity and origin, championing instead cultural hybridity - and sees national and ethnic identities as culturally produced. 'Post-postcolonial' criticism in Irish Studies seeks, it seems to me, an accommodation between postcolonialism and postmodernism: or, at the very least, it explores the encounter between the two. To do otherwise - simply to invest in notions of authenticity and origin - can produce some curious results. (Stephen Regan's essay here which interrogates essentialist notions of Celticism is instructive in this context.) A case in point: a recent collection of essays on Oscar Wilde seeks, according to the editor, to 'reinstate his spirit back in its own haunting grounds: to relocate its origins and its effects in its native Ireland and in that spiritual territory that Wilde himself understood as home to the collective unconscious of the race.'[5] One essay in the collection, for instance, interprets this brief by reclaiming Wilde for the ancient tradition of Irish oral story-telling.[6] This is Molly Mahood in reverse: the traditions might be different but the process of assimilation to them is the same. Wilde is bundled out of Mahood's select Reading Room, and into a shebeen.

One of the principal encounters we have engineered in this volume is that between the sharp theoretical focus of the essays mentioned above, and those which are fundamentally positivist in approach. In this respect, the collection deliberately mirrors an unresolved debate in contemporary Irish Literary Studies, which has perhaps been comparatively slow in acknowledging the usefulness of cultural theory in the analysis of Irish writing. In this second, less theoretically inflected, group of essays we might mention Michael Parker's painstakingly detailed analysis of the specific historical context for a selection of poems about the Troubles, Sarah Ferris's critique of John Hewitt's self-mythologising as political victim and Eileen Reilly's account of novelist James Owen Hannay's vicissitudes with the Gaelic League. Tessa Hadley's discussion of the characteristic 'incompleteness' of Elizabeth Bowen's narrative prose is similarly concerned to link text directly with political context and the crux of mutual incomprehension she identifies as symptomatic of Ireland at a specific historical moment: she does so by means of the fundamentally positivist technique of what Mahood would have called 'close and appreciative reading,' the technique also favoured by Gerwin Strobl in his essay on J.G. Farrell. Both Bowen and Farrell, of course, were acutely aware of the political symbolism of 'The Big House', and Julie Campbell gives us an account of its function in Beckett's *Watt* by means of a close comparison with the novel's early drafts.

Sarah Briggs and Siobhán Holland are concerned, however, with the immediacies of domestic politics: Briggs with the political and sexual economies which underpin Mary Lavin's short stories, and Holland with John McGahern's itemisation of the subtle and intimate strategies whereby patriarchy can be subverted in the home. For Briggs, the subversive potential of Lavin's fiction lies partly in the way it interrogates 'masculine' notions of Irish identity; for Barry Sloan, Protestant autobiography struggles to be similarly subversive, as writers such as Robert Harbinson and Forrest Reid find, respectively, legitimation and estrangement in their encounter with Protestant versions of history and individual identity. Sloan argues that Forrest Reid's autobiographical writing can be read as an attempt to escape the complexities of Irish politics; Richard Greaves reminds us that, for Yeats, such an escape was impossible and that autobiography was part of the material from which the poet could fashion his version of that inevitable encounter.

In effect, this collection of essays, in exploring encounters between the discourses of poetry, politics and prose in modern Irish writing, distributes itself across a series of debates and issues which define the state of contemporary Irish Studies: the nature of nationalism and postnationalism; the relevance of postcolonialism to the analysis of Irish culture; the construction - and deconstruction - of 'Irishness' from dissident perspectives, such as feminism; the usefulness of notions of cultural authenticity; the role of cultural theory in Irish Studies. That 'literary studies' find such parallels in broader 'cultural studies' in the Irish context suggests the limitations to Mahood's injunction that we should concern ourselves with 'the work of art as the figment of a particular sensibility'. Perhaps the most fruitful 'postcolonial encounter' we could explore is that between literary and cultural studies, an encounter which might transform both.

NOTES

1. M.M. Mahood, *The Colonial Encounter: a Reading of Six Novels*, London, 1977, p. 3.
2. Ibid., p. 2.
3. Kevin Barry, 'Critical Notes on Postcolonial Aesthetics', *Irish Studies Review*, 14, Spring 1996, p. 2.
4. See David Lloyd, *Anomalous States: Irish Writing and the Post-Colonial Moment*, Dublin, 1993.
5. Jerusha McCormack, ed., *Wilde the Irishman*, Yale, 1998, p. 59.
6. See Deirdre Toomey, 'The Story-Teller at Fault: Oscar Wilde and Irish Orality', ibid., pp. 24-25.

Colonial Violence, Imitation and Form:
Samuel Ferguson and the Phoenix Park Murders

Colin Graham

> Ethnographers have used [the term 'transculturation'] to describe how
> subordinated or marginal groups select and invent from materials
> transmitted to them by a dominant or metropolitan culture. While
> subjugated peoples cannot readily control what emanates from the
> dominant culture, they do determine to varying extents what they absorb
> into their own, and what they use it for.[1]

Mary Louise Pratt's *Imperial Eyes: Travel Writing and Transculturation* (1992)
is one of the most radical (and overlooked) critical excursions into post-colonial
and colonial discourse studies in the post-*Orientalism* era. Pratt's book asks
questions which are, as she says, 'heretical', in that she suggests that the
boundaries between coloniser and colonised are not only unstable but that
cultural forms move, migrate and transform across these demarcations of
identity; the colonised, in her carefully exemplified schema, are able both to pull
cultural resources from the colonising culture for the purposes of self-representa-
tion, and to use 'transculturating elements of metropolitan discourses to create
self-affirmations designed for reception in the metropolis'.[2] In the 'liminal
space'[3] of the Irish colonial encounter movements across cultures will,
necessarily, be complex and often submerged; but this recognition in itself
means that utilising the conceptual levers provided by research such as Pratt's
becomes all the more emphatically pressing in an Irish context.

This chapter attempts to build on Pratt's assumptions by examining a cultural
encounter, between what can only loosely be called England and Ireland, on the
apparently arcane level of poetic form. I will discuss two poems by the
nineteenth-century Irish poet Samuel Ferguson, 'At the Polo-Ground' and 'In
Carey's Footsteps', written as reactions to political murders in Phoenix Park
Dublin in 1882.[4] These poems, both imitations of Robert Browning's dramatic
monologues, reveal the politics of Ferguson's obsession with the imitation of
English poetic styles; and while these texts are intended by their author to act
as uncoverings of the ideological weaknesses of violent nationalism, they can
instead be understood (against their own intentions) as indicative of the elusive
nature of cultural imitation itself, revealing instabilities caused by their reliance

on the already ambivalent model of Browning's dramatic monologues. There is thus a potentially dissolving basis for outrage in Ferguson's poems, since his imitation of poetry which is prioritised as an 'English' model at this historical moment produces an ambiguity where moral certainty is intended.

The Phoenix Park Murders stand out in late nineteenth-century Irish history as a focal moment of the intertwining of land agitation and nationalism. On 13 October 1881 Charles Stewart Parnell, leader of the Irish Parliamentary Party and president of the Land League had been arrested and imprisoned in Kilmainham Gaol on the orders of the Chief Secretary of Ireland, Forster. Gladstone, then Prime Minister, had, partly out of necessity, begun to work more closely with Parnell on Irish issues, and was embarrassed and disadvantaged by Parnell's arrest. Parnell was then able to use these circumstances to negotiate changes to the Land Act of 1881, gaining concessions which protected tenants in arrears, and under what was known as the Kilmainham Treaty, Parnell was released in April 1882. Forster, as a result, resigned his post as Chief Secretary and Gladstone replaced him with Lord Frederick Cavendish. Cavendish, along with T.H. Burke, permanent Under-Secretary who had also served under Forster, arrived to take up his post on 6 May 1882. On the evening of 6 May, while walking in Phoenix Park, Cavendish and Burke were stabbed by members of a Fenian splinter group called the Invincibles who, according to one historian, had been attempting to track and murder Burke and the previous Chief Secretary Forster, for some time.[5] These murders had several important effects, both immediate and longer term. They shifted the political emphasis away from Parnell's perceived victory in negotiating the Kilmainham Treaty and they led to the false implication of Parnell in the murders themselves. For the participants the aftermath of the murders was as violent as the act; five of the Invincibles were executed and buried in Kilmainham Gaol. James Carey, who had acted as lookout for the Invincibles (and who speaks as monologist in Ferguson's 'At the Polo-Ground'), turned informer, was allowed to leave Ireland and travelled to South Africa. However, when the ship carrying him was off Cape Town he was shot, supposedly by an Irish American who happened to be on board and was outraged by Carey's 'betrayal'.[6]

The Phoenix Park murders thus represent a cycle of brutal violence which brings together, in potential ideological confusion, land agitation, political violence and a sense of historical momentum in nationalism. Before going on to examine Samuel Ferguson's poetic imitations in reaction to these events, it is important to examine how he might fit into the political difficulties raised by the murders and how his writing in imitation negotiates the culture and politics of nineteenth-century Ireland. Ferguson can be placed in that now apparently anomalous position, but one which in the nineteenth century was not unusual:

in political terms he was a Unionist, in cultural terms he believed in the difference of Ireland from other nations; this twinning of cultural nationalism with political unionism was an ambiguity not lost on Yeats, for example, whose obituaries for Ferguson deliberately play on the latter's cultural nationalism, implying its 'natural' dominance over his constitutional politics.[7] This awkward ideological layering of nationalism and unionism can be only partially resolved through its mere prominence in nineteenth-century Ireland; that Yeats is able to play off Ferguson's cultural politics against his constitutional politics is indicative of the gaps that remained in Ferguson's thinking. The conflictual trajectories of politics and culture which Ferguson embodies needed some explanation and can be seen explicitly covered in his imperialism, in which the notion of Ireland's parity with Britain, in a model reliant on fraternity as the cohesive power of empire, is assumed.[8] Describing the Phoenix Park murders themselves Lady Ferguson exemplifies this imperial trope as a means of blurring the potential critical distinctions between nation and nationalism, culture and politics. Of the murders Lady Ferguson says: 'four ruffians armed with knives...shocked not alone Dublin, but the empire'.[9] The conceptual movement here is crucial since it both omits and includes British opinion, which becomes subsumed within the entity of the empire; it is able to resolve, for itself at least, the necessity to address Britain by assuming a commonality of interest which includes Britain. In this there is the difficult irony which Ferguson's cultural politics has to deal with; partnership in the empire is not an adequate explanation for either political or cultural relations between British culture and Irish culture in the nineteenth century, yet it is conceptually crucial to the marrying of his intellectual dichotomies. While Ferguson developed strategies for combating this imbalance, those very strategies themselves were an admission of that imbalance. The sort of cultural fragmentation which underlies this assertion of shared interest returns when Lady Ferguson goes on to describe the poems her husband wrote in response to the Phoenix Park murders; they were, she says, 'written partly to show how readily Browning's mannerisms might be imitated'.[10] That she is able to shift her discursive register in one paragraph from 'ruffians' and 'miscreants still more guilty than those butchers'[11] to a literary discussion of how easy it is to imitate Browning may seem bizarre if not dextrous, and is certainly more revealing than Peter Denman suggests when he sees this as Lady Ferguson's 'genteel attempt to depoliticise' these texts.[12] An implication of her interwoven description of the violence of the murders with the manner in which Ferguson wrote is surely that imitation was appropriate at this point; an implication for the critic reading Ferguson from a post-colonial perspective must be that the parallels between the murders and the poetic text may be theorised in terms of the conceptual violence, or at least disruption, of the act of imitation itself. The cohabitation of outrage and polite literary comment is thus held together by an unacknowledged link in the use of forcefulness - and this in turn can help reveal the ideological disturbances apparently made quiet by the notion of 'not alone Dublin, but the empire'.

Beginning his essay 'Of Mimicry and Man: The Ambivalence of Colonial Discourse', Homi Bhabha quotes Jacques Lacan from *Of the Gaze*. Lacan says 'The effect of mimicry is camouflage...It is not a question of harmonizing with the background, but against a mottled background, of becoming mottled - exactly like the technique of camouflage practised in human warfare.'[13] That Lacan should choose to draw on images of violence and warfare in explaining the phenomenon of mimicry is useful here. More important is the seed of the assertion in what Bhabha quotes that mimicry produces *difference*. The effect of 'mottling' as Lacan calls it seems to produce something which is both different in its identity (and perhaps even status) from that which is mimicked, and which is also in some way blurred or made indeterminate by the process of mimicry. The crux of this process in Irish cultural terms will always be the imbalance of cultural power between Britain and Ireland - imitation and mimicry may assert difference by *not* being what is mimicked; they may give status to that which is mimicked; they may in a sense do violence to that which is mimicked by apparently changing it. The extent to which mimicry and imitation might work against standard notions of cultural power structures may well be the measure of the usefulness of examining the phenomenon of imitation in Irish cultural terms. Such complexities in the processes of literary imitation can usefully be seen played out and exemplified in an Irish context in Ferguson's epic poem *Congal* (1872). *Congal* has an interestingly long period of gestation and composition; Ferguson began researching the poem in 1842, the same year in which Tennyson published 'Morte d'Arthur' which was to be the first part of his pseudo-epic *Idylls of the King*. And Tennyson, having published *Idylls* in various serial forms over thirty years, believed that he had finished *Idylls* in 1872, the same year Ferguson published *Congal*. *Congal*'s parallels with Tennyson's *Idylls* are deliberate and important; while *Congal* is not 'in the manner of Tennyson' in the sense that the Phoenix Park poems are 'in the manner of Browning', it does insist on a paralleling which aids our understanding of the kinds of resonances we would expect to see in Ferguson's writing. *Congal* has a specific purpose, which is to raise the status of Irish culture by making it epic, showing that the material of 'Irishness' was researchable, that it could be catalogued and understood; above all the poem seeks to prove that Irish culture is historically verifiable *and* different. In this it challenges perceived English cultural attitudes to Ireland, insisting in a fractious way on the sort of cultural equity we have already seen implied in Lady Ferguson's notion of empire. *Congal* imitates *Idylls* in the sense that it attempts to put Irish culture through the same ideological, formal and literary processes which Tennyson attempted for (his version of) Englishness. Indeed *Congal* even includes a slyly disparaging reference to Tennyson's text and here the act of imitation flirts with a critique of what it imitates. Ferguson's desire to elevate Irish culture to an equal level with English culture invokes a resentful acknowledgement of power and a double-edged acceptance of the value of English imperial culture.[14]

Mimicry and imitation in such colonial circumstances are then, as Bhabha says 'constructed around an ambivalence; in order to be effective, mimicry must continually produce its slippage, its excess, its difference'.[15] While this might seem to be an always servile relationship, the gap between objects in mimicry does not necessarily sit within the hierarchical framework of established power relations: as Bhabha says, mimicry entails that the colonial subject 'becomes transformed into uncertainty' so that 'mimicry is at once resemblance and menace'.[16] These co-existing tropes usefully fix, in conceptual terms, the possible relationship between the apparently monolithic blocks of what can be labelled 'Irish' and 'English' during the process of cultural mimicry. The sense of resemblance, menace and irritation expressed in Ferguson's imitations is furthered by the ambivalence of his position in Irish cultural politics, so that a process transforming one entity and necessarily producing an ambiguity as a result will also be affected by the ambiguity Ferguson feels about that which is mimicked (the word 'mannerism', describing Browning, is hardly compliment- ary, for example). This seems to imply a framework for reading imitation across this particular colonial encounter; Ferguson's imitations of English poets (whatever the closeness of their mimicking) will both pay homage to and deride that which they imitate. By producing a copy and simultaneously asserting a difference from the original they reveal the crises afflicting Ferguson's dual cultural politics, and show the mechanics of the relationship between the metropolitan centre and the Anglo-Irish. To this extent such a framework is valuable, but it is worth further complicating the model before looking at the specific nature of the poems Ferguson wrote on the Phoenix Park murders. Lacan, writing about mimicry as 'mottling', suggests not only that that which mimics becomes 'mottled' (perhaps hybrid is a comparable term from post- colonial discourse) but that it does so to blend in with the mottling of that which it mimics. This draws attention to one over-assumption common to reading Irish cultural politics: that England, in its effect on Ireland and its cultural self- representation, can be understood as a single, unproblematic entity. This is certainly the case with, for example, Ferguson's own understanding of Tennyson, which in using *Idylls* as a model relies on the model's security of status. Ferguson's *Congal* is unintentionally ironic in that it conveys a stronger sense

9

of a coherent Irish politico-cultural nation, against the wishes of its author, than Tennyson's poem does for England (*Idylls of the King*, beginning as a statement of imperial strength, becomes a meditation on imperial loss).

With the Phoenix Park poems the same assumptions apply; there is an imitation of an English model which is intended to produce a secure version of Ireland. However, the imitation, for all its own ambiguities of process and politics, is still reliant on what it imitates being a stable entity. If this could be said to be arguable in the case of Tennyson, then Browning was in some ways the worst model to choose either as a representative English poet, or, as is necessary to Ferguson's project in the Phoenix Park poems, as a morally unshifting cultural figure. If Ferguson is, as Lady Ferguson suggests, adopting Browning's style simply to show how easily it may be imitated, and thus perhaps making a cultural statement about the nature of Englishness as constructed through supposedly 'great' poets, then he has paid interestingly little attention to Browning's reputation in England.[17] As many commentators have pointed out, Browning was deeply mistrusted as a deliberately obscure and at times immoral poet dealing in what the *Daily News* in 1873 called 'explorations in the mournful phantom-haunted borderland between Illusion and Guilt'.[18] In contemporary critical terms Sarah Gilead suggests that in Browning's poetry:

> The game that all the players within and without the poem play is the game of 'logos', the game that hides and seeks the signifier and its elusive capacity to point to ... 'The Way, the Truth, the Life'.[19]

Such moral and semantic slipperiness is ignored in Ferguson's notion of Browning; the mannerisms of Browning's dramatic monologues are imitated, the logical impact of those mannerisms is lost when the psychological terror of immorality is stabilised by outside agency. In writing the Phoenix Park poems Ferguson may believe that he is writing in the manner of Browning's 'humorous' dramatic monologues (such as 'Soliloquy of the Spanish Cloister' or 'A Bishop Orders His Tomb'), but behind Ferguson's poems are the more unsettling (indeed murderous) figures of the monologist of 'Porphyria's Lover', the speaker of 'My Last Duchess' and the various narrators of *The Ring and the Book*.

The first of the Phoenix Park poems, 'At the Polo-Ground', is spoken as a dramatic monologue by Carey who is later, appropriately for this confessional format, the informer at the trial of the Invincibles. In this poem Ferguson adopts some very obvious 'mannerisms' from Browning. There is, for example, a hesitancy of speech, and a conversational conveyance of the narrative process; thus Carey says 'Here I am/ Beside the hurdles fencing off the ground' and later 'No: not in sight. That man is not so tall'. These 'mannerisms' as they are called by Lady Ferguson are clear signals that Browning is invoked; Fra Lippo Lippi's final line 'There's the grey beginning! Zooks!' spoken of the dawn functions in a similar way, as does 'Gr-r-r - there go, my heart's abhorrence!' the first line of 'Soliloquy of the Spanish Cloister'. Such stylistic mannerisms are indicators (in both Browning himself and in Ferguson's imitations) of the potential of the mode of dramatic monologue. Lady Ferguson suggests that 'The analysis of Carey's hesitancies before he had given the fatal signal to the assassins is quite in Browning's manner'.[20] As this implies, Ferguson's primary interest in Browning's method is its potential for unintentional self-revelation on the part of the speaker; for example, Carey is made to indulge in a wonderful flight of fancy when he imagines that, after Parnell comes to power in a Home Rule Ireland, he (Carey) will rise from his status as a bricklayer to be made Lord Mayor of Dublin for life (in this his self-aggrandisement is closest to the speaker of Browning's 'A Bishop Orders his Tomb'). Carey's 'hesitancies', as Lady Ferguson calls them, go to the ideological crux of the act of imitation itself. Carey considers that he has left no evidence behind and cannot, he thinks, be linked to any crime. He goes on:

> But, somehow, these reflections make me pause
> And set me inly questioning myself,
> Is it worthwhile - the crime itself apart -
> To pull this settled civil state of life
> To pieces, for another just the same,
> Only with rawer actors for the posts
> Of Judges, Landlords, Masters, Capitalists?
> And then, the innocent blood. I've half a mind
> To trip across this elm-root at my foot,
> And turn my ankle.[21]

While the poem continues to imitate Browning's style at this point, it veers away from the processes Browning uses in similar circumstances. The murderers in 'Porphyria's Lover' and 'My Last Duchess' never show this degree of hesitation; they are terrifying for their certainty and for the internal logic of what they have done, so that Browning's monologists build an amorality out of the ideological assumptions of liberalism. As E.A.W. St George says:

> The Browning imagination always negotiates between the need to confess and the horror of exposure; it situates itself in the poems which typically feature acts of self-revealing or declaration; and it finds its voice in voices which mediate between assertion and confession. The imagination which creates, peoples and legislates the Browning world is essentially interactive, a dramatised process which draws speaker and listener together in a contract or a compact or a cabal.[22]

Ferguson's imitations break any 'compact' even suggested by their imitation of Browning, in that they deny the demand for negotiation inherent in Browning's 'cabal'. Ferguson will not allow Carey's self-justification to be solely self-revealing in the way St George describes; instead Ferguson uses the Browningesque not to comment on the ambivalences of moral certainties, but on the certainty that Carey was uncommitted. And Carey is of course the perfect figure for this function: confessor and informer in court, he becomes confessor through the dramatic monologue, with the same result in undermining the ideological solidity of the terrorist act.

'At the Polo-Ground' is followed in Lady Ferguson's biography by 'In Carey's Footsteps', another dramatic monologue this time spoken by a priest who walks in Phoenix Park after the trials of the Invincibles. In a way the priest figure is another ironic confessor, instead of listening to confession he begins the poem by making one:

A hideous thought. I'll walk a while in the Park
And rid my mind of it. I wish to God
I had not said it; though no man can say
I counselled or advised it: only this;
I did not, as I ought, advise *against* -
Express some detestation - say, at least,
Such crimes are cowardly, and Irishmen,
Having the true faith, should be bold to act
The manlier part.[23]

This priest then considers his guilt and implication in violent murders because he does not advise, or has not advised, against violent nationalism. Even more so here than with Carey the Browningesque uncertainty of the monologue is reversed in that phrase 'as I ought'; Ferguson turns what is at its extreme the self-revelation of Browning's monologists into a self-condemnation which accords with the position of the author rather than challenging the ideological assumptions of the reader. Later in the same poem the priest says:

Carey thought himself
So safe, he laughed and puffed his cigarette
Leaving the prison van. Well, what he did
At last was right
And what were right for me
To do at this conjuncture? Openly
Avow my sorrow that untimely words
Escaped me which some miscreant might wrest
To implication of assent to crime?
That were heroic, that were right indeed;
My conscience so inclines.[24]

12

Carey, now apparently murdered, was still right to confess, the priest suggests; here Ferguson turns the trope of confession to its final use as the priest's affirmation of the role of confession is shifted into legality while simultaneously enforcing the priest's own realisation of wrong.

The gap between Browning and Ferguson's imitation is then crucially maintained by Ferguson's desire to use Browningesque mannerisms as a method to uncover immorality rather than force standard socialised morality into ambiguity; yet this method also leads him to open the poem to sustained tracts of argument *for* Irish nationalism, and Ferguson at times appears to lose control of the morality which always threatens to disintegrate because of the impact of the Browningesque model he employs. More importantly the evidence of the gap between the imitated and the imitation, and the very necessity for the existence of that gap, indicates the instability of the relationship between English culture and the Anglo-Irishness Ferguson attempts to foster. Walking through Phoenix Park the priest says:

> I'm not for statues nor for works of art
> Reminding one at every step he takes
> In his own grounds, at home, that some one else
> Confers his culture on him from outside.[25]

The discomfort the priest reveals here with English influence on the Irish physical and cultural landscape is paralleled by Ferguson's cultural duality,[26] using and imitating English models, writing in the image of English culture but with the desire to assert difference. Ferguson's imitations of Browning are destabilised because of the ambiguities of the process of imitation itself (the violence they do to what they mimic circulates disconcertingly with the violence they attempt to control), and when control is apparently achieved, when morality is injected into the dramatic monologue, the gap between Browning and Ferguson, between English culture and Anglo-Irishness, is restated. If the colonial mimicking process is one of 'resemblance and menace', the example of Ferguson shows that in an Irish context the closeness of the participants in the colonial encounter can exaggerate both the similarities in cultural production and the disruption they uncover. The 'transculturation' of cultural forms in this context is explicit and fraught; cultural power structures remain, but their divisions are not absolute and the (Anglo-)Irish version of the 'English' form bristles uncomfortably in its deference and dependence. Ferguson's poems, as direct imitations, indicate how the processes of connection and colonialism in the Irish context might be disinterred from a stasis imposed by our own accumulated critical assumptions.

NOTES

1. Mary Louise Pratt, *Imperial Eyes: Travel Writing and Transculturation*, London, 1992, p. 6.

2. Ibid., p. 143.

3. For a fuller account of this notion see Colin Graham, '"Liminal Spaces": Post-Colonial Theories and Irish Culture', *The Irish Review*, 15 (1994), pp. 29-43.

4. These poems were first published in Lady [M C] Ferguson, *Sir Samuel Ferguson in the Ireland of His Day*, 2 vols., Edinburgh and London, 1896, Vol. II, pp. 257-67.

5. Tom Corfe, *The Phoenix Park Murders: Conflict, Compromise and Tragedy in Ireland 1879-1882*, London, 1968.

6. Though see John O'Beirne Ranelagh, *A Short History of Ireland*, Cambridge, 1994, p. 139, who reverts to a version contemporary with the events in which Carey is deliberately trailed and assassinated by the Invincibles.

7. W.B. Yeats, 'Irish Poets and Irish Poetry: The Poetry of Sir Samuel Ferguson', *Irish Fireside*, (9 October 1886), pp. 81-6, and W B Yeats, 'Sir Samuel Ferguson', *Dublin University Review*, 2 (1886), pp. 923-41.

8. Ferguson's poem 'The Widow's Cloak', which revolves around an extended metaphor of Queen Victoria's 'mantle' exemplifies this strand of his thought - despite its rhetoric of imperial fraternity and equality the poem is also careful to differentiate Ireland from the rest of the empire. See Sir Samuel Ferguson, 'The Widow's Cloak', *Blackwood's Edinburgh Magazine*, 122 (1877), pp. 742-3.

9. Lady Ferguson, *Sir Samuel Ferguson*, Vol. II, p. 258.

10. Ibid., p. 258.

11. Ibid., p. 258.

12. Peter Denman, *Samuel Ferguson: The Literary Achievement*, Gerrards Cross, 1990, p. 170.

13. Quoted in Homi K. Bhabha, *The Location of Culture*, London, 1994, p. 85.

14. See Sir Samuel Ferguson, *Congal*, London, 1872, pp. 67-9.

15. Bhabha, *The Location of Culture*, p. 86.

16. Ibid., p. 86.

17. In reviewing Elizabeth Barrett's poems Ferguson showed a similar lack of detailed awareness of her status and reputation. See Sir Samuel Ferguson, 'Miss Barrett's Poems', *Dublin University Magazine*, 25 (1845), pp. 144-54.

18. Cited in Clyde de L. Ryals *The Life of Robert Browning*, London, 1993, p. 196. Victorian views of Browning are collected and discussed in Colin Graham, 'Browning and His Critics', in Colin Graham, ed., *Robert Browning, Men and Women and Other Poems*, London, 1993, pp. 265-77.
19. Cited in Ryals, *Robert Browning*, p. 263.
20. Lady Ferguson, *Sir Samuel Ferguson*, Vol. II, p. 258.
21. From 'At the Polo-Ground', ibid., Vol. II, p. 261.
22. E.A.W. St George, *Browning and Conversation*, London, 1993, p. 1.
23. From 'In Carey's Footsteps', in Lady Ferguson, *Sir Samuel Ferguson*, Vol. II, p. 263.
24. Ibid., pp. 264-5.
25. Ibid., p. 263.
26. This paralleling itself alludes to a Browningesque characteristic. In 'Andrea del Sarto', for example, as with others of Browning's poems, 'works of art' are made to stand for Browning's poetic craft.

3

'A Noble Manliness':
Chivalry and Masculinity in
Bram Stoker's *The Snake's Pass*

William Hughes

Recent critical studies of Bram Stoker's first published novel, *The Snake's Pass* have concentrated primarily on the work's portrayal of Ireland and the Irish.[1] This critical preoccupation has arisen, arguably, in response to a perceived need, in part generated by the centenary of the first publication of *Dracula* in 1997, to relocate the author within an Irish context, to appropriate him, as it were, as a portrayer of the West Coast countryside in which he served, albeit briefly, as Inspector of Petty Sessions under British rule.[2] Such an appropriation, tempting as it is to the Irish tourist industry, is not unproblematic, and the potential cultural difficulties implicit in the author's Anglo-Irish background have in consequence been both recognised and developed in academic criticism.

If we accept W.J. McCormack's contention that as a writer Bram Stoker consistently identified himself 'with the London-based exiles ... as against the home-based revivalists', then we are forced to concede also that Stoker's perception of Ireland and the Irish is of necessity compromised by the need to construct the text through discourses acceptable on both sides of the Irish Sea.[3] Such discourses inevitably *exclude* certain readers through the same cultural and rhetorical processes by which they include others. Those excluded from participation in the discourse arguably become available to others *through* the discourse - they become objects of study, a subject people in an empirical as well as a political sense. Hence, for Nicholas Daly, *The Snake's Pass* may be read as both an 'adventure story' and a displaced 'imperial romance' written in the tradition of works which 'depict the mastery of overseas space by the reader's delegates within the text, the fictional explorers, hunters, soldiers and engineers who march relentlessly across trackless desert, jungle and veldt'.[4] By figuring County Clare as 'a vision of the colonial territory as a virgin page awaiting inscription', Daly forces an intimacy between the author and a readership whose discursive position permits an easy transition between the sites of colonialist endeavour.[5] This intimacy, though, privileges one discursive context - a context admittedly fashionable in modern Irish studies - at the expense of the other discourses which penetrate and support both the text and the concept of imperialism itself. To return to Daly's identification of *The Snake's Pass* as an adventure narrative, it may be argued that the novel embodies a series of parallel discursive signals which enables readers access not only to the imperial tradition but also to a vision of masculinity which contributes to that tradition the myth of the gentleman-adventurer. *The Snake's Pass*, in this respect, provides not merely an opportunity to explore the colonial status of Ireland but equally a forum within which the author might visibly proclaim to his readers an allegiance to a chivalric mode of behaviour which arguably informs the culture of both Anglo-Irish and English masculinity.

In his study of chivalry in modern culture, *The Return to Camelot*, Mark Girouard argues that the behaviour of the nineteenth century English gentleman was shaped not so much by a direct representation of a single knightly original but by an idealised, romanticised revision of prototypical chivalric relationships embodied in a variety of frequently-read texts:

> All gentleman knew that they must be brave, show no sign of panic or cowardice, be courteous and protective to women, be loyal to their comrades, and meet death without flinching. They knew it because they had learnt the code of the gentleman in a multitude of different ways, through advice, through example, through what they had been taught at school or by their parents, and through endless stories of chivalry, daring, knights, gentlemen and gallantry which they had read or been told by way of history books, ballads, poems, plays, pictures and novels.[6]

Chivalry, Girouard concludes, influenced 'all gentlemen ... even if they did not consciously realise it'.[7] *The Return to Camelot* concentrates primarily on the ideals of male behaviour in British society between the late-eighteenth century and the outbreak of the First World War and is, as Girouard admits, primarily a cultural rather than a literary study. These cultural ideals, however, are frequently replicated in the popular fiction of the period - in works as diverse, for example, as Thomas Hughes's *Tom Brown at Oxford* (1861) and Bram Stoker's *The Snake's Pass* (1890).[8] Hence, Arthur Severn, the gentlemanly and English first-person narrator of *The Snake's Pass* is consistently portrayed as engaging, apparently spontaneously and unthinkingly, with the modern chivalric discourse that permits him to comprehend and control his relationships with members of other social classes, people of different nationalities, and the opposite sex. This is arguably the same discourse which enables a proportion of the novel's readers to empathise with the central character and his subsequent actions in Ireland. Severn's response to a chance meeting with an Irish peasant girl on a hillside in County Clare thus rehearses not merely a series of conventional assumptions regarding how he, as a fictional hero, *should* react, but exposes also a fragment of the cultural, educational and behavioural assumptions that the text makes with regard to the reader. Severn recalls:

> She was so frank, however, and made her queries with such a gentle modesty, that something within my heart seemed to grow and grow; and the conviction was borne upon me that I stood before my fate. Sir Geraint's ejaculation rose to my lips:
>
> 'Here, by God's rood, is the one maid for me!'[9]

Full cognisance of Severn's allusion demands a certain standard in literacy as much as in social manners, as the text does not provide a source for the quotation. This knowledge is not essential, however, as Severn's romantic interest in the peasant girl, Norah Joyce, is comprehensible whether or not the reader is aware of the provenance of the narrator's remark. But the reader who recognises its source benefits from additional access to a series of less explicit chivalric and literary allusions throughout the novel. Arthur is quoting Tennyson's Arthurian Idyll, *The Marriage of Geraint*:

> He [Sir Geraint] found an ancient dame in dim brocade;
> And near her, like a blossom vermeil-white,
> That lightly breaks a faded flower-sheath,
> Moved the fair Enid, all in faded silk,
> Her daughter. In a moment thought Geraint,
> 'Here by God's Rood is the one maid for me.'[10]

Acknowledging this literary source, a number of parallels between the poem and the novel become available. Arthur's surname, for example, recalls the location of the feudal lands of Tennyson's errant knight, Sir Geraint, who originally dwelt on 'the shores/Of Severn'.[11] Both men initially hear rather than see the beloved, who possesses an explicitly 'sweet voice'.[12] Finally, Geraint and Severn both marry girls 'Of broken fortunes', whose fathers have been 'foully ousted' from their own property.[13] These marriages are the final reward in a masculine chivalric myth where the implicit duty of the errant male is, as Tennyson argues in 'Guinevere', 'To ride abroad redressing human wrongs'.[14]

Arthur's initial encounter with the unseen woman is particularly significant. He recalls the incident:

> As I got closer, I heard someone singing. 'By Jove,' I said to myself, 'the women of this country have sweet voices!' - indeed, this was by no means the first time I had noticed the fact. I listened, and as I drew nearer to the top of the hill, I took care not to make any noise which might disturb the singer. It was an odd sensation to stand in the shadow of the hill-top, on that September day, and listen to *Ave Maria* sung by the unknown voice of an unseen singer. I made a feeble joke all to myself:

'My experience of the girls of the west is that of *vox et praeteria nihil*' (p. 73).

Essentially, at this stage Norah represents nothing other than the concept 'woman', her most basic signification in chivalric terms. Being unseen, she evades any modifications which age, race or physical appearance may make to her status.[15] Arthur is thus able to approach the female at its most abstract and romanticised, as a prototypical knight should. His self-conscious Latin quotation establishes a further complicity between reader and author based upon classical education. Most women, as well as many non-Classically educated men, would be unable to fully appreciate the aptness of Severn's supposedly 'feeble joke'.[16] This encounter, however, initiates an interface in the novel between chivalry, embodied here in the discourse of modern courtly love, and the equally chivalric myth of the gentleman adventurer - a figure which may be easily appropriated by a political discourse. Arthur, significantly, continues his observation by reading into Norah's behaviour the suggestion of an unhappiness which will later enable him to reconfigure her as a modern 'damsel in distress'. He continues, 'There was an infinity of pathos in the voice - some sweet, sad yearning, as though the earthly spirit was singing with an unearthly voice - and the idea came on me with a sense of conviction that some deep unhappiness underlay that appeal to the Mother of Sorrows' (p. 73). His conviction is confirmed by her subsequent behaviour:

> The song died away, and then there was a gulp and a low suppressed moan. Her head drooped between her knees, her shoulders shook, and I could see that she was weeping.... The solitude, now that the vibration of her song had died out of the air, seemed oppressive (p. 74).

Severn is already beginning to appreciate the situation through the filter of a romanticised chivalric consciousness. Through the explicit solitude of the location, Norah has become the archetypal defenceless female, vulnerable and alone, encountered by the errant knight, to whose love, defence and cause he will consecrate his future life.[17] Severn's honour as a modern gentleman demands as a minimum that he attend to her immediate needs.[18] His initial attentions, in his own appreciation of her situation, succeed in superficially redressing her still unspecified unhappiness:

> One thing gave me much delight. The sadness seemed to have passed quite away - for the time at all events. Her eyes, which had first been glassy with recent tears, were now lit with keenest interest, and she seemed to have entirely forgotten the cause of her sorrow (p. 77).

Thus far the narrative remains a simple love-story with an Irish setting, for all Severn's attempts to manoeuvre himself into the position of knight errant.

The discovery, however, of the exact nature of Norah Joyce's complaint permits the chivalric discourse to combine not merely more forcefully with a complex conjunction of national identities and aspirations, but also with the manner in which these identities construct and value the female. Norah's 'broken fortunes' (to recall Tennyson's phrase) are a consequence of her father having fallen into debt through the agency of 'Black' Murdock, a local usurer or, to use the Irish phrase, Gombeen Man. To discharge his debt, her father has exchanged his productive lands with the Gombeen's sterile estate, the latter consisting largely of undrained bog. The fertile lands, now in the possession of Murdock, are left uncultivated as the Gombeen Man searches them for a chest of gold, buried there during General Humbert's invasion. The bog, however, carries an additional mythic signification. Local legend, as overheard by Severn, suggests that the bog is the form assumed by the King of the Snakes, who defied the command of St Patrick and remained in Ireland. The bog thus functions both as a popular local emblem of chaos, and as a literal source of infertility in the region.[19] The relationship between the protagonists and the omnipresent bog is, however, again rendered almost entirely through the medium of the chivalric discourse.[20] Through Arthur Severn's participation in the discourse, the waste of the land becomes embodied in a version of the Arthurian legend of the Fisher King.[21] Phelim Joyce, father of Norah and original owner of the more prosperous of the two estates, is, like the Fisher King, maimed. Joyce recalls:

> ... I rid all the way from Galway this blessed day to be here in time, but the mare slipped coming down Curragh Hill and threw me over the bank into the lake.... I was foreninst the Curragh Rock an' only got a foothold in a chink, an' had to hold on wid me one arm for I fear the other is broke
> (p. 32).

Though Joyce physically recovers, his new land, like the kingdom of the Fisher King, has implicitly remained fallow and unproductive during the time of his illness. Even after his recovery, the land presents a striking contrast to the fertility of that which he formerly owned (p. 53). At the same time, the hitherto fertile land is left unworked as Murdock searches it for the missing French gold.

The Arthurian legend is admittedly distorted here, but survives, encoded, in a 'modern' technological representation. The novel is explicit regarding both how the treasure is sought, and as to who seeks it. Dick Sutherland, a former schoolfellow of the narrator, employed by Murdock, explains to Severn:

> '... we have poles on opposite sides of the bog with lines between them. The magnet is fixed, suspended from a free wheel, and I let it down to the centre from each side in turn. If there were any attraction I should feel it by the thread attached to the magnet which I hold in my hand.'
> 'It is something like fishing?'

'Exactly.' (p. 62)

Murdock, though, is aided in his search by Arthur and Dick, both of whom frequently identify themselves with the cause of the displaced landowner, Joyce. Their rather surprising participation in the Gombeen Man's plans, however, can be explained through their often thinly-disguised desire to see him depart from both estates, which Arthur eventually purchases from Joyce and Murdock.

The textual construction of the narrator in *The Snake's Pass*, though, permits the legend of the Fisher King to combine with a more general or popular conception of knightliness. Severn's Christian name has resonances in kingship, fraternity and national unity - Arthur, too, was styled as a king upon whose presence the well-being of the land depended.[22] Moreover, by the late nineteenth century the mythical King Arthur had arguably already been appropriated as an emphatically *British* (rather than Welsh or Anglo-Welsh) popular signifier of unity and nationhood. In short, Arthur had become an alternative to St. George, mobilising not merely a similar range of nationalistic identities and aspirations, but much of the same iconography also.[23] *The Snake's Pass*, in this sense, reveals how easily these discourses may map over each other. The proximity of the equally evocative figure of St. Patrick in the novel demonstrates also how such a blurring of discursive boundaries may induce hierarchies among myths.[24] Essentially, in works such as *The Snake's Pass*, apparent inadequacies may be built into the textual construction of one mythological figure so that a rival mythological figure may successfully both fill in these apparent gaps, and ultimately overwrite the corresponding character. In *The Snake's Pass* this practice is realised not merely by the ease with which the 'kingdom' passes from the Fisher King (Joyce) to 'King' Arthur Severn, but by the manner in which the novel forwards a chivalric myth as a corrective to St. Patrick's apparent failure to drive the last and greatest of the snakes from Ireland. The key scene here is a dream sequence in which Arthur essentially reviews the whole history of the region from the legendary period associated with St. Patrick to its present day poverty through local debt and underdevelopment, by way of the mythical (and mythicised) figures who emblematise past and present. Arthur recalls:

I seemed to live over again in isolated moments all the past weeks; but in such a way that the legends and myths and stories of Knockcalltecrore which I had heard were embodied in every moment. Thus, Murdock had always a part in the gloomy scenes, and got inextricably mixed up with the King of the Snakes. They freely exchanged personalities, and at one time I could see the Gombeen Man defying St Patrick, whilst at another the serpent seemed to be struggling with [Phelim] Joyce, and, after twisting round the mountain, being only beaten off by a mighty blow from Norah's father, rushing through the sea to the Shleenanaher (p. 181).[25]

21

When voiced by Severn, the identification of the Gombeen Man with the King of the Snakes facilitates an intense pattern of signification. Immediately, it enables an easy transition to be made between the myth of King Arthur and that of St. George, in that both were popularly viewed as adherents of a similar code of chivalry, though only the latter slew a dragon. Again, the customary representation of the dragon in British art was coiled, scaly and snake-like.[26] This blurring of the boundaries of signification here permits Arthur to cross into a separate chivalric legend whilst retaining the cultural associations of his Christian name.

As a serpent, though, Murdock embodies a further series of associations that link him to the legendary expulsion of the snakes from Ireland. In this sense Murdock is *in* Ireland, though not *of* Ireland. He has become ostracised from the community because of his financial dealings with Catholic and Protestant alike. St. Patrick here functions primarily as a representative of Ireland rather than of God, in that in both the legend and the dream he attempts to cast out the undesired inhabitant and, implicitly, all that he stands for. If Murdock is the snake then, equally, his provincial tyranny and unregulated usury are the snake-like qualities which need to be driven out with him (p. 37). In Arthur's dream a rather inadequate St. Patrick fails to oust Murdock, though Joyce succeeds in driving out the Gombeen Man's serpentine *alter ego*. The implication is that chivalry, here embodied in the person of the regenerated Fisher King, may prove the more effective remedy. Beyond the dream, though, Joyce lacks the strength and qualities to defend more than his own person and daughter. It is thus left to the more heavily coded chivalric figure Arthur, who is by now capable of being read as both knight and saint, to compensate for the inadequacies of the past, and to drive the unacceptable from Ireland. Leaving aside his status as the representative of a unique form of usury which in itself signifies Irish backwardness and provincialism, Murdock is quite simply unacceptable to the gentlemanly discourse that supports the new power that is taking over the Snake's Pass through purchase rather than usury.

Though wealthy, Murdock is quite simply not a gentleman, as Arthur and Dick both suggest on more than one occasion. Dick, indeed, makes it clear that his employer's suspicions and frequent profanity fall below even the most basic standard of masculinity:

> Of course, I don't expect a fellow of your stamp to understand a gentleman's feelings - damn it! how can you have a gentleman's understanding when you haven't even a man's. You ought to know right well that what I said I would do, I shall do (p. 60).

As Dick's concluding remark indicates, the behaviour of the gentleman, unlike that of the Gombeen, is regular, reliable, and regulated by both written and ethical law. Murdock, however, goes so far as to question the most central touchstone of chivalrous masculinity, the essential purity of the feminine nature. When he says to Norah

> An' so ye have him at home already, have ye! An' yer father prisent too, an' a witness. It's the sharp girrul ye are, Norah Joyce, but I suppose this wan is not the first! (p. 170)

he is effectively profaning her more than he does when, finally, he strikes her. Arthur's physical response to the Gombeen Man's accusation of sexual impropriety on Norah's part represents more than merely a defence of her as his *fiancée*: quite simply, it emblematises how he *should* react to an insult tendered to *any* woman. As Stoker phrases it in an earlier work on American culture, 'Such a thing as a woman suffering molestation or affront, save at the hands of the criminal classes - which are the same all the world over - is almost unknown, and would be promptly resented by the first man coming along.'[27] Unquestioning opposition to figures such as Murdock thus represents a cause that all gentlemen may recognise and empathise with.

It would be easy at this juncture to suggest that Arthur's knightliness, supported by that of Dick, emblematises a blatant contrast between English chivalry and Irish anarchy in the novel. The political script of *The Snake's Pass*, which in many respects is attached to the nationalistic aspirations embodied in some versions of the chivalric discourse is, however, more complex than this. The 'natural' chivalry displayed by Joyce, who is, in Arthur's words 'manly and handsome' (p. 164) certainly disperses the notion that all Irishmen are 'cunning' and duplicitous (p. 118). This is the type of classless and at times internationally recognised chivalry which Baden-Powell was later to celebrate as a model for the Boy Scout movement (p. 191).[28] Elsewhere, the Irish lawyer Mr Caicy emblematises sound and reliable legal practices, even when burdened by, to quote Arthur, 'the endless formalities and eccentricities habitual to a country whose administration has traditionally adopted and adapted every possible development of all belonging to red-tape' (p. 191).[29] The suggestion of a common standard in chivalry reaches its most acute expression, however, in an exchange between Arthur and his car-driver, Andy Sullivan, whose concern for Arthur's interest in Norah Joyce is based not on the latter's nationality, but on his social class. Andy questions Arthur:

> 'Surr, there can be only one harrum to a girrul from a gintleman,' he laid his hand on my arm, and said this impressively - whatever else he may have said in jest, he was in grim earnest now - 'an' that's whin he's a villain. Ye wouldn't do the black thrick, and desave a girrul that thrusted ye?' (p. 97)

Arthur's uncompromising reply affirms a common standard between the two men, who stand here as representatives of different social positions and supposedly inimicable cultures. Essentially, once the practices and individuals unacceptable to the common standard that binds Arthur to his Irish associates are driven out, an ordered and regulated society, based on the chivalric practice that already implicitly permeates society on both sides of the Irish Sea, may be developed. Dick Sutherland's vision of the Snake's Pass as a regenerated community, with an outward-looking harbour and stone buildings 'with proper offices and farmyards' (p. 203) is really not very far, in intellectual terms, from Rugby, the colony of 'muscular young gentlemen and honest English yeomen' founded in Tennessee by the professed 'Muscular Christian' and author of *Tom Brown's Schooldays*, Thomas Hughes.[30]

The gentleman, it would seem, stands in opposition to all that is not ordered. *The Snake's Pass*, in this sense, rather modifies the cultural image of the gentleman adventurer through its specific application to the Irish environment. Stoker's novel presents a more complex vision of the interaction of the English gentleman with the alien terrain than, for example, Carlyle advances in *Past and Present*:

> It is for ever indispensable for a man to fight: now with Necessity, with Barrenness, Scarcity, with Puddles, Bogs, tangled Forests, unkempt Cotton.... Here too thou shalt be strong of heart, noble of soul; thou shalt dread no pain or death, thou shalt not love ease or life; in rage thou shalt remember mercy, justice; - thou shalt be a Knight and not a Chactaw, if thou wouldst prevail![31]

Arthur, of course, is recognisably all of these things - a tenacious combatant against literal and figurative morasses, a defender of women, a loyal friend, and one who both warns and forgives Murdock, a mortal foe, at a moment of combined personal anger and impending danger. But Carlyle's binary opposition between the Knight and the 'Chactaw' does not function with any certainty in *The Snake's Pass*. The bog, which is simultaneously a sterile restriction on the ecological growth of the area and (through the association with the King of the Snakes and, therefore, Murdock also) a symbol of the stagnant and provincial practices which equally inhibit local fiscal regeneration, may here be almost wholly identified with the chaotic and unchivalric 'Chactaw.' At the close of the novel Murdock's house sinks into the swollen and unstable mass of the bog. The Gombeen Man, his ill-gotten gains, and the morass that symbolises both then make a rapid, sinuous exit through the Snake's Pass to their final destruction in the breakers of the Atlantic Ocean. The chaos that is left behind becomes a site for redevelopment and exploitation, as Arthur and Dick had always planned. Their final struggle, though, is here scripted as a purely physical one against the environment. As Arthur notes, among the local populace (other than Murdock) he has always found at minimum 'a good feeling and kindness of heart' (p. 244). At best, in the person of Andy, he has found a rudimentary chivalry and consistency of behaviour. *The Snake's Pass* is, in this sense, not a straightforward *Boy's Own Paper* adventure or empire narrative, in that, in its closing fantasy about the regeneration of Ireland, there are no savage natives to be forcibly civilised, no murderous or duplicitous activities to be suppressed. The fantasy here, indeed, consists of the possibility that the Irish peasantry is, when given a chance to express itself, a rudimentary version of the naturally chivalric English yeoman classes. This idealised view of the Irish peasantry, it may be concluded, arguably owes more to the sentiments that established Toynbee Hall and the University Settlements in the East End of London, than it ever could to the Anglo-Irish manifestation of the chivalric discourse, grounded as that latter is within a racially as well as socially-divided society.[32]

NOTES

1.   See, for example, Nicholas Daly, 'Irish Roots: The Romance of History in Bram Stoker's *The Snake's Pass*', *Literature and History*, 4 (1995), pp. 42-70; William Hughes, '"For Ireland's Good": The Reconstruction of Rural Ireland in Bram Stoker's *The Snake's Pass*', *Irish Studies Review*, 2:12 (Autumn 1995), pp. 17-21.

2.   See, for example, Leslie Shepard, *Bram Stoker. Irish Theatre Manager and Author, with information on where to visit the Dublin Locations associated with Bram Stoker*, Dublin, 1994, pp. i, 1, 10.

3.   W.J. McCormack, 'Irish Gothic and After, 1820-1945', in Seamus Deane, ed., *The Field Day Anthology of Irish Writing*, Vol. 2, Derry, 1991, p. 845.

4.   Daly, 'Irish Roots', pp. 42-3.

5.   Ibid., p. 43.

6.   Mark Girouard, *The Return to Camelot. Chivalry and the English Gentleman*, New Haven, 1981, p. 7.

7.   *Ibid.*, 'Preface', p. v.

8.   See, for example, Thomas Hughes, *Tom Brown at Oxford* (1861), London, 1880, p. 99.

9.   Bram Stoker, *The Snake's Pass* (1890), Dingle, 1990, p. 77. All further references will be included parenthetically in the text.

10. Alfred, Lord Tennyson, 'The Marriage of Geraint' (1857), *Tennyson: Poems and Plays*, London, 1965, p. 323.

11. Ibid., p. 318.

12. Ibid., p. 322.

13. Tennyson, 'The Marriage of Geraint', pp. 318, 324.

14. Tennyson, 'Guinevere', ibid., p. 430.

15. Compare here the rather unchivalric response of Walter Hartright to the silhouetted Marian Halcombe in Wilkie Collins's *The Woman in White* (1860), London, 1994, p. 24.

16. Literally translated, the quotation reads 'A voice and nothing more'. For further information on the gender and class implications of a Classical education see: J.R. de S. Honey, *Tom Brown's Universe*, London, 1977, pp. 130-3.

17. This is, of course, the basic plot of Tennyson's *The Marriage of Geraint*, and explicitly forms part of the conduct expected of 'the knighthood-errant of this realm' by King Arthur. The theme, though, informs a wide range of other nineteenth century texts, including Millais' 1870 painting *The Knight Errant* (Tate Gallery), and Collins's *The Woman in White* (1860).

18. See Girouard, *The Return to Camelot*, p. 260; see also Robert Baden-Powell, *Scouting for Boys. Boys Edition* (1908), London, 1947, pp. 171-3; Robert Baden-Powell, *Rovering to Success. A Book of Life-Sport for Young Men*, London, pp. 110-111.

19. As a signifier in a wider cultural context the bog also carries a burden of topographical and racial prejudice with regard to the portrayal of Ireland and the Irish. See Hughes, '"For Ireland's Good"', pp. 18-9.

20. Beyond the historical and mythical narratives of the bog supplied by the peasants encountered by Severn in a local shebeen, the narrator's close friend, the Englishman Dick Sutherland, attempts elsewhere to describe the terrain in scientific terms (p. 59).

21. See R.S. Loomis, *The Grail*, Princeton, 1991, pp. 36-40.

22. For a contemporary rendering of the legend, see Alfred Nutt, *Studies on the Legend of the Holy Grail*, London, 1888, pp. xi-xiv.

23. See the iconography of illustration 127, and plates XXIV, XXV, and XXVIII, in Girouard, *The Return to Camelot*, pp. 195, 241-2, 277.

24. Note, for example, Simon Fowler's caption to the 1874 poster, *God Save Ireland*, reproduced in Simon Fowler, '"Lend us your Eyes": The Irish in Britain Travelling Exhibition', *Irish Studies Review*, 2:16 (Autumn 1996), p. 30.

25. The name 'Knockcalltecrore' here refers to the mountain which fringes the bog, where the 'Shleenanaher' is the Snake's Pass of the title. Severn again pictures the Gombeen as the King of the Snakes in a later dream (pp. 205-6).

26. See Edward Burne-Jones's 1868 gouache, *St George and the Dragon* (William Morris Gallery, Walthamstow) and Adrian Jones's (c.1919) memorial to the Cavalry of the Empire (Hyde Park, London), reproduced in Girouard, *The Return to Camelot*, p. 292.

27. Bram Stoker, *A Glimpse of America*, London, 1886, p. 23.

28. Baden-Powell, *Scouting for Boys*, p. 167.

29. The almost imperceptible irony of this specific remark may be read though its connection to the author's own contribution to the administration of Ireland, *The Duties of Clerks of Petty Sessions in Ireland*, Dublin: Printed for the Author by John Falconer, 1879.

30. Girouard, *The Return to Camelot, Tom Brown's Schooldays* (1857), with its now-forgotten sequel *Tom Brown at Oxford* (1861), proved highly influential in the popularising of chivalric as well as so-called 'Muscular Christian' doctrines amongst young men during the later nineteenth century: see Girouard, *The Return to Camelot* pp. 166-8.

31. Thomas Carlyle, *Past and Present* (1858), A.M.D. Hughes ed., Oxford, 1927, p. 172.

32. Girouard, *The Return to Camelot*, p. 250.

4

The Celtic Spirit in Literature:
Renan, Arnold, Wilde and Yeats

Stephen Regan

Ernest Renan's *La Poésie des Races Celtiques* was a potent and influential source for Irish nationalist sentiment in the late nineteenth century. The book directs its scholarship towards recognising the Celts as a cultured race, thereby displacing the old charges of barbarism. Renan's assertions of Celtic 'imaginative power' and 'infinite delicacy of feeling' are powerful counter images of national identity. Similarly, Renan attempts to give a more positive dimension to the old colonial model of Ireland as a dependent woman by identifying the vital creativity of the Celts as a feminine characteristic: 'If it be permitted us to assign sex to nations as to individuals, we should have to say without hesitance that the Celtic race ... is an essentially feminine race.'[1] It is important to stress how persistent Renan's ideas were, not least because they were later recycled by Matthew Arnold. *The Poetry of the Celtic Races* did not appear in English translation until the early eighteen nineties, giving a fresh impetus to the book's ideas, and Renan was himself still actively propagating ideas of national essence in the later part of the century. In his lecture 'What is a Nation?', delivered at the Sorbonne in March 1882, Renan inveighs against the error of confusing race with nation. A nation, he insists, can no more be founded on race than it can on language, religion, commerce or geography. What, then, is a nation? As Renan sees it, a nation is 'a living soul, a spiritual principle'.[2] This definition was to prove a powerful impulse behind the Irish Literary Revival in the 1890s, but it also signalled just how precarious and vulnerable the principle of nationhood was.

Renan, writing as a Celt, creates an appealing image of a noble people, gently modifying the traces of barbarism into something akin to primitive simplicity. In mid-Victorian England, however, many of the old stereotypes still pertained and were given a new and vicious import by political events in both England and Ireland. Strongly negative images of the Irish were, to some extent, the product of religious and class prejudice shown to Irish Roman Catholics by middle-class Victorian Protestants. Irish, in this respect, was synonymous with Papist and peasant. The most intriguing shift in representations of the Irish national character occurred, however, because of the unusual

28

convergence of Fenianism with the heated debate over *The Origin of Species* in the 1860s. The consequence was a widespread propagation of the idea that Irish Fenians and anthropoid apes were closely related. Later, in the 1880s, this notion of the simian Celt was combined with the idea of the Irish as white negroes and also with prevailing nineteenth-century stereotypes of criminals, assassins, revolutionaries and gypsies. Images of this kind appeared frequently in the British press, one obvious source being John Tenniel's cartoons of the Irish in *Punch*. The fullest study of this debasement of the Irish character is L.P. Curtis's book, *Apes and Angels: The Irishman in Victorian Caricature* (1971), which examines physiognomy in cartoons of the Irish and argues that the process of simianizing the Celt took place roughly between 1840 and 1890, with the 1860s serving as 'a pivotal point in this alteration of the stereotype'. The main concern of the book is 'the gradual but unmistakable transformation of Paddy, the stereotypical Irish Celt of the mid-nineteenth century, from a drunken and relatively harmless peasant into a dangerous ape-man or simianized agitator'.[3]

One of the obvious consequences of Fenian agitation in the 1860s was the resurgence of the claim that the Irish could never be properly civilised and that they possessed a temperament fundamentally unsuited to English ideals of restraint and stability. The image of Ireland as a female body was also revived in the 1860s and took a very specific form. This was the representation of Erin or Hibernia as the beautiful suffering sister of Britannia. Erin was frequently portrayed in flowing robes embroidered with shamrocks, with a harp in her arms and an Irish wolfhound at her feet. One variant of this idea in cartoons in the 1860s suggests that Fenianism is the Beast that lurks within the Irish character. Beauty, in the form of Erin or Hibernia, is rescued from the clutches of the Fenian Beast by a handsome Prince or by Saint George (both images of English law and order). As Fenian activities continued, the English image of the politicised Paddy became increasingly bestial, while Fenianism became identified with anarchism to the point where the two terms were interchangeable.

The line from Ernest Renan to Matthew Arnold is unmistakable but in some respects unlikely, given that what preoccupies Arnold in the 1860s is not so much Celticism as Fenianism. The Fenian - a debased form of the Celt - is associated in Arnold's mind with anarchy: so much so that at one level culture and anarchy function as descriptive terms for England and Ireland respectively. The breaking down of the railings at Hyde Park during working-class demonstrations is clearly associated in Arnold's mind with another disturbing instance of anarchic tendencies: the invasion of the Home Secretary's office on 18 November 1867. On this latter occasion a group of demonstrators protested against the death sentence imposed upon those Fenians held responsible for the murder of a police sergeant during an attempt to free two inmates from Manchester Prison. It is worth noting what Arnold has to say about the Irish Fenian:

> The difference between an Irish Fenian and an English rough is so immense, and the case, in dealing with the Fenian, so much more clear. He is so evidently desperate and dangerous, a man of a conquered race, a Papist, with centuries of ill-usage to inflame him against us, with an alien religion established in his country by us at his expense, with no admiration of our institutions, no love of our virtues, no talents for our business, no turn for our comfort![4]

Arnold is unremitting in his view that Fenianism should be met with over-whelming force, and yet he does go some way towards recognising the source of Irish grievances against the English, even appearing to sympathise with the Fenian disdain for English institutions, values and business. The ironic self-criticism in these lines is in keeping with Arnold's view of the Irish question in a series of lectures titled 'On the Study of Celtic Literature'. Like the lectures which came to form *Culture and Anarchy*, these Irish lectures were first delivered in Oxford in the 1860s and demonstrate Arnold's increasing concern over the widespread agitation for political reform.

Throughout his writings on Ireland, Arnold's attention is directed - as it is in *Culture and Anarchy* - at deficiencies in the English national character. The dullness and insensility of the English 'type' provoke Arnold into a declaration that 'We in England have come to that point when the continued advance and greatness of our nation is threatened by one cause, and one cause above all'. The cause Arnold is referring to here is Philistinism, and as an antidote to its worst effects he prescribes 'the greater delicacy and spirituality of the Celtic peoples'. Arnold's appraisal of the Celtic spirit owes much to Renan: the Celt possesses 'the power of quick and strong perception and emotion' but is wanting in 'balance, measure and patience'. In short, the Celtic temperament has 'love of beauty, charm and spirituality for its excellence, ineffectualness and self-will for its defect'.[5]

What Arnold claims to be studying, however, is Celtic *literature*, and what is most striking in these lectures is their assertion that the Celtic people can be *known* through their language and literature: 'To know the Celtic case thoroughly, one must know the Celtic people; and to know them one must know that by which a people best express themselves, - their literature'. Arnold's method is to bring 'the Celt and sound criticism together'. Convinced that a nation expresses its 'very self' through the forms of its language, Arnold believes that the Celt can be 'truly known' through 'a disinterested, positive and constructive criticism' of Celtic literature. In addition, Arnold believes that there is a Celtic element in English literature. This Celtic inspiration gives English poetry its 'natural magic', its facility for 'catching and rendering the charm of nature in a wonderfully near and vivid way'. The evidence of Celtic Genius in English poetry is evidence enough for Arnold that there are Celtic traces in the English national character. In this respect, both Keats and Shakespeare have elements of Celtic genius. What makes Arnold's pursuit of the Celtic spirit unusual is his assertion that if the English can but recognise the Celt in themselves they may yet become 'more intelligent, more gracious, and more humane'.[6] Arnold does not appear to be promoting intermarriage, as some commentators have supposed. His ideal is one of *cultural* unification, as it is for Yeats later in the century.

Arnold responds in an awkward and hesitant way to the suggestion that the Celts are essentially a feminine race: 'Some people have found in the Celtic nature and its sensibility the main root out of which chivalry and romance and the glorification of a feminine ideal spring; this is a great question, with which I cannot deal here.' This does not prevent Arnold, though, from claiming just a few lines later that 'the sensibility of the Celtic nature, its nervous exaltation, have something feminine in them, and the Celt is thus peculiarly disposed to feel the spell of the feminine idiosyncrasy; he has an affinity to it; he is not far from its secret'. It is not entirely clear what Arnold means by 'the spell of the feminine idiosyncrasy'; it is, after all, meant to be a secret. The effect, though, is to render the Celt unfit for self-government, just as 'his want of sanity and steadfastness' in other respects have 'lamed him on the world of business and politics'. There is, in the end, a stubborn political statement in Arnold's musings on the Celtic spirit: the English must *know* the Celt in order to govern Ireland more effectively and efficiently. There is never any question of separation since the Celts are our 'brothers in the great Indo-European family'. What Arnold asks of his English readers is that they recognise the Celt in themselves, allowing it to mingle with the Germanic and Norman elements in their own natures. In a vocabulary strongly reminiscent of 'Dover Beach' Arnold complains that we are 'blindly and ignorantly rolled about by the forces of our nature', with 'one part clashing with another'.[7] As with *Culture and Anarchy*, Arnold's ideal is one of cultural improvement and cultural renovation, and just as Oxford is the true home of sweetness and light, so too should it become the home of a new Chair of Celtic Studies.

Arnold is frank about the extent of English misgovernment and injustice in Ireland, even acknowledging the Philistines as 'the guilty authors of Fenianism'. He is adamant, though, that the remains of the Celtic kingdom, with the exception of Brittany, belong to an *English* Empire: 'we have Ireland, the Scotch Highlands, Wales, the Isle of Man, Cornwall. They are part of ourselves, we are deeply interested in knowing them, they are deeply interested in being known by us'.[8] The suggestion that England's interest in other territories is largely academic cannot quite disguise the crude expression of ownership ('we *have* Ireland'). Arnold's policy is to quell the tide of Irish nationalism through a process of amelioration or, as Seamus Deane puts it, a process of 'killing Home Rule by kindness'.[9] Arnold did, in fact, oppose the Home Rule Bill in 1886. Deane claims further that the salient features of Arnold's response to Ireland were taken direct from Edmund Burke. In 1881 Arnold produced an anthology of Burke's writings on Irish affairs, and in 1882 he opened his volume of *Irish Essays and Others* by exhorting his readers to seek out 'every essay, letter and speech of Burke on the subject of Ireland'. The principal essay of that 1882 volume, 'The Incompatibles', was written by Arnold during the preparation of the Irish Land Bill and its sentiments are much more blunt and overt than Arnold's reflections in the earlier lectures on Celtic literature. The Irish, he maintains, must be brought to 'cordial acquiescence' in English affairs, but Arnold does not rule out 'coercion' when the Irish are 'disorderly'.[10]

What Seamus Deane points out is that Arnold's search for some unifying principle based on national characteristics proves, in the end, to be divisive and sectarian. The obvious reason for this is that racial differences slide all too easily into religious differences, so that Celtic and Catholic become synonymous. One obvious example can be found in Arnold's assertion that just as Celtic and Catholic France was able to attract and pacify Germanic and Protestant Alsace, so should Germanic and Protestant Great Britain have sought the acquiescence of Celtic and Catholic Ireland. Arnold claims to be seeking 'healing measures' but the effect of his statement is to give a new political and cultural prominence to a specific religious community. What Deane claims is that 'the romanticizing of the Celt becomes, in effect, the romanticizing of the Irish Catholic'.[11] Arnold, in this respect, exacerbates sectarian tension in Ireland by giving tacit recognition to one distinctive religious and racial grouping. Unexpectedly, then, Arnold not only prepares the ground for some of the most heated debates about Irish nationality in the 1890s but also helps to sustain one of the most potent nationalist myths: that of a primary and essential Celtic Catholic Ireland.

Arnold is instrumental in bringing about what becomes, in the 1890s, a very common distinction between cultural nationalism and political nationalism. Characteristic of his stance on this particular issue is his remark in the essay 'From Easter to August', published in *The Nineteenth Century* in September 1887, that Ireland should be 'a nation poetically only, not politically'.[12] Unlike Renan, Arnold refuses to contemplate the idea that the Celt might one day be capable of 'getting the upper hand' over the English. Twenty years after Arnold's lectures 'On the Study of Celtic Literature', however, the theory of an eventual Celtic triumph was still in circulation. It was to be found, among other places, in an essay titled 'The Celt in English Art' which appeared in *The Fortnightly Review* in February 1891. The author of this essay was Grant Allen, an anthropologist who was sympathetic to the Irish nationalist cause. Adopting Arnold's distinction between Celtic and Teutonic characteristics, Allen welcomed what he called the 'return-wave' of Celtic influence. What is most interesting about Allen's essay in the context of the 1890s is that it clearly recognises the opportunity for fusing Celticism with aestheticism and socialism:

> The great and victorious aesthetic movement ... may be regarded in its wider aspect as just a particular part of the general racial, political and social return-wave. It is a direct result, I believe, of the Celtic reflux on Teutonic Britain, and of the resurgence of the Celtic substratum against Teutonic dominance ... The Celt comes back upon us with all the Celtic gifts and all the Celtic ideals - imagination, fancy, decorative skills, artistic handicraft; free land, free speech, human equality, human brotherhood.[13]

Among the writers Allen acknowledges for their part in fusing 'the connexion between the decorative revival and the Celtic upheaval of radicalism and socialism' are William Morris and Oscar Wilde. 'Mr Oscar Wilde', he remarks, 'whom only fools ever mistook for a mere charlatan, and whom wise men know for a man of rare insight and strong common-sense, is an Irishman to the core'. Wilde read Allen's essay; it would have been surprising if he hadn't, since it appeared in the same issue of *the Fortnightly Review* as 'The Soul of Man Under Socialism'. Significantly enough, the opening lines of Wilde's essay pay tribute to 'the fine critical spirit' of M. Renan, one of many references to Renan in Wilde's critical writings. The week in which the two essays appeared in *the Fortnightly Review*, Wilde wrote to Allen to congratulate him for his 'superb assertion of that Celtic spirit in Art that Arnold divined, but did not demonstrate, at any rate in the sense of scientific demonstration, such as yours is'. That Wilde concurred in the idea of aestheticism as a blossoming of the Celtic spirit is evident in 'The Critic as Artist', published in two parts a few months later in 1890. Here Wilde blends Allen's scientific racialism and Walter Pater's *Studies in the History of the Renaissance*:

> And though the mission of the aesthetic movement is to lure people to contemplate, not to lead them to create, yet, as the creative instinct is strong in the Celt, and it is the Celt who leads in art, there is no reason why in future years this strange Renaissance should not become almost as mighty in its way as was that new birth of Art that woke many centuries ago in the cities of Italy.[14]

There has been, in recent years, a very noticeable revival of interest in Wilde as an Irish writer. Terry Eagleton, in his preface to *Saint Oscar*, writes about 'the

Irish Oxfordian socialist proto-deconstructionist Oscar Wilde', giving Wilde all the credentials of an Irish Roland Barthes.[15] Wilde's destabilising ironies and contradictions are seen to emerge from his experience of colonialism. For Declan Kiberd, introducing a section on 'The London Exiles' in the controversial *Field Day Anthology of Irish Writing*, 'Wilde was, to the end of his days, a militant Irish republican'. Kiberd reminds us that after the Phoenix Park murders in 1882, when even the more militant Irish commentators denounced the killings, Wilde remarked laconically to an American audience that 'England is to blame. She is reaping the fruit of seven centuries of injustice'. Kiberd's argument, though, rests mainly on Wilde's explosion of the antithesis of England and Ireland. He claims that this antithesis was particularly intense in the later nineteenth century because it allowed the Victorian Englishman to attribute to the Irish all those emotions and impulses he had repressed in himself:

> Thus, if John Bull was industrious and reliable, Paddy was held to be indolent and contrary; if the former was mature and rational, the latter must be unstable and emotional; if the Englishman was adult and manly, then the Irishman must be childish and feminine. So the Irish joined hands with those other two persecuted minorities, women and children; and at the root of many an Englishman's suspicion of the Irish was an unease at the woman or child who lurked within himself.

Wilde's Englishness was essentially a theatrical performance, a way of parodying the very notion of Englishness: 'By becoming more English than the English, Wilde was able to invert, and ultimately to challenge, all the time-honoured myths about Ireland'.[16] Kiberd's assertions are difficult to substantiate in terms of what Wilde actually wrote, though there is clear evidence of Wilde's republicanism in a little-known review of J.A. Froude's *The Two Chiefs of Dunboy* which Wilde submitted to the *Pall Mall Gazette* in April 1889.

Wilde introduces Froude's novel as a parliamentary Blue Book, implying (as he does in 'The Decay of Lying') that fiction of this kind is deficient in imagination. In such records of Irish life, he tells us, England has 'written down her indictment against herself, and has given to the world the history of her shame'. What stirs Wilde's indignation is that Froude 'admits the martyrdom of Ireland, but regrets that the martyrdom was not completely carried out'. His criticism of the book suggests that Froude's understanding of events is a weak version of Arnold's thoughts on national characteristics. The Irish had, according to Froude, 'disowned the facts of life'; the English had been 'unable to tolerate anarchy so near their shores', and eventually the Teutonic power failed to impose law and order on the Celtic people. Wilde exposes the shallowness of Froude's book simply by listing the platitudes and stereotypes of English-Irish relations which fill its pages:

Irish society grew up in happy recklessness. Insecurity added rest to enjoyment. Too close a union with the Irish had produced degeneracy both of character and creed in all the settlements of English. We age quickly in Ireland with the whisky and the broken heads ... The Irish race have always been noisy, useless, and ineffectual. They have produced nothing, they have done nothing which it is possible to admire. What they are that they have always been, and the only hope for them is that their ridiculous Irish nationality should be buried and forgotten. The Irish are the best actors in the world. The animal spirits of the Irish remained when all else was gone, and if there was no purpose in their lives they could at least enjoy themselves.

Wilde's final paragraph involves a comic dismissal of Froude's tedious account of Irish life, but in a more serious way it invokes a new ideal of Irish national pride and strength:

It is dull, but dull books are very popular at present, and as people have grown a little tired of talking about 'Robert Elsmere', they will probably take to discussing 'The Two Chiefs of Dunboy'. There are some who will welcome with delight the idea of solving the Irish question by doing away with the Irish people. There are others who will remember that Ireland has extended her boundaries, and that we have now to reckon with her not merely in the Old World but also in the New.

At an immediate level Wilde recognises the importance of a transatlantic relationship in Ireland's social and political development. In a more general way he suggests that the experience of exile has galvanised Irish nationalism. Behind both of these perceptions is the figure of Parnell, whom Wilde refers to as 'an Irish American' (on the grounds that Parnell's mother was American). Wilde appears to be drawing a parallel between his own career as a writer in London and that of Parnell as an Irish politician in the English parliament. He remarks of the Celtic intellect, for instance, that 'At home it had but learned the pathetic weakness of nationality; in a strange land it realized what indomitable forces nationality possesses'.[17]

It is in the writings of W.B. Yeats rather those of Oscar Wilde, however, that Arnold's notion of 'the Celtic element in literature' is given extended life. One indication of this can be found in a series of fourteen articles written for *The Boston Pilot* in the early 1890s and signed by Yeats 'The Celt in London' (later 'The Celt in Ireland'). The repeated theme of these pieces is that 'There is no great literature without nationality,no great nationality without literature'.[18] *The Pilot* was an Irish Catholic weekly newspaper (formerly *The Jesuit*), under the management of a well-known Fenian, John Boyle O'Reilly, to whom Yeats had been introduced by John O'Leary. Yeats clearly enjoys playing 'The Celt in

London' to an American audience and occasionally panders to O'Reilly's Fenian sympathies, referring to London, at one point, as 'the capital of the enemy'.

If there is still a tendency in English literary criticism to underplay or marginalise the Irish cultural context of Yeats's work, there is also a tendency to overstate the nature of Yeats's nationalist commitment. The recent temptation has been to situate the work of Yeats within the broad terrain of 'post-colonial discourse' where some monolithic version of nationalism is pitted against some global notion of colonialism. Edward Said encourages this kind of procedure when he argues that Yeats is one of the great nationalist artists of decolonisation and revolutionary nationalism, along with Cesaire, Senghor, Darwish and Neruda. Said stakes his claims on those early poems of the 1890s which are concerned with the recovery or repossession of colonized territory through the act of imagination.[19] While this claim gives a new political import to a poem such as 'The Lake Isle of Innisfree', it fails to engage with two important and related contradictions which eventually undermined the force of Irish cultural nationalism at the turn of the century. The first of these contradictions is that much of the impetus behind the Irish Literary Revival came from Irish Protestants such as Lady Gregory, George Russell and Yeats himself. The Anglo-Irish or Protestant Ascendancy had begun to feel increasingly isolated and insecure in the wake of the Land Wars and the push for Home Rule in the 1880s. Many members of this community looked to culture in the Arnoldian sense as a healing measure for the nation. But the more 'revolutionary nationalism', since Said uses that term, was to be found in the Irish Ireland movement which, under the vigorous leadership of D.P. Moran, insisted that Ireland was an exclusively Gaelic and Catholic nation. To state the obvious, there was clearly more than one 'nationalism' at work in Ireland in the 1890s. The second contradiction is that although many of the theories of national identity in the nineteenth century rested upon the idea that the essence or spirit of the nation could be transmitted through language, the Irish Literary Revival attempted to forge a new sense of Irish identity through the *English* language. The opposing position was that Gaelic was crucial to Ireland's survival as a distinctive nation, and even Douglas Hyde, a leading Protestant thinker, supported this position in his 1892 lecture, 'The Necessity for De-Anglicising Ireland'. Yeats's response to Hyde's lecture was to ask, 'Can we not build up a national tradition, a national literature, which shall be none the less Irish in spirit from being English in language?'[20] Not surprisingly, one of the most intense cultural debates of the time centred on the act of translation and raised some intriguing questions about whether translation into another language might preserve the Celtic spirit.

If, as Said claims, Yeats's nationalism can be observed in his reclamation of the land, it is also the case that in the act of recovery Yeats repeats and perpetuates many of the myths and stereotypes already noted in the writings of Ernest Renan and Matthew Arnold. Yeats's 1897 essay 'The Celtic Element in Literature' acknowledges that tradition without essentially altering it. Not only does Yeats feminize Ireland - most emphatically in the figure of Cathleen ní Houlihan - he also constructs an archaic, spiritual, peasant Ireland which seems designed, in close consultation with Matthew Arnold, as an antithesis to modern, commercial, urban Britain. What Yeats wished to reveal through myth was an ideal of Ireland and Irishness that *preceded* the colonial disputes and sectarian divisions of its more recent history. Not surprisingly, perhaps, Yeats was sharply opposed by more radical nationalist thinkers such as D.P. Moran and Padraic Pearse. Nationalism came into conflict with internationalism, as well as with socialism. James Connolly, for instance, reminded the Irish people in 1897 that nationalism, in itself, would not bring an end to oppression. It is difficult within this larger context to sustain Said's belief that Yeats's Celtic phase was one of *revolutionary* nationalism.

There are serious problems in simply acknowledging Yeats as a nationalist writer without proper regard for the contradictions and complexities of that specific *version* of Irish nationalism that was fostered within a particular phase of the Literary Revival. In many ways, Yeats and his Revivalist companions repeated and reinforced the Celtic ideals of Renan and Arnold, and did so at a time when they claimed to be seeking a new and vital cultural transformation. So often, Yeats's early nationalist ideals are aestheticised in a way that renders such characters as 'The Fisherman' politically inert and picturesque. In this respect, Yeats would seem to share Arnold's conviction that Ireland should be 'a nation poetically only, not politically'. There seems to be little evidence to suggest that Yeats ever seriously entertained the idea of Ireland's political separation from Britain.

Luke Gibbons has argued persuasively that 'many of the concepts requisitioned by nationalist propagandists in defence of Irish culture are, in fact, an extension of colonialism, rather than a repudiation of it'. This suggestion throws into doubt the kind of nationalist resistance that Said detects in the early writings of Yeats. Gibbons maintains that the Celtic revival owed as much to 'the benevolent colonialism' of Matthew Arnold as it did to 'the inner recesses of the hidden Ireland'. He shows how readily the Arnoldian stereotype was taken to heart by the Irish revivalists and how, even now, historians like Sheridan Gilley continue to regard that stereotyping as benign. As a valuable antidote to the pervasive Celticism of the late nineteenth century, Gibbons cites the work of George Sigerson, who 'sought to remove the racial epithet "Celtic" entirely from the cultural canon, arguing that Irishness incorporated the residue of several cultural or "racial" strains, as befitted a country exposed to successive waves of invasion and internal strife over the centuries'.[21]

Celticism, like nationalism, is an untrustworthy essence and yet it continues to exert a powerful cultural appeal. It is an irony frequently associated with national and cultural identities that Celticism can function variably as both the construct of the oppressor and as an authentic sign of selfhood. Like those other identities, Celticism has often invited antagonism, relying upon continued opposition for any secure definition of itself. One set of images begets another; one mythology competes with another. Declan Kiberd's magisterial book *Inventing Ireland* (1995) shows all too clearly how the strategy of occupying and reclaiming existing images of identity and nationality can have both positive and negative consequences. The Irish encounter with the Celtic spirit has been an enchanting source of inspiration, but it has also had its disabling and alienating effects. Any new and lasting definition of Ireland and Irishness must reach beyond the potent myths on which the mystique of Celticism has been nourished and sustained.

NOTES

1. Ernest Renan, *The Poetry of the Celtic Races*, London, 1896, p. 8.
2. Ibid., p. 80.
3. L.P. Curtis, *Apes and Angels: The Irishman in Victorian Caricature*, Newton Abbott, 1971, pp. vii, 19.
4. Matthew Arnold, 'Culture and Anarchy', in R.H. Super, ed., *Complete Prose Works*, Ann Arbor, 1965, pp. 349, 395.
5. Arnold, 'On the Study of Celtic Literature', in *Complete Prose Works*, pp. 349, 395.
6. Ibid., pp. 303, 361, 395.
7. Ibid., pp. 347, 302, 383.
8. Ibid., pp. 386, 384.
9. Seamus Deane, *Celtic Revivals*, London, 1985, p. 25.
10. Arnold, 'English Literature and Irish Politics', in *Complete Prose Works*, pp. 246, 262.
11. Deane, *Celtic Revivals*, p. 27.
12. Arnold, 'From Easter to August', *The Nineteenth Century*, 22 September, 1887, p. 321.
13. Quoted by Michael S. Helfand and Philip E. Smith in 'Anarchy and Culture: The Evolutionary Turn of Cultural Criticism in the Work of Oscar Wilde', *Texas Studies in Literature and Language*, 20 (1978),

    p. 203.

14.   Ibid., pp. 203-4.

15.   Terry Eagleton, *Saint Oscar*, Derry, 1989, p. viii.

16.   Declan Kiberd, 'The London Exiles: Wilde and Shaw', in Seamus Deane, ed., *The Field Day Anthology of Irish Writing*, Derry, 1991, Vol. II, pp. 373-75.

17.   Oscar Wilde, rev. *The Two Chiefs of Dunboy* by J A Froude, reprinted in *The Field Day Anthology of Irish Writing*, Vol. II, pp. 380-3.

18.   W.B. Yeats, eds. George Bornstein and High Witemeyer, *Letters to the New Island*, London, 1989, p. 30.

19.   Edward Said, *Yeats and Decolonization*, Derry, 1988, p. 8.

20.   John Kelly and Eric Domville, eds., *The Collected Letters of W B Yeats*, Vol. I: 1865-95, Oxford, 1986, p. 338.

21.   Luke Gibbons, 'Race Against Time: Racial Discourse and Irish History', *Oxford Literary Review*, 13 (1991), pp. 104-5. Gibbons (both here and in *The Field Day Anthology of Irish Writing*) argues that Sigerson's influence should not be underestimated. It is clearly evident, for instance, in Thomas MacDonagh's *Literature in Ireland*, published posthumously after the author's execution as one of the leaders of the 1916 Rising.

5

W B Yeats:
Poetry, Politics, *Responsibilities*

Richard Greaves

Seamus Heaney speaks in *The Redress of Poetry* (1990) of the claims made by poets for poetry set against Plato's 'calling into question whatever special prerogatives or even useful influences poetry would claim for itself within the *polis*'.[1] Poetry faces the problem of maintaining a position where it is treated seriously while keeping that distance from society which allows it to offer difference, to operate as a sort of counter-reality. The other side to this is that Liberal society can *contain* poetry by an acceptance of the poet's right to say what others cannot. The granting to poetry of its freedom entails its social neutralisation: it is entitled to its different view because it is *merely* poetry. It is worth remembering here Donald Davie's point about the awarding of the Bollingen prize to Pound for *The Pisan Cantos*, that it confirmed American society's recognition of 'an absolute discontinuity between the life of the poet and the life of the man', and that the privilege so extended to the poet is 'the privilege of the pariah'.[2] As Adorno said of art: 'If it lets go of autonomy it sells out to the established order, whereas if it tries to stay strictly within its autonomous confines it becomes equally co-optable, living a harmless life in its appointed niche.'[3] The problem of what J.M. Bernstein calls 'aesthetic alienation' is only half the problem, or really, is only half a *problem*. According to Bernstein,

> Modernity is the separation of spheres, the becoming autonomous of truth, beauty and goodness from one another and their developing into self-sufficient forms of practice: modern science and technology, private morality and modern legal forms, and modern art.[4]

But if society is to escape the constant regeneration of the same, then this capacity of art to be other is necessary.

In *Poems Written in Discouragement*, a small pamphlet of five poems composed in response to the Hugh Lane gallery controversy, Yeats's concern that art should present an ideal to which the world might aspire is clear. 'To a Wealthy Man' and 'To a Shade' suggest that through exposure to the best art can offer, society can transcend itself. In taking part in a public controversy, Yeats establishes himself as a poet who insists on the right of art to affect society in the way proper to art. Art has the potential to transform reality by maintaining both its difference from and its relation to reality. In dealing with public affairs and yet steadfastly maintaining his personal vision, Yeats believed in this potential of art. This stance is, of course, fundamentally undemocratic, and can be said to insist on the right of an elite to dictate to the masses because the elite knows what is best for all. Yeats's espousal of the Anglo-Irish 'Big House' in the form of Coole (note, for instance, the elitist tone of a poem like 'Upon a House shaken by the Land Agitation') makes him vulnerable to the charge that the *noblesse oblige* kind of view is self-deluding. As Michael North points out, 'What the aristocracy gives had first to be taken, and the material independence of the class is not in fact the basis of its service to the community but rather a result of its exploitation.'[5] So, the aristocrat merely gives back by his grace and favour a little of what his ancestors appropriated in the first place. Heaney, in his 1978 lecture 'Yeats as Example?', defends Yeats: 'he donned the mantle - or perhaps one should say the fur coat - of the aristocrat so that he might express a vision of a communal and personal life that was ample, generous, harmonious, fulfilled and enhancing'[6]:

> But it is a later comment of Heaney's which I want to take up: in terms of the writer conducting himself in a politicised milieu, I think Yeats becomes important within that milieu not so much for what he says as for who he is. Within a culture the most important thing for the poet is to establish authority, and Yeats had the gift of establishing authority: first of all by achievement, but secondly by a conduct which was 'majestic' in some kind of way and overbearing to some extent but based upon a belief in the culture. He could rebuke the culture because he was its most intense representative to some extent. And I think that the poet has not to get caught in a position where he is answerable to the politician but where in some way the politician is under his spiritual gaze. Now that is what is exemplary about Yeats, but also what is very difficult to achieve for a writer in contemporary Ireland.[7]

'Most intense representative' strays towards fascist theory, and we should not forget, when pondering the influence Yeats may have had in Ireland, just how unpopular he was there at times. But the point here is that the effect of the poetry is not totally contained within the words on the page. Yeats's position as a man in relation to his society (as well as to literary culture) contributes to the effect of his poetry, and since this position was consciously achieved, constitutes part of the work. The difficulty Heaney notices is that which the writer faces in trying to bring the force of symbolic capital to bear outside the sphere of art. On one hand, late twentieth-century criticism is not to be fooled by the artist's claim to disinterestedness; on the other, the recognition of the

41

political element in all social matters can promote politics to a position where art becomes marginal and trivial. At the same time, the discrediting of the concept of authority and leadership by fascist politics and their culmination in the Holocaust renders the authority of the poet suspect, even as an aim.

There is a retrospective element to Heaney's comment. Hostility to Yeats in the Irish nationalist press in the early years of this century shows how difficult it is for the poet to maintain the necessary distance from society. The response to his work is something over which he does not have control, though he may try to manipulate it. If his work is to be vital, it will touch on social and political realities, and people will respond in terms of these, refusing, as they would see it, to allow the licence demanded by the artist. D.P. Moran in the *Leader* indicates a strong feeling that Yeats was peddling a form of pseudo-Irishness to an English audience.[8] Even Standish O'Grady was upset:

> You are at one with me about the iniquity of the tourist movement and the exploitation for commercial purposes of the beauty of our country. Yet holding such opinions you bring us all - we who in some poor way stand for Ireland - over to London and trot us round for the delectation of your clever London friends whose favourable opinion we don't want and can do very well without.[9]

The delightfully named Eugenia Brooks Frothingham's response to Yeats's visit to America in 1903 shows that Irish people had a right to be suspicious about the encouragement of stereotypes by Irish writers selling to a foreign market: 'The Irishman is a creature of delicious extravagance, who has always cultivated the lovely folly at the expense of the potato patch. May he long continue to do so!'[10]

A 1903 article in the *Leader* points to a difference between Yeats's claimed idealism and the reality of his commercially motivated practice in reproducing in *Ideas of Good and Evil* articles previously published in London reviews. Part of its complaint is that Yeats is accepted abroad as representative of Ireland. The article refers to a review of *Ideas of Good and Evil* in the *Saturday Review*:

> It is not at all mortifying to find the giant labours of the Gaelic League not merely ignored, but apparently not so much as known; to find a 'movement' conducted exclusively in the English language, and to no slight degree in the London press, posing and passing as an 'Irish Keltic' movement! This is one of the things that come from having a group of over-adroit literary self-advertisers and 'movement' exploiters frisking about on the fringe of our forces. But an indication like this of the *Saturday* man's has its uses. It teaches us how much is really known about Ireland over-sea, and shrewdly instructs us in a sense of the value of letting Mr Yeats mix himself up with us.[11]

42

The difficult relationship of art with the world in which it is produced is indicated in the method of this article's attack. To accuse Yeats of commercial motivation diminishes his claim to credit as an artist. Yeats's own realisation of the need of the artist to distance himself from commercial considerations is shown by his comments on the necessity of leisure to art and his ideas on patronage. The imputation to Yeats of commercial motivation in his publishing practice threatens the symbolic capital he has accumulated by his refusal to seek commercial success through deliberately catering to a mass audience.[12] Further, the separation of poetry from the 'real world', its trivialisation as entertainment (probably for a London drawing-room), was a means of marginalising Yeats which, if he sought to maintain the claims of art dependent on its distance from the imperatives of political expediency, it was difficult for him to defend himself against.

The poem 'To a Wealthy Man' was published first in the *Irish Times*. The influence of Yeats's visit to Italy and his reading of Castiglione is clear. The wealthy man is attacked partly for his refusal of that element of risk involved in *sprezzatura*, and his care for the judgement of those who are not his equals. He betrays his position as leader by seeking to follow the opinion of the masses, who should be led. The anti-democratic note of the poem is one that highlights Yeats's view that democratic art is impossible. 'What the blind and ignorant town. Imagines best to make it thrive',[13] cannot be what is best for it, since it is not only ignorant, but also fallen into the materialism and the seeking of an immediate goal which makes impossible the realisation in the future of any goal not currently visible: the exclusive pursuit of the immediately attainable renders impossible the improvement, the transcendence, of present culture. This transcendence may be possible through the aspiration towards that imaginative ideal which the best art places before society.

Yeats, to some extent, fixed the context of his poem. He suggested to Joseph Hone the lines of an article which Hone wrote and which appeared on the opposite page.[14] Hone's article claimed that the gallery project gave 'the gentlemen of Ireland' an opportunity to show leadership. The idea, shared by Synge, that the old politically ascendant class could and should assume cultural leadership now that their political power had waned is evident in Hone's piece.[15] It is also possible to see in the article one of Yeats's developing narratives, that of the decline of the Anglo-Irishry which had its glorious moment in the eighteenth century, but has the opportunity of taking the lead in something which rises above the 'filthy modern tide' of mass nationalist politics and bourgeois commercialism. Underneath the poem is a list of further subscriptions to the gallery and a letter supporting the project. The publication of 'September 1913' in the *Irish Times* was a similar case, with a supportive editorial (arising from an interview between Yeats and Hone) appearing opposite the poem, and two letters of support underneath. A letter opposing the gallery from the dreaded William Martin Murphy (an enemy of Yeats) is bumped onto the following page.[16]

It was impossible by this time for Yeats to have identified himself completely with the mass nationalist cause. In 1912, for instance, Yeats asked Edward Martyn if a *rapprochement* with the Roman Catholic Church was possible. Martyn thought not.[17] In any case, this would, in his terms, to have been to make of his poetry an abstraction, the expression of a cause, the thought common to many rather than the expression of the individual. Yet by establishing *himself* as a public figure, involved in controversy, and by maintaining the link between himself and the figure of Yeats who inhabits the poems, he was able to mediate between the world of art and the everyday world while retaining the necessary distance between them. Through his poetry and his involvement in public controversy Yeats created *himself* as a figure embodying particular values. In constructing this public figure of the poet, Yeats is true to his idea of the poet in an earlier lecture:

A poet is by the very nature of things a man who lives with entire sincerity, or rather the better his poetry the more sincere his life; his life is an experiment in living and those that come after have a right to know it. Above all it is necessary that the lyric poet's life should be known that we should understand that his poetry is no rootless flower but the speech of a man.[18]

But the reader now encounters these poems as part of *Responsibilities*. The volume's opening poem, 'Pardon, old fathers' addresses as one possible audience the poet's ancestors.[19] He distances himself from the lower middle class which he despises, distinguishing between the 'merchant' and 'traders' from whom he is descended, and the huckster by whose type his blood has not been tainted. Although the poem is an apology to his ancestors, there is a hint of equivocation between life, represented by procreation, and the work, represented by the book. The volume continues to establish an unresolved debate between the virtues of life and those of art, and between life limited by mortality and eternal life. In the Cuala Press *Responsibilities*, 'Pardon, old fathers' and the closing 'While I, from that reed-throated whisperer' are distinguished from the rest of the volume by red italics, providing a personal frame which dramatises the volume as the utterance - the performance - of the poet they construct. 'Pardon, old fathers' addresses Yeats's ancestors, but particularly *his* conception of them, with an emphasis on how he would like to see them, and an effort to identify them - and so himself - with a particular class, and so with a particular set of values. There is a willed quality to the past from which he wants the figure created in the

44

poems, and identified with himself, to be descended. The past is itself a projection associated with his history, built from the material of his history, but suffused with, and inspired, by a set of values consciously arrived at.

In the *Responsibilities* volume, two long poems, 'The Grey Rock' and 'The Two Kings' follow 'Pardon, Old Fathers', immediately preceding the five *Poems Written in Discouragement*. 'The Grey Rock' dramatises its poet in italicised passages which are frankly personal.[20] The creation in this way of a second level recalls 'The Old Age of Queen Maeve' and 'Baile and Aillinn', but in addressing the poem to his former companions in the Rhymers' Club, Yeats identifies the dramatised poet more closely, more clearly, with himself. The poem gains poignancy from the emphasis on the poet's aloneness as survivor of his poetic generation. The sacrifice of easy friendship for the sake of that association with immortality which contributing to true art confers is heightened for Yeats because the friends who shared his artistic standard are dead.

Some difficulty in finding a satisfying reading of the poem arises from the obvious appeal of the heroic action of the warrior Aoife loves. But the appeal to this form of the heroic is the popular appeal the poet rejects: in allowing his story to do justice to the appeal of physical heroism, the poet stresses the difficulty of this rejection. The poem compares Maud Gonne with Aoife, and so the poet keeps faith with his muse, with art, rather than being seduced by the appeal of the heroic, which would have kept him in better repute with the mass of the people. The keeping of faith with art and with his nationalism can be reconciled, in fact are one, provided it is remembered that the mass nationalist cause is something different again. The poem gains a sense of nobility from the integrity shown in keeping faith with a love that has been, in a physical sense, 'a barren passion', and with an ideal nationalism, closely tied to art, which means the rejection of popular appeal and the acceptance of ill-fame. The need the eternal world has of the temporal and the attraction the temporal world holds for the eternal is illustrated in Aoife's complaint of the mortal love who has accepted his mortality and rejected her.

'The Two Kings' tells the story of the conflict of King Eochaid and his wife Edain with a figure who had been her husband in her former, supernatural existence. Eochaid battles this figure in the form of a white stag, which vanishes once he has overcome it.[21] Edain debates the relative merits of love in the temporal and the eternal worlds with her former husband, arguing that love must be built on the risk of loss if it is to be love. She uses a spatial metaphor for time:

What can they know of love that do not know
She builds her nest upon a narrow ledge
Above a windy precipice?[22]

Love must be founded above (in a sense, necessarily in spite of) the void of ultimate nothingness. This is its miraculous quality. Love gains intensity from the limitation of time in the mortal world, from the inevitability of its passing. Yet that possibility of ultimate nothingness must be acknowledged, confronted.

'The Grey Rock' and 'The Two Kings' both concern the contact of the mortal and immortal worlds. In the first poem, the poet tells a story of commitment to the mortal world, and the value conferred on life by heroic death, by the acceptance of risk and the refusal of the immortal lover. Having told this story, the poet affirms his own commitment to the eternal. 'The Two Kings' similarly tells the story of commitment to the mortal world, this time on the part of Edain, and the value conferred on love in the mortal world by the inevitability of death, by the limit placed on its duration which is the source of its intensity.[23] In the second poem there is no second level in which the poet rejects this commitment to the mortal world. In allowing the claims of the mortal to prevail, the poem effectively takes the opposite stance to that of 'The Grey Rock'. The mortal and immortal worlds are shown as antithetical in both poems, and this continues a theme begun much earlier. Taken together the poems indicate the attraction exerted on the poet by mortal and immortal, and his need to create his work from the tension and conflict generated by these opposite forces of attraction. The poet is a creature of the margins, caught between two worlds.[24]

The poet's ultimate commitment is to his poetry, and this must contain the antithesis generated by mortal and immortal - or perhaps not 'contain', but allow the play of - and between life and art. To claim an absolute correspondence between the immortal world and art would be to oversimplify, but the association of the two suggests an interesting consequence of the view of the poet as inhabiting the space between opposing worlds. The poet must feel the claims of art *and* life. Though he cannot allow the values of art to be subject to worldly values, he cannot allow that art is entirely autonomous, completely separated from the life which is the source of its intensity. Yet he must also be aware of the incompatibility of the values of art and worldly values. The reconciliation of these opposing sets of values would deny the power of art to indict the world for its narrownesses, its failure to allow full play to human potential. But from *The Wanderings of Oisin* on, the theme of the other, immortal, world is not a utopian theme; Yeats seems always to acknowledge the possibility that it is empty, that it merely has a pernicious effect on happiness in the mortal world. On a personal level, the poems cannot be read as literal autobiography, but this is not to say that they have no connection at all with the poet's biography. The relationship between the poet's art and his biography is problematic: it is not an exact correspondence, nor is it non-

46

existent. The two narrative poems at the head of *Responsibilities* establish a debate which finds no resolution. They cast a light by which other poems in the volume can be read.

NOTES

1. Seamus Heaney, *The Redress of Poetry*, Oxford, 1990, pp. 1-2.
2. Donald Davie, *Ezra Pound: Poet as Sculptor*, New York, 1964, p. 242. See also Humphrey Carpenter, *A Serious Character: The Life of Ezra Pound*, London, 1988, p. 792.
3. T.W. Adorno, trans. C Lenhardt, eds. Gretel Adorno and Rolf Tiedemann, *Aesthetic Theory*, London, 1984, p. 337.
4. J.M. Bernstein, *The Fate of Art: Aesthetic Alienation from Kant to Derrida and Adorno*, Cambridge, 1992, pp. 5-6.
5. Michael North, *The Political Aesthetic of Yeats, Eliot, and Pound*, Cambridge, 1991, p. 41.
6. Seamus Heaney, *Preoccupations: Selected Prose 1968-1978*, London, 1980, p. 108. The fur coat refers to George Moore's attack on Yeats's scorn of the middle class, to which, Moore points out, he belongs. See Moore, *Hail and Farewell: Ave, Salve, Vale.* ed. Richard Cave, Gerrards Cross, 1976, pp. 540-1.
7. Quoted by Ronald Schuchard, from a conversation with Richard Ellmann filmed by radio Telefis Eireann for their programme 'Joyce, Yeats and Wilde' (1982), in his introduction to Heaney, *The Place of Writing*, Atlanta, 1989, p. 11.
8. See, for instance, 'At the Abbey Theatre', *Leader*, 7 January 1905, pp. 330-1.
9. O'Grady, editorial comment following Yeats's 'A Postscript to a Forthcoming Book of Essays by Various Writers', *All Ireland Review*, 1 December 1900, p. 6.
10. E. Brooks Frothingham, 'An Irish Poet and His Work', *The Critic*, New York, 4:1 (1904), pp. 26-31, 27.
11. 'Imaal', 'A Rather Complex Personality', *Leader*, 26 September 1903, p. 72.
12. See also Pierre Bourdieu, trans. Richard Nice, 'The Field of Cultural Production, or: The Economic World Reversed', *Poetics*, 12 (1983), pp. 311-56.
13. *The Variorum Edition of the Poems of W B Yeats*, Peter Allt and Russell K Alspach, eds., New York, 1957, p. 287.

14. Joseph Hone, 'Art and Aristocracy', *Irish Times*, 11 January 1913, p. 6. Yeats indicated in a letter to Lady Gregory dated 14 January 1913 that he had 'suggested ... the lines of' the article. See 'Some New Letters from W B Yeats to Lady Gregory', in Donald T Torchiana and Glann O'Malley, eds., *A Review of English Literature*, 4 (1963), pp. 9-47, 16.

15. See Synge, 'Good Pictures in Dublin', *Manchester Guardian*, 24 January 1908, collected in Alan Price, ed., *Collected Works*, London, 1966, pp. 390-2.

16. *Irish Times*, 8 September 1913. See also Torchiana and O'Malley, 'Some New Letters' p. 40.

17. See James W. Flannery, *W B Yeats and the Idea of a Theatre: The Early Abbey Theatre in Theory and Practice*, New Haven and London, 1976, p. 337.

18. From Yeats's notes to his lecture 'Friends of My Youth', ed. Joseph Ronsley, in Robert O'Driscoll and Lorna Reynolds, eds., *Yeats and the Theatre*, London, 1975, pp. 60-81, 74. The lecture was given on 9 March 1910.

19. *The Variorum Edition of the Poems of W B Yeats*, pp. 269-70.

20. Ibid., pp. 270-6.

21. Ibid., pp. 276-86.

22. Ibid., p. 285.

23. Yeats's source for the story of 'The Two Kings' was 'The History of Ailell and Etain', trans. and ed. Eduard Muller, *Revue Celtique*, 3 (1876-8), pp. 355-60. This version places more emphasis on Etain's wish to stay with Eochaid than does Lady Gregory's 'Midhir and Etain' in her *Gods and Fighting Men*, London, 1904, pp. 88-100.

24. See Warwick Gould, 'An Empty Theatre? Yeats as Minstrel in 'Responsibilities', in Jacqueline Genet, ed., *Studies on W B Yeats*, London, 1989, pp. 79-118, 89.

6

'The Very Best Kind of Fiction': James Owen Hannay, 'George A Birmingham', and the Gaelic League

Eileen Reilly

An examination of the numbers of novels produced in Ireland at the turn of the century gives a clear indication of a literate market and an appetite for fiction.[1] This appetite was catered for by numerous Irish novelists publishing romantic fiction, humorous stories, historical and political novels. For many the urge to write and publish fiction was an economic one - a viable means of supplementing salaries, and in the case of women writers, of establishing an independent income.[2] In addition to the economic incentive, many writers indulged their desire to preach, to moralise, to direct and to instruct. The novel was perceived as an ideal medium to examine contemporary issues of politics, identity, society and culture. James Owen Hannay writing as 'George A Birmingham' was one such author.[3] His first novels clearly demonstrated the desire to write fiction with contemporary resonance. Dealing with politics, religion and society, these novels caused great controversy: this resulted in what Hannay saw as the baser side of Irish life attacking him personally and unfairly for his assessments of Irish society. The discord caused by his novels had larger ramifications. It provoked a crisis within the Gaelic League, an organisation which was founded upon the principles of maintaining a non-sectarian and non-political position in its drive to resurrect the Gaelic language. Birmingham's novels led directly to a campaign by members of the Catholic clergy to drive him out of the League. They succeeded. His experience revealed the hollowness of the non-sectarian stance; the Catholic clergy threw down the gauntlet and the League refused the challenge. Douglas Hyde, the President of the Gaelic League, was dismayed by the Hannay controversy and feared its consequences; he believed that offering a challenge to the Catholic priests would split the movement and end the chance to revive the language. Hyde urged Hannay to resist such a confrontation for the sake of the League's survival. While doubting the wisdom of strategic retreats, he obeyed and let the issue dissipate. The significance of this controversy lay not only in exposing the League as a body which tacitly admitted the power of the Catholic clergy and could not defend its principle of non-sectarianism, it also revealed the impact and power of the novel.

From an Ulster unionist background, James Owen Hannay had emerged at the turn of the century as a decisive commentator on, and supporter of the ideals of the Gaelic League. Hannay described himself at this point in his life as a cultural nationalist: one who believed in the essential uniqueness of Irish culture but had little difficulty in reconciling that with the larger political union of Great Britain and Ireland. This did not exclude support for a limited measure of home rule. He believed that Ireland suffered from twin tyrannies: the despotism of the Catholic church and the autocracy of the political demagogue. It was his ardent hope that movements such as the Gaelic League and Arthur Griffith's Sinn Féin would result in a greater independence of thought and action leading to religious and cultural harmony among the Irish people. As a clergyman in the Church of Ireland Hannay was in a prime position to defend the League from suspicion and criticism among his co-religionists. He energetically repudiated Protestant censure of the League within the *Church of Ireland Gazette* and soon entered the fray in other publications. His enthusiasm for the League and its ideals soon earned him the sobriquet of Hyde's 'lieutenant'. Hannay's early secular writings were limited to journalistic forays on behalf of the League but growing experience and confidence led him to comment upon varied subjects such as the agricultural problems of the west of Ireland, and economic and social issues. His journalism was prolific, popular, and an important part of his career throughout his life, but he is best remembered as the novelist 'George A Birmingham'.

The publication of his first novel, *The Seething Pot*, in 1905 was an important advance for Hannay. His apprenticeship in journalism had resulted in a seasoned assurance in his writings and he was determined to comment at length upon Irish society through the popular medium of the novel. A more practical reason for a clergyman in a poor parish with a growing family was the financial emolument. Although Hannay had written numerous articles under his own name he chose to publish his first novel under the pseudonym 'George A Birmingham', in order to keep distinct his church life from his life as an author. It may be that he astutely assumed a second identity in anticipation of a reaction to his novels, but it is unlikely that he had any inkling of the controversy they would cause. The first three novels, *The Seething Pot*, (1905), *Hyacinth*, (1906), and *Benedict Kavanagh* (1906) were intended as serious commentaries upon Irish society and politics.[4] His primary motive in writing them is clear from his anxiety that his first manuscript had elevated the political text at the expense of plot and character. He was amply reassured by his brother-in-law F.E. Wynne who wrote that the manuscript of *The Seething Pot* was a commendable novel while simultaneously praising him for the political nature of the fiction:

The character of the hero, the dilemma which you construed for him ... and the use you make of the actually existing cross-currents of political thought in Ireland are all the very best kind of fiction. Of course it solves no problem; its strength is that it does not attempt to. But it is an altogether admirable 'enunciation' of the problem that waits solution.[5]

The Seething Pot diagnosed political and cultural problems but did not offer a panacea. Its primary theme was the illustration of a double dilemma: the persistent decline of paternal authority on the part of the Irish ascendancy, leaving a political and ethical vacuum which the clergy of the Catholic church were aggressively occupying. Pessimistic in its conclusion, it averred that political initiatives were futile given the power of clericalism and the discord among contending forces at work in the country. With his first serious attempt at writing fiction, Hannay had produced a novel which assessed the inflexibility of a society based on class and religion. His personal experiences were soon to illustrate clearly to him just how intractable that society could be. His next novels, *Hyacinth* and *Benedict Kavanagh* were more contemporary in their settings and more optimistic in their treatment of Irish society. Politics were abandoned in favour of themes of national regeneration and reconciliation as the fruit of a new spirit informing Irish society, that of the Gaelic League. Hannay had considered introducing the League or at least its philosophies to *The Seething Pot*, but hesitated to misplace it in an earlier era and was anxious that, as his first novel was decidedly political in subject and treatment, the League with its non-political character would have been well and truly excluded. Both *Hyacinth* and *Benedict Kavanagh* reflected the non-sectarian and non-political stance of the League in the quest for an auspicious accord between all Irish people. Although Hannay was seeking a somewhat utopian Irish society in his fiction, confidently expounding his vision of an order informed by the enlightened ideals of the League, his own personal experiences were a direct result of his novels and revealed a truly intractable reality.

The identity of the enigmatic 'George A Birmingham' had largely remained unknown with the exception of some close friends like T.W. Rolleston. Exposure was inevitable; with the imminent publication of *Hyacinth*, Hannay was unmasked at a gathering in Dublin where he had spoken on the subject of Irish fiction. Censure and recrimination followed. At first the controversy was localised in Hannay's parish of Westport and took the form of attacks in the local newspaper from the parish priest, MacDonald. The latter was incensed by the character of the priest in *The Seething Pot* whom he believed was a vulgar caricature of himself. Claiming the credit for unmasking Hannay as the

51

nefarious author of 'gross libels' and 'virulent attacks', MacDonald dominated
the local newspaper, the *Mayo News*, with letters and articles expressing his fury
at Hannay's 'calumny' upon himself and attacks 'on the position and influence
of the Catholic Church in Ireland' which MacDonald was sure any 'intelligent
reader' would recognise as vitriolic.[6] Intelligent readers were lacking. What
was clear in the ensuing crusade against Hannay was the pride taken by his
antagonists in claiming that they had not read the books. Rather, they relied
upon the extracts quoted by MacDonald and reiterated his criticisms. MacDonald's articles were followed by resolutions from the local government boards
demanding his resignation from his position as chaplain to the local workhouse.
Various members of these boards made fiery speeches calling for action
including pitching him in the local river. The resolutions and the language in
which they were expressed placed the local conflict in a wider arena. Charles
Craig, Member of Parliament for Antrim asked the Chief Secretary for Ireland
in the House of Commons if Hannay would be dismissed as chaplain and if it
was advisable to offer him police protection. The press in England and Ireland
began to cover the controversy. Many of the Irish newspapers agreed with
MacDonald that the novels were sectarian attacks on the Catholic church, but
many saw that Hannay, while certainly critical of the Catholic clergy, was also
openly censorious and satirical in his treatment of his own class and creed.
What was more significant was the defence of Hannay and his novels offered
by those who disagreed with him but supported the right to free speech. In the
preface to *Benedict Kavanagh*, published towards the end of 1906, Hannay
commented upon the controversy making particular reference in this issue:

> Shortly after the publication of my last novel I received a letter from a wise
> friend who had read the book. 'They will blast your Hyacinth', he wrote,
> 'by setting its roots in a Seething Pot.' The prophecy was half fulfilled.
> The roots were set in a pot seething with acrimonious controversy. But the
> plant itself survived. It even benefited by the treatment. The outpourings
> of angry men were not unlike a fertiliser, unsavoury to handle, but beneficial
> to the life of the plant. I suffered for a time from a fear that I had been
> guilty of exaggerating the grotesqueness of the baser side of Irish life. I now
> know that neither I nor anyone else could be guilty of such an exaggeration.
> But there is another side of Irish life which is not base. The controversy
> over my books has helped me to realise more clearly than ever before how
> fine a love of liberty, how broad a tolerance for honest opinion, there is
> among Irishmen of to-day. In papers which represent the opposite poles of
> opinion my books were dealt with freely and critically. The *Church of
> Ireland Gazette* and the *United Irishman*, the *Northern Whig* and the *Irish
> Peasant* are miles apart from each other in policy. The writers of their

reviews and articles were all of them out of sympathy with much that I wrote. But they and many other admitted frankly the principle that an author should have freedom to express his opinions.[7]

Hannay had optimistically lauded what he saw as love of liberty and tolerance in Irish life but it was another aspect of Irish life which continued to rear its head. Previously confined to the printed word, the controversy assumed a more personal character. Hannay wrote to a friend that MacDonald had organised men to heckle him at a local League feis. Priests ostentatiously ignored him. While MacDonald and his supporters certainly made life unpleasant for Hannay and his family the larger significance of the conflict with the clergy lay in the implications it held for the Gaelic League. It was imperative for the survival of the movement in Hyde's view to ward off any confrontation with the priests. Although ostensibly a non-sectarian body, in reality the influence of the Catholic clergy could make or break the League. Hyde anxiously advised Hannay:

If the status quo could be sustained for another five years, how strong we would be then to fight if a breach *should* come ... They are and will be for the next fifty years (unless a strong Home Rule Bill is passed) the dominating factor in Irish life ... Make them feel that the League is theirs and do nothing to frighten them off ... avoid all friction for as long as possible.[8]

Hannay's reply to Hyde affirmed his obedience in matters pertaining to the League. He was anxious himself to minimise his experiences and to avoid provoking a power struggle. While agreeing with Hyde that the priests were a powerful clique, he voiced doubts at the feasibility of Hyde's policy. 'Your policy is no doubt the right one. But can you carry it out? In the long run the two forces must clash ... I trust and hope that in this matter I am a fool but frankly I don't believe it is possible'.[9] Despite his best efforts to avoid confrontation the crux came at the end of September at a League meeting held in Claremorris to arrange the 1907 Connaught Feis. Twenty-two delegates attended; of these five were Catholic clergymen including the chairman, Canon Macken of Tuam, a close friend of MacDonald's. As a member of the central executive, the Coisde Gnótha, Hannay also attended the meeting. Mr Hamilton of Tuam proposed that all present together with one representative from each branch, two from each Coisde Ceanntair, and two from each Feis committee not represented form the executive Committee. Macken objected but refused to give a reason. An amendment was subsequently proposed which had the direct effect of excluding Hannay from the Executive Committee. When members insisted on an explanation Macken stated that he could not work with Hannay. This was a direct breach of the League's constitution as many of the members there indignantly pointed out. Macken was adamant; he declared that he did not hold himself 'bound down in matters of principle by the constitution of the Gaelic

League. There is a higher constitution which I look to'. He accused Hannay of trampling 'on the deepest sentiments and aspirations of Catholics and Irishmen ... That is my reason for objecting'.[10] The subject of this heated debate attempted gracefully to defuse the situation by supporting the amendment which was carried with two dissenters, both of whom were Catholic priests enraged by Macken's action. The conflict did not end there despite Hannay's best efforts. It was the latest in a series of clerical incidents which had occurred over the previous two years. Could the League in the light of this most recent incident refrain from addressing the problem of clerical power?

The *Peasant* felt the answer was obvious. If Canon Macken did not consider himself bound by the constitution of the League, he should not be a member of that body. The official organ of the League, *An Claidheamh Soluis*, was more emphatic. 'We should be untrue to ourselves and to the trust reposed in the organisation if we did not protest with all the vehemence of which we are capable'.[11] The editor of the latter, Patrick Pearse, had not consulted with the League's president before taking this stance. Hyde's policy was one of caution and conciliation despite the long-term implications of succumbing to clerical autocracy. While careful not to dictate a course of action he made his wishes clear to Hannay:

With regard to his action I agree with you that he had no right to take the chair and to say that he was a law unto himself. I hope Gaelic Leaguers will never give him the chance again. Of course I would not dream of presuming to advise you what to do in this matter, but if I consulted my own wishes and feelings I would be glad if the affair were not pushed, for many reasons. *First* there is a growing feeling of lay liberty in all affairs, you can see it yourself, but a vehement struggle over this question now will make people take sides and harden into parties, much to Ireland's detriment ... This incident certainly gives good grounds for raising the whole question of clerical tyranny, but I would sooner not see it raised all the same.[12]

Hannay was angry and hurt. Privately, he felt that the issue had gone beyond simple personal hostility and that it was 'in reality a question between the fundamental axes of Protestantism and Romanism'. No longer was it solely a conflict centred on his books or opinions for which he had been criticised by 'my own clergy and people'. Those criticisms had been based on what his detractors regarded as the unjustifiable nature of his opinions. The attacks by the Catholic clergy he regarded as blatant sectarianism. Despite his personal feelings he recognised Hyde's position although privately he doubted the 'wisdom of retreating from point to point ... it is ill fighting with soldiers who have got into a fixed habit of making strategic movements to the rear'.[13]

Publicly, Hannay was most unwilling to play the role of sectarian martyr and depreciated the seriousness of the issue to the point of joking about it in the press.[14] Even if Hannay's public persona was unsuccessfully trying to belittle the significance of the conflict, other members of the League were outraged and horrified by the incident. The controversy raged among Gaelic Leaguers, between nationalists and unionists, and in the English and Irish press. Horace Plunkett, Francis Sheehy Skeffington, Peadar McGinley and Alice Stopford Green wrote to Hannay expressing their support. McGinley was most indignant: 'It is still too easy to get up a sectarian cry in Ireland'.[15] Many newspapers and journals seized on the proceedings to argue that the League was riddled with intolerance and sectarianism; the *Daily Express* argued that Hannay's case proved that it was impossible to be a member of the Gaelic League and preserve 'liberty of thought, action, or criticism'.[16] Hannay attempted to alleviate the situation despite his misgivings about Hyde's policy by voluntarily resigning from the Coisde Gnótha. He also wrote a letter to the *Church of Ireland Gazette* asserting that Macken did not represent League opinion. He agreed with Sinn Féin that what was under attack was the principle of free speech and that the Gaelic League had been basely used as the instrument of the attack. He appealed to the public, and most pointedly to Irish Protestants, to read a selection of Irish papers and to judge the incident for themselves.[17] Initially Hannay was hopeful that public outcry would persuade Hyde and the executive committee of the League to take definite action against Macken and the ecclesiastical tyranny which he represented. Hyde obstinately remained committed to his cautious policy of circumvention. His tactic was to wait until the issue had waned and dissipated; the central executive at its meeting to discuss the issue agreed to postpone action for a year. In Hyde's view the policy was vindicated. As emotions cooled, interest and pressure declined until it was all but forgotten. Hyde had successfully evaded challenging the clergy and provoking an inevitably damaging, perhaps fatal, split. The only casualty was Hannay. Despite his public support of the League and Hyde's policy, Hannay felt personally betrayed and pessimistic regarding the future of the once promising movement. At the height of the controversy he wrote despondently to Stephen Gwynn that he had 'been mistaken about the meaning of the constitution and [should] retire, if not from the organisation, at least from taking any active part in its work'.[18]

Ada, Hannay's wife, expressed the full extent of her anger in a letter to Hyde. She pointed out that her husband had sacrificed a great deal in supporting the League with the result that 'he is now practically an outcast, an object of suspicion in his own Church'. Above all they both regretted, Ada wrote, that the result of the whole controversy was the 'sad fact ... that the League does not now provide a platform broad enough for anyone to stand on who is not *persona grata* with the Roman Catholic priests'.[19] Hyde in his reply assured Ada that he appreciated Hannay's unselfish action in preventing a split in the League and expressed his sorrow at the outcome. Hannay continued publicly to support the ideals of the League although his private conviction was that it was doomed if it continued to avoid challenge and allow the Catholic clergy to dominate its course. Shortly after the shelving of the issue by the executive committee, Hannay spoke to a meeting of the Protestant Young Men's Association stressing the positive aspects of the League's aims and work, urging them as Irish Protestants to take their part in Irish life and culture, at the peril of leaving clerical tyranny unchallenged. His bitterness at his treatment by the League did not appear in his writing until as an elderly man he wrote his autobiography, *Pleasant Places*, in which he scornfully made a casual reference to his youthful follies as a nationalist. Yet even in his letters shortly after the controversy there is a tone of despondency:

> I am not so hopeful about the Gaelic League as I was two years ago. I thought then that it was setting the people ... free from the twin tyrannies which are crushing our lives ... the tyranny of the priest and the tyranny of the political boss. I still believe it has done this to some extent and is doing it by awakening the intellect of the people and setting them thinking. In my own personal experience I have come across so many instances of independent thought and courage created by the League's teaching that I shall always, I hope, remain a member of the League and support its work. But I find of late that some of the leaders of the movement are becoming cowardly and are truckling to priests and politicians.[20]

Hannay continued to comment on Irish society and politics in newspapers and journals. He also persevered in writing fiction but there was a perceptible change in his approach. Indulging his gift for biting satire, he produced superficially comic portrayals of Irish life which proved immensely popular especially among British readers: a fact which did little to endear him to many in Ireland. Yet even at home these comic novels were more acceptable because they were so farcical and far fetched. Hannay, while utilising to some degree the traditional stage Irishman, was careful to make his facetious characters Protestant as well as Catholic - the recurring character of Reverend J.J. Meldon, a Church of Ireland curate is just one example. Occasionally he returned to serious topics, such as the rebellion of 1798 in *The Northern Iron* which explored the Protestant aspect of the rebellion in Ulster. *The Red Hand of Ulster*, while a novel with a serious angle on civil war in the event of home rule, was also a farcical portrayal of imaginary events in Ulster, although the original ending of the novel was amended on the advice of his publisher and the

Foreign Office who believed the denouement was a little too close to what might follow in Ulster in 1912. Yet despite Hannay's determination to steer clear of provocative realistic fiction in favour of satire, his work still caused controversy. Hostility towards Hannay survived in Westport long after the original controversy was forgotten by the rest of the country. When his play, *General John Regan*, based on an earlier novel of the same name, toured Ireland it met with little reaction until it arrived in Westport where it resulted in riots. Those who stormed the stage chanted MacDonald's name and denounced Hannay. Ironically, at the same time as the riots were raging, Hannay was giving a lecture in Manchester in which he commented on the *Playboy* riots of 1907 and spoke of the danger of becoming too self-conscious - a danger he perceived in Ireland where people were losing their capacity for healthy laughter at themselves.

NOTES

1. For an indication of the range of fiction published in this period see Stephen J. Brown, S J, *Ireland in Fiction: A guide to Irish novels, tales, romances and folklore*, Dublin, 1919; Brown also gives a list of periodicals and newspapers which published fiction in an appendix to this work; much research in this subject has been carried out by Rolf Loeber and Magda Stouthamer-Loeber in 'Literary fiction as a mirror of the times. A guide to Irish fiction published in Europe, North America and Australia before 1900', (unpublished manuscript, Pittsburgh, PA); also see Eileen Reilly, 'Fictional histories; an examination of Irish historical and political novels, 1880-1914', D.Phil, Oxford University, 1997.

2. Hannay, among others, wrote fiction to supplement an income and this was particularly the case for women writers; see Gaye Tucheman, *Edging Women Out: Victorian Novelists, Publishers and Social Change*, London, 1989.

3. Reverend Canon James Owen Hannay, MA D.Litt, 'George A Birmingham', 1865-1950, published sixty novels and collections of short stories, and two plays, numerous volumes of essays, travel books, theological and biblical works, and an estimated five hundred articles for newspapers and periodicals.

4. George A Birmingham, *The Seething Pot*, London, 1905; the plot centred on the fate of Sir Gerald Geoghan and his involvement in nationalist politics which results in his ostracisation by his own creed and class, and rejection by the parliamentary nationalists. In *Hyacinth*, London, 1906, the hero embodies the ideals of the Gaelic League in working for the

regeneration of the national character and reconciliation of classes and creeds; the portrayal of a fictional convent, 'Robeen', identified by many as the Providence Mills at Foxford caused much criticism. 'Robeen' was depicted as sweating its workers, ruining competition by undercutting other industries due to the government subsidy it received, and pouring the profits of the mill into material goods for the beautification of the convent. *Benedict Kavanagh*, London, 1906, has a similar plot to *Hyacinth*, chronicling the progression of the hero towards working for Ireland according to the ideals of the League regardless of creed or politics.

5. F E Wynne to Hannay, 25 October 1904 T[rinity] C[ollege] D[ublin], Hannay papers, MS 3454, fo. 174.

6. *Mayo News*, 28 April 1906.

7. *Benedict Kavanagh*, pp. 7-8.

8. Douglas Hyde to Hannay, 16 July 1906, T.C.D., Hannay papers, MS 3454, f 316.

9. Hannay to Hyde, 16 July 1906, N[ational] L[ibrary of] I[reland], Hyde papers, MS 18, 2252, fo. 5.

10. *Evening Mail*, 29 September 1906.

11. *Peasant*, 6 October 1906; *An Claidheamh Soluis*, 5 October 1906.

12. Hyde to Hannay, 1 October 1906, T.C.D., Hannay Papers, MS 3454.3, fo. 321.

13. Hyde to Hannay, 28 September 1906, N.L.I., Hyde papers, MS 18,252, fo. 4.

14. *The Northern Whig*, August 1906.

15. Peadar McGinley to Hannay, 2 October 1906, T.C.D., Hannay papers, MS 3454, fo. 323.

16. *Daily Express*, 29 September 1906.

17. *Church of Ireland Gazette*, 12 October 1906.

18. Hannay to Stephen Gwynn, 17 October 1906, T.C.D., Hannay papers, MS 3454, fo. 343.

19. Ada Hannay to Hyde, April 1907, N.L.I., Hyde papers, MS 21099, fo. 3.

20. Hannay to Montgomery, 29 May 1907, T.C.D., Hannay papers, MS 3454, fo. 405b.

7

Postcolonial Joyce?

Willy Maley

Gentes and laitymen, fullstoppers and semicolonials, hybreds and lubberds! (*Finnegans Wake*)

Can one speak of postcolonial Joyce, given that postcolonialism is seen as a field confined to the post-war period? Is postcolonialism, as Lyotard has argued of postmodernism, and as Derrida claims of deconstruction, a principle of destructuring inherent in a system rather than an historical moment or process? It could be argued that Joyce cannot be punctuated, and that he belongs, like the best writers, to more than one period. Joyce painstakingly undoes the (false) opposition between close and contextual reading by breaking the distinction between form and content, and by showing the textuality (fictionality) of history, which can no longer be thought of as 'background'. We cannot speak of Joyce's period, because his writing punctures periodisation. Joyce's period is ours, and it has been remarked that his work lends itself to the kind of attention to language fostered by post-structuralist theories of literature. Joyce has had a special relationship to post-structuralism, and in particular to deconstruction. Margot Norris, in her reading of *Finnegans Wake*, drew on Derrida's 'Structure, Sign and Play'[1]; she was interested specifically in the critique of structure and in a particular philosophical tradition. I shall draw too on the same essay, and another by Derrida, in order to suggest that Derrida's thoughts on humanism and nationalism offer a cautionary note, if not for Joyce, then for Joyce's critics, post-structuralist and nationalist alike. There is an underlying complicity between both groups that does not do justice to Joyce. I should say at the outset that I think Joyce's treatment of nationalism is more complex than either side appreciates or envisages. The view of Joyce as an exemplary humanist and anti-nationalist has had a fairly wide circulation. Bloom's fart at the end of 'Sirens' has been seen as a colophon, the last word on nationalism, a release from closure that, ironically, in turn closes debate.[2] Betrayal, a key theme in Joyce, is what I suspect is taking place with respect to his critique of nationalism.[3]

Emer Nolan's recent book - *James Joyce and Nationalism* - complicates this view, but Nolan sees 'post-structuralism' as the natural ally of the anti-nationalist perspective, and she regards deconstruction as being akin to revisionism, implacably averse to nationalism. In fact, as I shall argue, Derrida takes the (common) ground away from under so-called nationalists and post-structuralists alike. I shall argue here that a deconstructive approach to nationalism challenges those who wish to see Joyce as somehow opposed to nationalism in any simplistic sense. Post-colonial theorists are divided between those who see humanism and modernity as incomplete projects that can be improved and extended, and those who take up vehemently anti-enlightenment and anti-humanist positions.[4] For Frantz Fanon, for example, colonialism contradicts humanism, and anti-colonialism prefigures a new humanism. Henry Gates writes: 'Fanon's vision of the New Man emerges as a central tableau in identity politics, for us as for him. At the intersection of colonial and psychoanalytic discourse, Fanon wonders how to create a new identity.'[5] Fanon's was a theory of connections, interdependence and implicatedness: 'The future of every man today has a relation of close dependency on the rest of the universe. That is why the colonial peoples must redouble their vigilance and their vigour. A new humanism can be achieved only at this price.'[6] Of Fanon's demand for a new or real humanism, Said writes: 'How odd the word "humanism" sounds in this context, where it is free from the narcissistic individualism, divisiveness, and colonialist egoism of the imperialism that justified the white man's rule.'[7] It may be that Fanon's devotion to culture and faith in the humanist project prevented him from seeing a deeper complicity between that universalism and the colonial enterprise itself.

Jacques Derrida offers an instructive reading of the quandary facing modern critics, when in the conclusion to 'Structure, Sign, and Play', he says:

There are ... two interpretations of interpretation, of structure, of sign, of freeplay. The one seeks to decipher, dreams of deciphering, a truth or an origin which is free from freeplay and from the order of the sign, and lives like an exile the necessity of interpretation. The other, which is no longer turned toward the origin, affirms freeplay and tries to pass beyond man and humanism, the name man being the name of that being who, throughout the history of metaphysics and ontotheology - in other words, through the history of all of his history - has dreamed of full presence, the reassuring foundation, the origin and the end of the game. The second interpretation of interpretation, to which Nietzsche showed us the way, does not seek in ethnography, as Lévi-Strauss wished, the 'inspiration of a new humanism'.[8]

Since Stephen Dedalus claims that literature is 'the eternal affirmation of the spirit of man', it is not surprising that James Joyce should be a 'battlefield' for such debates. Critics of Joyce arguing for or against Irish nationalism assume that he found it narrow and rejected it, but they often do not devote the attention to defining the nation or nationalism that Joyce demands. In *Ulysses*, Leopold Bloom, tackles the question of nationality and Irishness:

A nation? says Bloom. A nation is the same people living in the same place.

- By God, then, says Ned, laughing, if that's so I'm a nation for I'm living in the same place for the past five years.

So of course everyone had a laugh at Bloom and says he, trying to muck out of it:

- Or also living in different places.

- That covers my case, says Joe.

- What is your nation if I may ask, says the citizen.

- Ireland, says Bloom. I was born here. Ireland.[9]

Bloom's difficulty in defining a nation is, I would argue, our difficulty. How do we construct a notion of national identity that is inclusive rather than exclusive? And if inclusive, how to avoid incorporation and a repetition of the colonial/imperial project? The nationalist citizen in this section of *Ulysses* is more willing to allow that the Irish abroad belong to Ireland than he is to accept that Bloom, a Jew, has a right to claim Ireland as his home: 'We have our greater Ireland beyond the sea', says the citizen, and yet his anti-semitism shows that he has a lesser Ireland in his own mind.[10]

Bloom is all too aware, as was Joyce, of the risks of racism and xenophobia that could flow from too narrow a definition of 'the nation'. Bloom reminds the Irish nationalist citizen who would exclude him from his vision of Irish identity of the fact that the Irish are not the only race to suffer. 'I belong to a race too, says Bloom, that is hated and persecuted. Also now. This very moment. This very instant'.[11] Bloom's double sense of belonging, living in Ireland, as a Jew, exposes the poverty of a concept of national identity that refuses to be open to the other, to other races, and that thinks it has a monopoly on the experience of repression or discrimination. As Fanon once remarked: 'The native is an oppressed person whose permanent dream is to become a persecutor.'[12] There are further links between Fanon and Joyce that could be pursued. Postcolonial theory depends upon the very notions of ambivalence and hybridity that deconstruct binary oppositions like English/Irish. The term Anglo-Irish is freighted with conflictual histories. 'Hyphen' comes from Greek 'huphen', 'together', compounded of two words, 'hupe', under, and 'hen', one. Under one. That is what it means to be hyphenated, whatever the apparent duality. To be 'under one' is to be lost in the hyphen of history. In spite of all its talk of 'plurality' and 'multiplicity' much postcolonial theory depends upon a narrow oppositional model of positive and negative poles. 'Ambivalence' is an unashamed double bind. There is little room for a third term. 'Hybridity' can mean more than two, but that meaning is seldom thought through or worked out.

Perhaps 'heterogeneity' is a better expression. Otherwise we get not only nothing but the same old story, more of the same. Ireland itself is only just allowed entry to the post-colonial field. The rest of the 'Celtic Fringe' is deemed irremediably imperialistic. Ashcroft, Griffiths and Tiffin, in *The Empire Writes Back*, distinguish between 'dominated' and dominating' societies, drawing on the work of Max Dorsinville. They discuss the constituent parts of the British state and conclude: 'While it is possible to argue that these societies were the first victims of English expansion, their subsequent complicity in the British imperial enterprise makes it difficult for colonized peoples outside Britain to accept their identity as post-colonial.'[13] Leaving aside the problematic status of inside/outside, what is meant by 'complicity' here? And what is the relationship between that process of incorporation and subordination, union and plantation, conquest and colonisation that saw the British state formed, and 'the British imperial enterprise'? The problem of periodisation is crucial, especially if one takes a starting-point that naturalises one historical domination and alienates another. It could be argued that some post-colonial theorists are determined to keep the British state intact, since this monolith suits their purposes, and since they cannot tell the difference between England and Britain, and would prefer not to take the trouble to read up on the histories of the various nations of which the British state is composed.[14] All those whom Joyce called 'fullstoppers and semicolonials' might find it convenient to punctuate the discourse of post-colonialism, but in order to cross borders, we have to be able to count beyond two, to 'think two thinks at the same time'. Historical hyphens have to be negotiated, not in order to return to some unique origin or essence, but, rather, to arrive at a politics of plurality and difference rather than polarity and deference.

Joyce was certainly devoted to breaking out of the double bind of victor and victim, and dedicated to destroying the myth that in any conflict there was only one victim and only one perpetrator. Where is home for Joyce? The obvious answer is Ireland, but Joyce's relationship with Ireland is a vexed one, both in the sense that he was an exile from Ireland, and in terms of his apparent rejection of the demands of his nation. You can take Joyce out of Ireland, but you can't take Ireland out of Joyce. The idea of escaping from Ireland to Europe or the so-called 'New World' permeates Joyce's work. *Dubliners*, for example, is full of dreams of leaving, the desire for adventure and romance, for escape to the 'Wild West', to Buenos Aires. The desire for exile is found throughout Dubliners. In 'An Encounter', we learn that 'real adventures, I reflected, do not happen to people who remain at home: they must be sought abroad'.[15] In 'A Little Cloud', Little Chandler reflects: 'There was no doubt about it: if you wanted to succeed you had to go away. You could do nothing in Dublin.'[16] In *Exiles*, the writer Richard Rowan has returned to Ireland to face a dilemma, whether to stay at home or escape once more. Ireland itself faces a dilemma in Joyce's drama. It must choose between England and Europe. Richard's counterpart, Robert declares: 'If Ireland is to become a new Ireland she must first become European ... Some day we shall have to choose between England and Europe.'[17] It would be tempting to see in these lines Joyce's favouring of the latter, but the stage direction and opening segment of this speech undercuts the illusion of choice. Robert is handed a Virginia cigar by Richard, and says: 'These cigars Europeanize me'. Walter Raleigh went from England to Ireland to Virginia to get the tobacco that made them, thus proving that there is nothing outside of Europe, not the so-called 'New World', whether conceived of as Ireland or America, and certainly not England.

Yet despite the fact that Ireland is in Europe, there is a tradition of seeing Joyce as either a provincial Irish intellectual, an Irish nationalist, or as a cosmopolitan author, self-exiled, and rejecting Irish nationalism and with it the Catholic Church. Of course it has been argued that Joyce became more Irish and more Catholic for these repudiations. In *A Portrait*, Cranly tells Stephen: 'It is a curious thing, do you know ... how your mind is supersaturated with the religion in which you say you disbelieve.'[18] Bloom says: 'It's a patent absurdity on the face of it to hate people because they live round the corner and speak another vernacular, so to speak.'[19] There is more than one way to be Irish, and one is always more than just Irish. There is also more than one way to be a nationalist, and, again, national identity is only one identity, one group or category to which one can belong, though, as I shall suggest, it is more pervasive than is sometimes allowed. It is when nationalism is being denied that it is most assuredly at work. As soon as we speak, even if we open our mouths to deny our national identity, or to say, 'I am not a nationalist', the language in which we speak betrays the hold that a nation has over us. As soon as I start to speak, no matter what I say, I say something else. I affirm something. There are times at which even to speak is an act of national defiance, an assertion or affirmation of identity.

'Post-structuralists' and 'Irish nationalists' (both terms are fraught) agree broadly on what nationalism is, that is, something narrow. From both sides, as it were, assumptions are made about nationalism, Irish and otherwise. Seamus Deane writes: 'The most appealing and dangerously seductive form of solidarity in Irish conditions was that offered by Irish nationalism, in all its variant forms, from the United Irishmen of 1798 to the Young Ireland movement of the 1840s and the more recent Fenian and Home Rule movements.'[20] Irish nationalism, 'in all its variant forms', is here rather narrowly conceived. Deane adds: 'Exile safeguarded independence; cosmopolitanism helped to avoid provincialism.'[21]

Thus 'the narrowness of Irish nationalism is satirized and yet its basic impulse is ratified.'[22] 'If Ireland could not be herself, then, by way of compensation, the world would become Ireland.'[23]

According to Klaus Reichert, Joyce 'had become thoroughly dissatisfied with Ireland, whose atmosphere of nationalist parochialism had become distasteful to him.'[24] Reichert asks: 'What was the good of the rising nationalism that turned out to be as authoritarian and intolerant as the oppressors from which it had set out to liberate its people.'[25] According to deconstruction, there is always the risk of becoming (like) the thing you ostensibly oppose. This is the risk that so much post-structuralist criticism of nationalism takes. For nationalism is not an entity. There is not one nationalism. Deane reminds us that Joyce saw Ireland as caught between 'two imperialisms, British and Roman Catholic',[26] and adds: 'Nor did he believe that nationalism was anything other than an extension of those imperialisms, despite its apparent antagonism to them ... he could find no alternative to imperialisms and nationalism other than an attitude of fierce repudiation.'[27] It is a question of reversal and displacement, and of the necessary precedence of the former. Internationalism is not anti-colonialism. Joyce's critique of xenophobia, sentiment and romance in 'Cyclops' is less a parody of nationalism than a pastiche of nationalist discourses. If we, as Derek Attridge enjoins us, appreciate 'the many-sidedness of language and story-telling' then we must look at nationalism with two eyes, not one.[28] Nor can we oppose the Panopticon of humanism to the Cyclops of nationalism. Attridge praises Joyce's 'inconclusiveness', and this is where the semi-colon comes in.[29] To repudiate Catholic Ireland in the name of a new humanity is simply to replace one national humanism with another.[30] Attridge writes of Joyce's 'fiercely-felt rejection of the narrowness and sterility of Ireland's political, religious, and cultural life; his fantasies and fabrications that were to contribute to two world wars'.[31] Forgeries, fantasises and fabrications. In the name of a progressive European cultural outlook all kinds of atrocities have been committed. How can one oppose a theory of progress or Europe to what underpinned the two world wars?

Joyce's Irishness, like his Catholicism, his nationalism, his politics, and all his other identities, is far from simple. In his introduction to *The Essential James Joyce*, Harry Levin suggests that Joyce was 'all too Irish', and 'all the more Irish', because he was a 'wild-goose', because of his exile and travels.[32] Expatriate Irishness, 'that greater Ireland beyond the sea', one argument goes, preserves aspects of cultural identity which can be diluted in the metropolis. As Deane puts it: 'Joyce became the professional exile from a home he never, imaginatively speaking, left.'[33] Levin, having suggested that Joyce's status as an exile made him all the more Irish, says: 'From first to last, his underlying impulses were those of his racial endowment: humour, imagination, eloquence, belligerence.'[34] There is a risk here of stereotyping, and of substituting for the old image of the stage Irishman, a new image of the literary Irishman. Joyce himself, in *A Portrait*, seems to endorse Levin's statement, before going on to complicate and perhaps contradict it. In an exchange with Davin, the Irish nationalist, Stephen Dedalus first asserts his Irish identity: 'This race and this country and this life produced me ... I shall express myself as I am.' Pressed further by Davin, Stephen says: 'My ancestors threw off their language and took another ... They allowed a handful of foreigners to subject them. Do you fancy I am going to pay in my own life and person debts they made? What for?' 'For our freedom', Davin replies. Stephen's response is crucial: 'No honourable and sincere man ... has given up to you his life and his youth and his affections from the days of Tone to those of Parnell, but you sold him to the enemy or failed him in need or reviled him and left him for another.' Having acknowledged that he is a product of his country, Stephen now says: 'You talk to me of nationality, language, religion. I shall try to fly by those nets.'[35]

Joyce spoke of Oscar Wilde in terms of 'his own distinctive qualities, the qualities, perhaps, of his race - keenness, generosity, and a sexless intellect'.[36] But to speak of national characteristics or racial endowments is not necessarily to analyse the philosophy of nationalism. Derrida, in a little-known essay entitled 'Onto-Theology of National Humanism (Prolegomena to a Hypothesis)', argues that:

> a national identity is never posited as an empirical, natural character, of the type: such and such a people or such and such a race has black hair or is of the dolicelaphic type, or else we recognise ourselves by the presence of such and such a characteristic. The self-positing or self-identification of the nation always has the form of a *philosophy* which, although better represented by such and such a nation, is none the less a certain relation to the universality of the philosophical.[37]

Derrida goes further - in what should be a warning to all those who wish to oppose universalism or cosmopolitanism to the bad example of nationalism:

> Not only does nationalism not happen like an accident or evil to a philosophy supposedly a stranger to it and which would, by essential vocation, be cosmopolitan or universalist, it is a philosophy, a discourse which is, structurally, philosophical. And it is universalist or cosmopolitan ... Nationalism never presents itself as a particularism but as a universal philosophical model, a philosophical *telos* ... always philosophical in essence, even in its worst and most sinister manifestations, those that are the most imperialistic and vulgarly violent.[38]

The risk that must be avoided at all costs is that of seeing the Holy Trinity of humanism, internationalism, and revisionism as examples of post-nationalist discourse when they remain irredeemably caught up in the net of nationalism. Deane describes Joyce as a 'cosmopolitan', but cosmopolitanism is no solution to nationalism; in fact, as Derrida points out, its often the guise in which nationalism presents itself. Those who seek to avoid or evade or oppose nationalism through cosmopolitanism and universalism risk succumbing to a nationalism of the most insidious kind. We must fly by those nets. Internal colonialism - indigenous indigestion, as I prefer to call it - cannot be conjured away with a wave of a wand.

Derrida also says that nationalism is a philosophy of life - a biologism - as opposed to death, so maybe Joyce, as a philosopher who interprets for the dead, is not a nationalist after all. Derrida says a little later:

> this essentially philosophical nationalism (as I believe every nationalism is philosophical, and this is the main point I wanted to emphasise at the outset) claims to be totally foreign to any naturalism, biologism, racism, or even ethnocentrism - it does not even want to be a political nationalism, a doctrine of the Nation-State. It is, further, a cosmopolitanism, often associated with a democratic and republican politics, a progressivism, etc.[39]

Derrida then argues that this philosophy of life is a biologism of sorts, before adding, 'as for cosmopolitanism, this is a fearfully ambiguous value: it can be annexationist and expansionist, and combat in the name of nationalism the enemies within'. Citing Marx, Derrida then points out the links between a humanist teleology and a philosophical nationalism.[40] He writes:

> Nationalism, once more, does not present itself as a retrenchment onto an empirical particularity, but as the assigning to a nation of a universalistic, essentialist representation.[41]

Nationalism 'always presents itself as a nationalism not of a nation, of a nationality, as one would naturally be tempted to think, taking its word for it, but as the discourse of man on man himself'.[42]

In 'A Mother', the third last story in *Dubliners*, we are told that Mrs Kearney 'respected her husband in the same way as she respected the General Post Office, as something large, secure and fixed'.[43] Published two years before that structure was shaken to its core, this tale, dealing as it does with an outstanding bill, is a timely reminder of the fact that the post is no more secure or fixed than the past. We may think the account has been closed, but we're still paying the national debt. Even as we write off older varieties of nationalism, we must guard against buying into the neo- that comes in the name of the post-. Nationalism is a dead letter only insofar as it is unclaimed, or undelivered. Between the pen and the post lies the possibility that a letter might not reach its destination. Ancient salt is best packing, as Yeats well knew. The classical humanist project is bound up with a discourse of nationalism. The openness that we accord Joyce, and that we constantly find in his work, must be extended to what, for the sake of convenience, without reading, that is, we call 'nationalism': not an openness to nationalism, but an openness to the nationalisms that may present themselves as something new or different. We must beware a second coming of nationalism in the guise of its demise. This does not call for renunciations or repudiations, solutions or conclusions, but for an interminable openness and vigilance - equivocation, hesitation, indecision, negotiation, and vacillation - all the things that Derrida and Joyce teach us to practice. It calls, in short, not for the closure of a period, but for the intermediary of a semi-colon.

NOTES

1. Margot Norris, *The Decentred Universe of Finnegans Wake: A Structuralist Analysis*, Baltimore, 1974, p. 121.

2. Emmit's epitaph after all was *pre*-nationalist in a sense. For a marvellous discussion of this episode see Emer Nolan, *James Joyce and Nationalism*, London, 1995, pp. 67-8. See also James Fairhall, *James Joyce and the question of history*, Cambridge, 1993.

3. It is a commonplace to see betrayal as central to Joyce's approach to gender and nationality. As Seamus Deane writes, 'wherever he looked, in Irish political or literary history, he found that the master-theme was betrayal'. See S. Deane, 'Joyce the Irishman', in D. Attridge, ed., *The Cambridge Companion to James Joyce*, Cambridge, 1990, p. 32.

4. See Homi Bhabha, '"Race", Time and the Revision of Modernity', *Oxford Literary Review*, 13 (1991), pp. 193-219.

5. Henry Louis Gates, Jr., 'Critical Fanonism', *Critical Inquiry*, 17 (1991), p. 469.

6. Frantz Fanon, 'First Truths on the Colonial Problem', in trans. Haakon Chevalier, *Toward the African Revolution*, London, 1967, p. 126.

7. Edward W Said, 'Resistance and Opposition', *Culture and Imperialism*, London, 1993, p. 325.

8. See Jacques Derrida, 'Structure, Sign and Play in the Discourse of the Human Sciences', in K. Newton, ed., *Twentieth-Century Literary Theory*, London, 1988, p. 153.

9. Joyce, *Ulysses*, Harmondsworth, 1982, pp. 329-30.

10. Ibid., p. 328.

11. Ibid., p. 331.

12. Frantz Fanon, *The Wretched of the Earth*, London, 1967, p. 41.

13. See Bill Ashcroft, Gareth Griffiths and Helen Tiffin, *The Empire Writes Back: Theory and practice in post-colonial literatures*, London, 1989, p. 33.

14. My own work has attempted to problematise notions of Britishness. See for example 'Rebels and Redshanks: Milton and the British Problem', *Irish Studies Review*, 1:6 (Spring 1994), pp. 7-11; 'Varieties of Englishness: planting a new culture beyond the pale', in *Salvaging Spenser: Colonialism, Culture and Identity*, London, 1997, pp. 48-77.

15. Joyce, 'An Encounter', *Dubliners*, in Harry Levin, ed., *The Essential James Joyce*, London, 1983, p. 30.

16. Joyce, 'A Little Cloud', in Levin, ed., *The Essential James Joyce*, p. 65.

17. Joyce, *Exiles*, in *The Essential James Joyce*, p. 388. There is also of course the moment at which Stephen in *A Portrait* places Europe beyond Ireland, and beyond the world: 'The Europe they had come from lay out there beyond the Irish Sea, Europe of strange tongues and valleyed wood-begirt and citadelled and of entrenched and marshalled races ... A voice from beyond the world was calling' (p. 300).

18. *The Essential James Joyce*, p. 355.

19. Joyce, *Ulysses*, p. 564.

20. Deane, 'Joyce the Irishman', p. 32.

21. Ibid., p. 39.

22. Ibid., p. 44.

23. Ibid., p. 50.

24. Klaus Reichert, 'The European background of Joyce's writing', in D. Attridge, ed., *The Cambridge Companion to James Joyce*, Cambridge, 1990, p. 55.

25. Reichert, 'The European background of Joyce's writing', p. 55.

26. Deane, 'Joyce the Irishman', pp. 34-5.

27. Ibid., p. 35.

28. D. Attridge, 'Reading Joyce', in D. Attridge, ed., *The Cambridge Companion to James Joyce*, p. 8.

29. Ibid., p. 6.

30. Deane, 'Joyce the Irishman', p. 31.

31. Attridge, 'Reading Joyce', p. 9.

32. Levin, *The Essential James Joyce*, p. 11.

33. Deane, 'Joyce the Irishman', p. 39.

34. Levin, *The Essential James Joyce*, p. 11.

35. Ibid., p. 327.

36. Cited in Deane, 'Joyce the Irishman', p. 35.

37.   Jacques Derrida, 'Onto-Theology of National Humanism', *Oxford Literary Review*, 14 (1992), p. 10.

38.   Ibid., pp. 10-11.

39.   Ibid., p. 16.

40.   Ibid., p. 17.

41.   Ibid., p. 19.

42.   Ibid., p. 20.

43.   *The Essential James Joyce*, p. 114.

8

Landscape and land ownership in Elizabeth Bowen's *The Last September*

Tessa Hadley

One of the ways in which contemporary literary criticism is busy revising
and renewing itself is in relation to the kind of challenges thrown out by Edward
Said in *Culture and Imperialism*:

> Western writers until the middle of the twentieth century, whether Dickens
> or Austen, Flaubert or Camus, wrote with an exclusively Western audience
> in mind, even when they wrote of characters, places, or situations that
> referred to, made use of, overseas territories held by Europeans. But just
> because Jane Austen referred to Antigua in *Mansfield Park* or to realms
> visited by the British navy in *Persuasion* without any thought of possible
> responses by the Caribbean or Indian natives resident there is no reason for
> us to do the same. We know now that these non-European peoples did not
> accept with indifference the authority projected over them, or the general
> silence on which their presence in variously attenuated forms is predicated.[1]

Fictions which had long been interpreted by criticism as offering universal and
unaltering truths fall into new contexts and are subject to new ways of seeing.
As all sorts of 'silences' upon which so many certainties had been predicated are
broken, we learn to re-think Sir Thomas Bertram's family matters in the light
of his other role as slave-owner, to re-visit the Africa in *Heart of Darkness* with
Chinua Achebe's protests to guide us.

At first sight - choosing a passage from the opening pages almost at random
- Elizabeth Bowen's *The Last September* (1929) might seem to demonstrate
itself a casualty of this new upheaval of perspectives. How can this be County
Cork in 1920? The Irish are at war: and Lois is anxious over her flower-
arranging. The novel's action is to consist of a tennis party, a dance at a
barracks, some very well mannered love affairs that do not go beyond a kiss or
two, and much leisured, agonised hyper-reflectiveness on the part of its Anglo-
Irish protagonists. Lois is anticipating that for want of much better to do, she
may fall in love with Mr. Montmorency, a married man, when he arrives for a
long visit. (She doesn't, as it turns out):

> [Lois] yawned with reaction. It was simply the Montmorencys who had
> come; whom one all day had been expecting. Yet she had been unable to

read, had scattered unfinished letters over her table, done the flowers atrociously. Sweet-peas had spun and quivered between her fingers from their very importance ... 'I apologise for the mauve sweet-peas,' she would have liked to be able to say to Mr Montmorency. 'I don't care for the mauve myself. I can't think why I ever picked them; there were plenty of others. But as a matter of fact I was nervous.' And - 'Nervous?' she would wish Mr Montmorency to ask her searchingly, 'why?' But she had her reserves, even in imagination; she would never tell him.[2]

Bringing almost any degree of historical awareness of the Irish context to an initial encounter with this novel is very likely to evoke - ought to evoke - something like protest. What silences is this novel's world predicated on? Who and what is missing from this text? How can we be seriously asked to think Lois's flower arranging - or her love affairs - matter: when outside the gates of the Danielstown demesne lorry-loads of Black and Tans are prowling the countryside by night, and sick and old women and children are being thrown out of their beds while soldiers search for the men who are hidden up in the hills? What I want to argue in this chapter, using *The Last September* as my focus, is that an incompleteness of perspective need not necessarily operate as a disabling closure in a fiction. Might it not even be possible for a fiction to be constructed around its omissions, be predicated upon the irony of its own incompleteness? And wouldn't one expect to find such a nervous and self-criticising fiction, if it *were* possible, at just such a crux of mutual cultural incomprehension as Ireland in 1920?

The gauzy foreground fabric of *The Last September* (sweet-peas, high ceilings, old portraits, *eau de Cologne*, umbrellas, family recipes for chocolate cake) is rent in several significant places by intrusions from another Ireland which the novel cannot represent full on, and doesn't pretend to speak for. Wandering idly alone in the Danielstown shrubbery one night, remembering foxtrotting down the avenue in the arms of the English subaltern Gerald she (again) can't quite convince herself she is in love with, Lois hears footsteps, a man passes 'within reach of her hand, with the rise and fall of a stride':

It must be because of Ireland he was in such a hurry; down from the mountains, making a short cut through their demesne. Here was something else that she could not share. She could not conceive of her country emotionally: it was a way of living, an abstract of several landscapes, or an oblique frayed island, moored at the north but with an air of being detached and washed out west from the British coast.

Quite still, she let him go past in contemptuous unawareness. His intentions burnt on the dark an almost visible trail; he might well have been a murderer he seemed so inspired. The crowd of trees, straining up from passive disputed earth, each sucking up and exhaling the country's essence - swallowed him finally. She thought: 'Has he come for the guns?' A man with a trench-coat had passed without seeing her: that was what it amounted to (p. 33).

The guns she wonders if he has come for are rumoured to be buried in the plantation; it's one of those pieces of recurrent tea-table conversation about 'the troubles' which the family pass around and handle like old silver forks, refusing them their threat. A guest suggests that the plaster casts at the Irish art schools ought to be searched for weapons: 'you could keep a good deal inside the Venus of Milo' (p. 173). Castle Trent has been raided for arms: they took some boots away.

What impresses Lois most about the intruder is his 'contemptuous unawareness': but how can *un*awareness be contemptuous, how can this non-encounter be a significant event? And yet the man's obliviousness - of her concerns and her family's concerns and all her ways of thinking about the land they seem to be co-existent on - is a defining irony in *The Last September*, something which it sustains, as if from outside, against its own fabric.

In a reversal of the normal relationship between foreground and background in a fiction, all the really significant moments in the development of *The Last September* are non-encounters like this one, intrusions into a static foreground from a dynamic background ('his intentions burnt on the dark') which we can't enter. Lois and Marda find a sleeping fugitive with a pistol in the ruined mill. We never know where the fugitive is coming from or going to. Gerald, Lois's subaltern, is meaninglessly shot dead in an ambush. The novel surrounds these rents in its own fabric, it concentrates its attention and its energy around the edges of them, and peers through. This play of irony in the novel around its own incompleteness is apparent especially in its treatment of land and landscape. Landscape is problematic and potent, rather than reassuring and consolidating. It won't cohere into a continuity: in a sense it is another kind of non-event. The view offers itself up to Lois driving home with Mr Montmorency from Mount Isabel to Danielstown (two of the triumvirate of Big Houses that preside over the novel):

Hugo debating if she were subtle or very stupid, Lois busy with melodrama, they drove home briskly. To the south, below them, the demesne trees of Danielstown made a dark formal square like a rug on the green country. In their heart, like a dropped pin, the grey glazed roof reflecting the sky lightly glinted. Looking down, it seemed to Lois they lived in a forest; space of lawns blotted out in the pressure and dusk of trees. She wondered they were not smothered; then wondered still more that they were not afraid. For from here too, their isolation became apparent. The house seemed to be pressing

72

down low in apprehension, hiding its face, as though it had her vision of where it was. It seemed to gather its trees close in fright and amazement at the wide, light, lovely unloving country, the unwilling bosom where it was set. From the slope's foot, where Danielstown trees began, the land stretched out in a plain flat as water, basin of the Madda and Darra and their fine wandering tributaries, till the far hills, faint and brittle, straining against the inrush of vaster distance, cut the droop of the sky like a glass blade. Fields gave back light to the sky - the hedges netting them over thinly and penetrably - as though the sheen of grass were a shadow on water, a breath of colour clouding the face of light. Rivers, profound in brightness, flowed over beds of glass. The cabins lifting their pointed white ends, the pink and yellow farms were but half opaque; cast doubtfully on their fields the shadow of living.... Only the massed trees - spread like a rug to dull some keenness, break some contact between self and senses perilous to the routine of living - only the trees of the demesne were dark, exhaling darkness (p. 66).

The very names are active in the energy field of this landscape in process: Madda and Darra the rivers, presumably Irish names; then the bland assertion of Englishness and ownership in Danielstown, and that significant feudal survival, the *demesne*, instead of the *park* more usual in England. Park with its suggestions of pleasure and the chase - almost of nature, enclosed - is euphemistic besides all that *demesne* suggests of legalism and possession.

The contrast dwelled on, between the open country and the thickly treed demesne is objectively 'real' enough: the Anglo-Irish plantations of magnificent old trees, often rare horticultural specimens, set down distinctively in spare open country, remain today. But transparency and opacity are not in this passage aesthetic contrasts composing a whole aesthetically free from its socio-historical underpinning. We are not inclined to call this 'nature', because it's such a human-saturated scene: we don't see a tree without having an idea who planted it, or a mountain without an idea who's hiding on it. We can't see the land without acknowledging who 'owns' it, and on what terms. Lois wonders the Danielstown inhabitants 'were not smothered; then wondered still more that they were not afraid'. The landscape is circumstance, not backdrop.

It may only be in reacting to the resistance of the landscape here that we realise how used we are to the invocation in novels of Nature as reinforcing background, reassurance, a place for the subjective to take refuge. To use only one - canonical - example in contrast, here are the significantly named Red Deeps in *Mill on the Floss*:

Just where this line of bank sloped down again to the level, a by-road turned off and led to the other side of the rise, where it was broken into very capacious hollows and mounds by the working of an exhausted stone-quarry

- so long exhausted that both mounds and hollows were not clothed with brambles and trees, and here and there by a stretch of grass which a few sheep kept close-nibbled. In her childish days Maggie held this place in very great awe, and needed all her confidence in Tom's bravery to reconcile her to an excursion thither, visions of robbers and fierce animals haunting every hollow. But now it had the charm for her which any broken ground, any mimic rock and ravine have for the eyes that rest habitually on the level, especially in summer, when she could sit on a grassy hollow under the shadow of a branching ash, stooping aslant from the steep above her, and listen to the hum of insects, like tiniest bells on the garment of Silence, or see the sunlight piercing the distant boughs, as if to chase and drive home the truant heavenly blue of the wild hyacinths.[3]

It's interesting how differently the exhausted quarry is operative there from how the ruined mill works in *The Last September*. Industrial intrusion into nature and the fall-out from its cessation are relegated in the Red Deeps into a past distant enough for there to be nothing painful left in the ruin's reminder; they have been assimilated in fact into natural process, grown over with brambles and trees. The Irish mill, on the contrary, bristles with resentful unfinished business even before Marda and Lois stumble into the pistol-toting fugitive inside who recommends they give up their country walks ('If you have nothing better to do,' he says, 'you had better keep in the house while y'have it'). The place is a 'dead mill - the country was full of them, never quite stripped and whitened to skeletons' decency' and Mr. Montmorency exclaims 'Another of our national grievances', and complains about English law (pp. 123-5).

The reassuringness of George Eliot's Nature is constructed as maternal, tending - the tree that 'stoops aslant', Silence that wears a garment. It is rhythmically incantatory, rhetoricised ('aslant' and 'like tiniest bells') in a way that signals safety, consoles, surrounds from above. And the architecture of the passage which links Maggie's own history and subjectivity to this Nature, links Nature beyond itself to some transcendent value: this 'real' place which feels home-like as Maggie sits in it, exists in iconographic relationship to another home, a greater tenderer Nature, signed for us by the hyacinths' heavenly blue. In *The Last September* if the land is a mother it's not for the inhabitants of Danielstown: 'It seemed to gather its trees close in fright and amazement at the wide, light, lovely unloving country, the unwilling bosom whereon it was set' (p. 66). Lois has an intimation, even, that the Danielstown element in the landscape, that rug of trees, represents an evasion, some deliberate failure of experience, of self-knowledge: 'the massed trees - spread like a rug to dull some keenness, break some contact between self and senses perilous to the routine of living' (p. 66). The depth the trees create around the house, if it's a refuge, is a consoling illusion; the Danielstown trees turn their back on the light and openness of the land. If Danielstown stands, for its inhabitants, for a 'routine of living', that routine depends on preventing contact between self and senses which have got separated somehow. The landscape is a field of energy, dynamically charged, and its Danielstown elements need to be insulated from what's outside to avoid shock, violence. The consummation can't but be desired (Lois cannot but want that 'keenness', a wholeness of self and senses) and dreaded (the end of the routine of living). Ironically, far from offering a refuge, the Danielstown trees make Danielstown itself conspicuous. The possibility of the land as hiding-place is very active in the novel, but it is the 'wide, light' landscape which is saturated invisibly with men in hiding, who - from their perspective 'outside' - render the sheltered inhabitants of the Big Houses ever more exposed. We're never 'with' the hidden men, we never 'see' them, yet throughout the novel they 'see' us. This is Laurence, Lois's 'political' Oxford cousin, walking into the garden after making tea at Mount Isabel:

> A sense of exposure, of being offered without resistance to some ironic uncuriosity, made Laurence look up at the mountain over the roof of the house. In some gaze - of a man's up there hiding, watching among the clefts and ridges - they seemed held, included and to have their only being. The sense of a watcher, reserve of energy and intention, abashed Laurence, who turned from the montain. But the unavoidable and containing stare impinged to the point of a transformation upon the social figures with their orderly, knitted shadows, the well-groomed grass and the beds, worked out in this pattern (p. 119).

It is an ironic *un*curiosity: piquant, agitating, to have the fabric of a novel presided over by a stare essentially uninterested in its protagonists. It is this surely that helps to empty poor Lois's *amours* of conviction. In fact in a curious displacement all high drama and passionate feeling is purged from the foreground and only able to re-insert itself into the text through the descriptive passages. The foreground is comic, dry, reserved, a world in which Lois's remark after her first kiss with Gerald is 'Oh, but look here ...'; or in which this exchange is possible, the same lunchtime:

> Going out through the hall Laurence offered Gerald a cigarette. 'American - extra mild.'
> 'Thanks - I -'
> 'How is your jazz band?'
> 'Very little practising; not much time, you see.'
> 'Do tell me: did you kill anybody?'
> 'How much?' said Gerald, startled.
> 'Anybody last night?'

'Oh, good Lord, no!'

'Isn't that why you go out?'

'We were looking for arms, really. And nights you find the most surprising people at home. We were after a fellow called Peter Connor: we got him. He was at home, in bed. These blighters think we are greater fools than we are.'

'Very cynical of him ... Oh, I say, Uncle Richard, Lesworth has captured Peter Connor.'

'I'm sorry to hear that,' said Sir Richard, flushing severely. 'His mother is dying. However, I suppose you must do your duty. We must remember to send up now and inquire for Mrs Michael Connor. We'll send some grapes. The poor woman - it seems too bad.' He went off, sighing, into the library. Gerald was horrified. His duty, so bright and abstract, had come suddenly under the shadowy claw of the personal. 'I had no idea,' he exclaimed to Laurence, 'these people were friends of yours' (p. 92).

Meanwhile, behind, mountains heave with melodrama, sunsets are overwritten: 'Evening drenched the trees; the beeches were soundless cataracts. Behind the trees, pressing in from the open and empty country like an invasion, the orange bright sky crept and smouldered' (p. 22). Outside the primary space of the novel, things are happening which are not provided for in the language of the Big House. No one who belongs to the House could find the words, as old Dannie Regan does when Marda and Mr. Montmorency drop in on his cottage, to say that 'this was young Mr Hugo, wasn't he the lovely gentleman, as fine and upstanding as ever. And here was his wife he'd brought with him, the beautiful lady ... He declared that she brought back the sight of youth to his eyes' (p. 86). The fragments of Irish voices in the text associate themselves with the ripe poetry of the natural descriptions.

One self-limiting discourse, deadpan, sophisticated, understating, can gesture outside itself - and in a characteristic movement of self-irony - to a world of other ways of seeing. This need not be a blithely optimistic gesture: as it happens, old Dannie is virtually blind and Marda isn't Mr. Montmorency's wife. The novel isn't optimistic: that fracture and that potential for shock and violence which Lois intuits in the landscape finds its fulfilment on the last page, when, without warning - except that we've been expecting it all through - anonymous visitors slide out through the Danielstown gates at night in cars without lights, leaving the house ablaze and Sir Richard and Lady Naylor, 'seeing too distinctly', with nothing left to say. It is interesting that Elizabeth Bowen describes the landscape, that last night of the fire, in words that suggest some kind of resolution - violent resolution - to the discontinuity of earlier accounts: 'It seemed, looking from east to west at the sky tall with scarlet, that the country

76

itself was burning ... not a tree, brushed pale by wind from the flames, not a cabin pressed in despair to the bosom of the night, not a gate too starkly visible but had its place in the design of order and panic' (p. 206). And if there is a case to be made for *The Last September* as that 'fiction predicated upon its own omissions' I proposed at the beginning of this chapter, then surely it is that out of whatever incompleteness such a fiction can contemplate its own extinction - the extinction, effectively, of its perspective - with, not enthusiasm, but at least clear-eyed recognition. Perhaps it is important to assert in a period of critical re-thinking that complex fictions, rather than being contained within finite intellectual systems, may contain within themselves the signs which, activated in a new perspective through cultural upheaval, recover meanings for them and re-equilibrate them in new readings. To assert this is to put the emphasis on the second part of Said's formulation here (my italics): 'In order more accurately to read works like *Mansfield Park*, we have to see them in the main as resisting or avoiding that other setting, *which their formal inclusiveness, historical honesty, and prophetic suggestiveness cannot completely hide*'.[4]

NOTES

1. Edward Said, *Culture and Imperialism*, London, 1994, p. 78.
2. Elizabeth Bowen, *The Last September*, London, 1987, p. 8. All further references will be included parenthetically in the text.
3. George Eliot, *The Mill on the Floss*, London, p. 393.
4. Said, *Culture and Imperialism*, p. 115.

9

Beckett and the Big House:
Watt and 'Quin'

Julie Campbell

This chapter will focus on Beckett's novel *Watt* in terms of the Anglo-Irish tradition of Big House Fiction: this kind of treatment of the text has been a fairly rare phenomenon in Beckett criticism. *Watt* has been written about extensively and in many ways: for instance, in terms of a philosophical enquiry (Jacqueline Hoefer's convincing consideration of the text in terms of Wittgenstein), or as a religious quest (David Hesla draws links with Dante, as does Eugene Webb).[1] Certainly the idea of a quest is very often given prominence. Here, for example, is Webb's description of *Watt*: 'The story of Watt's journey to Knott's house is the story of man's quest for some kind of absolute knowledge that will bring him peace.'[2] Other critical studies concentrate on the epistemological quest; in Ann M. Trivisonno's words: 'Watt in search of the whatness of things encounters Knott or nothingness.'[3] Many formalist studies emphasise the experimental aspects of the narrative structure and the narrative voice - such as those by Eric P. Levy, H. Porter Abbott and Steven Connor.[4]

In considering the text's Anglo-Irish context, John Chalker, in the 1970s, made links between the narrative playfulness of *Watt* and that of Laurence Sterne and Jonathan Swift, placing it firmly within an Anglo-Irish literary tradition of playing with, rather than conforming to, existing narrative conventions.[5] But it has been rare in the past to have the text treated in terms of its Irishness, although this is changing as Irish academics are beginning to claim Beckett as one of their own.[6] Eoin O'Brien in *The Beckett Country: Samuel Beckett's Ireland* links descriptions of place in Beckett's work to actual places in Ireland - often, possibly, a little too directly.[7] He considers that 'Cooldrinagh serves as the model for ... Mr Knott's house' and later states that 'Boss Croker's house [Glencairn] ... lends some of its features ... to the extraordinary establishment run by Mr Knott in *Watt*.'[8] 'Run' seems an inappropriate word here, for whatever Mr. Knott does he certainly doesn't seem to 'run' his establishment in any way.[9] James Knowlson, in his new biography of Beckett, *Damned to Fame*, explains that Cooldrinagh, the family house in Foxrock, was named after an authentic Big House: 'a very grand house, almost a mansion'. This was Beckett's mother's family home, and perhaps Beckett had this 'grand house' in

78

mind when writing *Watt*.[10] An important study which concentrates on Beckett's Irishness is John P. Harrington's *The Irish Beckett*.[11] He writes of *Watt* in terms of the Big House genre, a discussion which is convincing in itself, but which lacks the extra evidence which can be gleaned from the earlier unpublished material out of which *Watt* emerged.[12] Recently Terence Brown has also spoken of Beckett's work alongside Irish literary traditions, including that of the Big House, and I shall be returning to his discussion a little later.[13] I will be examining certain elements of earlier manuscript and typescript versions of *Watt* in order to show that the narrative began its life with many elements that are recognisable as belonging to the genre of Big House Fiction. I shall show the different way Beckett approaches the genre; Brown describes the tone of writers on the demise of the Big House as 'variously nostalgic, angry, or even gratified' otherwise it is viewed as 'tragedy, [whereas Beckett] has a peculiar philosophic mordancy all his own'.[14] Beckett approaches the genre from a sceptical position: there is some mockery and a certain scorn detectable, but a great deal of humour and playfulness, and a sustained ambivalence which prevents any easy positioning of the text's allegiances, or lack of them.

The best way to begin my own exploration of *Watt* and the earlier typescript version 'Quin' in relation to the Big House novel is by looking at how the Big House has been delineated by some other writers, and pointing to some of the connections that can be made with Beckett's work. Elizabeth Bowen, for instance, describes the 'real' Big House, rather than the genre (interestingly in an article that was published in 1942, the year in which Beckett began to write *Watt*).[15] In 'The Big House' Bowen begins by foregrounding the importance of point of view, the question of where the teller is situated vis-à-vis the Big House:

> Big houses in Ireland are, I am told, very isolated. I say 'I am told' because the isolation, or loneliness, of my own house is only borne in on me, from time to time, by the exclamations of travellers when they arrive. 'Well,' they exclaim, with a hint of denunciation, 'you are a long way from anywhere!' I suppose I see this the other way round: everything seems to have placed itself a long way from me.[16]

Here Bowen stresses the importance of point of view. The Big House will have a very different aspect according to 'who tells' (the position of the narrative voice), and also according to 'who sees' (the position of the focaliser). The reader has two very different points of view suggested here, depending on whether the Big House is described and seen from the inside (Bowen) or from the outside (visitor, 'travellers'; 'they'). 'Who tells' and 'who sees' are elements that are problematised in *Watt* and have a central importance in that narrative. This description of Bowen's also recalls the image of the centre and the circumference described in *Watt*, where a centre and its circumference seem to have become separated from each other.[17] Here the Big House, which was situated at the centre of things (and still is for Bowen), is now in isolation because the 'everywhere', or the circumference, has moved away. The Big House has become marginalised, separated (isolated) from the world in which it placed itself as central. This declares an intriguing active/passive reversal; its displacement is not due to any activity on the part of the centre; the circumference has, in a sense, got up and left it where it stands, alone.

When Bowen places herself in the double position of both insider and visitor she notices the mysteriousness of these houses: 'When I visit other big houses I am struck by some quality that they all have - not so much isolation as mystery. Each house seems to live under its own spell, and that is the spell that falls on the visitor from the moment he passes in at the gates' (p. 195). A strong sense of mystery is conveyed by the descriptions of Knott's house, and this mystery envelopes Watt, Knott's servant, from the moment he arrives; he is, in a sense, under its spell. Bowen goes on to describe the circles within circles within which the Big House is situated: first 'the demesne wall' and within this 'the ring of woods', and 'inner circle of trees', each circle having its gate. These circles are part of the spell: they are of course the barriers to keep out the peasantry; a defence system and a line of demarcation, dividing 'them' and 'us.' As Guy Felhmann describes it: 'The high walls of the Big House were to separate for seven centuries the Gaelic population from the English invaders and this partition gave birth to two separate worlds, both perfectly alien and yet close to each other.'[18] Within the circles described by Bowen there is the significant centre; without the marginalised Other. With the decline of the Big House the situation is reversed as the significance moves to 'everywhere,' beyond the demesne walls, and the Big House, in its turn, becomes the marginalised Other. Bowen considers that the separation of the house from its surroundings had a weakening effect which contributed to the decline: 'the big house people were handicapped, shadowed and to an extent queered - by their pride, by their indignation at their decline and by their divorce from the countryside in whose heart their struggle was carried on' (p. 197). They were 'quite ignorant of the outside world' (p. 197). The many critical discussions of Mr. Knott as a godlike being may be difficult to square with this idea of ignorance, handicap and queerness, but in the early typescript version the master is much more in line with this description. Traces remain of the rather bumbling, foolish master of the original version, as when he is described 'stumbling in the dark, seeking high and low the water-closet' ('Quin' p. 203). The original 'Quin' has a conversation with Arthur, his valet, concerning not being able to find the privy ('Quin' p. 10). (Certainly an unlikely situation for a deity to find Himself in.) His exclamations - 'Exelmans! Cavendish! Habbakuk! Ecchymose!' (p. 209) - included 'Kakaka!' and 'Gagaga!' in an earlier version[19] Bowen sees the separation of the Big House people from the Irish people as tending 'to exaggerate, to the point of absurdity, the family's individual point of view: there are a thousand legends of eccentricity' (p. 198). Knott certainly fits this characterisation: he is an eccentric figure in his dress and in his behaviour. The eccentricity of Big House occupants is well attested to both in actual experience and literary example, from Maria Edgeworth to Somerville and Ross, and in even more recent writers such as Aidan Higgins, Molly Keane, J.G. Farrell and John Banville. Eccentricity might include dress, conduct and beliefs, extravagance, wildness, etc. Of course the majority of Big House owners were Protestants while those 'outside' were mostly Roman Catholics.[20]

Another aspect Bowen calls attention to is the sense of the past the Big House manifests:

> The indefinite ghosts of the past, of the dead who lived here and pursued this same routine of life in these walls add something, a sort of order, a reason for living, to every minute and hour. This is the order, the form of life, the tradition to which big house people still sacrifice much (pp. 198-99).

The Big House history is usually the history of generations, and this links with the stress upon series which is so insistent in *Watt*. For instance, Mr Graves's father and his father's father had worked for Mr. Knott (p. 142). It clearly shows the kind of 'tradition' based solely on what has 'always been' that Beckett is mocking in his narrative: 'And in this long chain of consistence, a chain stretching from the long dead to the far unborn, the notion of arbitrary could only survive as the notion of a pre-established arbitrary' (p. 132).

Bowen, one of the 'big house people' herself, is celebrating the Big House in her article, and hopes for its survival. This is of course in the face of its decline: soon after the publication of this article she was forced to sell Bowen's Court which was then demolished. John M. Synge had a far more ambivalent attitude to the Big House, this is made clear in 'A Landlord's Garden in County Wicklow' as he charts the decline of the Big House people and terms it at first tragic and then less so, and then even less so:

> Everyone is used in Ireland to the tragedy that is bound up with the lives of farmers and fishing people; but in this garden one seemed to feel the tragedy of the landlord class also, and of the innumerable old families that are quickly dwindling away....The broken greenhouses and moth-eaten libraries ... are perhaps as mournful in the end as the four mud walls that are so often left in Wicklow as the only remnants of a farmhouse. The desolation of this life is often of a particularly local kind.[21]

81

Here the 'tragedy' seems to be captured by harnessing the 'big house people' onto the lot of the ordinary Irish people who had been involved in rural activities. This is the time, of course, when 'real' Irishness is being located in rural areas and in rural activities. What is tragic is the 'dwindling away' of a general Irish past: the 'old families' alongside the 'farmers and fishing people'. He continues in a less 'mournful' vein: 'The owners of the land are not much pitied in the present day, or much deserving of pity, and yet one cannot quite forget that they are the descendants of what was at one time, in the eighteenth-century, a high-spirited and highly-cultivated aristocracy.'[22] Here it is another aspect which is brought to the fore, and this is their separateness; they are, as Bowen put it, 'divorce[d] from the countryside'. Synge is here foregrounding the Otherness of these landowners. One must question just how far the 'alien' ancestry of so many of the 'high-spirited' and often wholly absent landlords could be relied upon to invoke the absent pity: Felhmann called them 'English invaders', an example of a point of view certainly shared by many. Clearest of all is the fact that these owners are not the 'high-spirited and highly-cultivated aristocracy' they once were a hundred years earlier. And in a few more words, which in the event he decided to cut from the published piece, Synge's tone becomes far more disparaging, suggesting that this is not a tragedy, that they deserve their demise: 'Still, this class, with its many genuine qualities, had little patriotism in the right sense, few ideas, and no seed for future life, and it has gone to the wall.'[23] He charges these 'big house people' with obtuseness and impotency. The sentiment and tone of this excised sentence is not so very far from that of Beckett's narrator at the beginning of the original version of *Watt*:

James Quin. The Name. Still standing among the ruins.

James or Jim, 'twas all the same to him.

The last to desert, said Quin to himself, the last to relent. They will stand on my headstone in lead letters if my wishes are respected, but they are going from me.

He raised his head and turned it to the window, he looked out blankly with his weak eyes through the streaming window at the indistinct scenes of his childhood. Another sweet April shower, said Quin to himself, lasting but another hour, on the violets plucked and the violets unplucked. In this month, in this house, I was born.

Living mildly retired nicely within his income from the world which, if it had not made, had left him as he was, seeing none but his numerous purveyors, speaking the strict minimum to same exclusively the strictly necessary, hearing no voice but theirs, he calculated that the powers remaining to him of hearing speech, sight and endurance, considered as aids to intercourse, never his forte, might maintain the same steady movement of decline in which for as long as he could remember they had been involved and the curtain fall without his having been occasioned, from the point of view of the inevitable little daily give-and-take, any serious inconvenience ('Quin' pp. 1-2).[24]

The sense of decline, and the impotence Synge points to, is evident here, as is the separation from the surrounding world outlined by Bowen. Intriguingly, of course, Quin (the ur-Knott) is the focaliser here, at the centre of the narrative world, and the narrator is (presumably) external to the narrative world. Bowen and Synge are Anglo-Irish writers who are discussing the 'real' situation of the Big House vis-à-vis the Ireland in which they were erected and the ambivalence of their status in this world; I want to also consider the Big House as a genre, and as a myth, rather than as a 'reality'.

Terence Brown speaks of the Big House as a metaphor born out of the 'anxiety of caste.'[25] He describes it as a 'pseudo-tradition invented in retrospect'. This retrospective valorisation of a past era is, as W J McCormack writes, 'a recurrent Anglo-Irish complaint':

the Gold Age always existed before some movable disaster, before the Union, before the Famine, before the Encumbered Estates Court, the Land War, Parnell, the Rising, the Troubles, an accelerating succession of unfortunate falls each one briefly inaugurating some (retrospectively acknowledged) idyll which is soon dissolved by the next disaster. Ascendancy is the principle medium by which this fleeting vision of a stable, prelapsarian order is imposed on the insolence of fact and circumstance.[26]

McCormack is surely a little unfair to suggest that this kind of nostalgic myth-making is an affliction only belonging to the Anglo-Irish, although perhaps their peculiar position between two worlds, both Irish and not Irish, must make them particularly susceptible to the kind of anxieties Brown refers to, and to the kind of retrospective construction of a lost idyll characterised by McCormack. The 'pseudo-tradition [is] invented in retrospect' because that is when its existence is deemed necessary. As Felhmann observes 'it was not until it was on the verge of total disappearance that the Big House became a major theme in Irish literature'.[27] Myths are created after the conditions on which they are (loosely) based are disappearing. They are created out of an intense yearning for what the 'pseudo-tradition' represents, a yearning created out of loss of status, fear of the future and resistance to change. These myths become the narratives of resistance; the fantasies that are haunted by the past, unreal but potent, as a myth, when it is believed, becomes, for the believer, a fact. In *Translations* Brian Friel has a character observe that 'it is not the literal past, not the "facts" of history, that shapes us, but the images of the past embodied in language'.[28]

Bowen writes about the haunted quality of the Big House:

The indefinite ghosts of the past, of the dead who lived here and pursued this same routine of life in these walls add something, a sort of order, a reason for living, to every minute and hour. This is the order, the form of life, the tradition to which big house people still sacrifice so much (pp. 198-99).

This was written just before Bowen lost her own Big House, and after many Big Houses had been burnt, demolished, left derelict. In Brown's characterisation of the genre ghosts and the past haunt the Big Houses. 'A sort of order' is just what the western psyche seems to seek in the nostalgic myths of a lost Eden, a lost garden, a lost childhood. 'Order' and 'form' become '*the* tradition' (my italics), both a 'reason for living' and a formula to live by. The unrealisable dream is of fixity, of a world without change to set against an anxious world of too many changes. According to Bowen, the Big House, safe within its inner circle of trees and its outer wall, 'enclosed in a ring of almost complete silence' (p. 195) creates a potent image of a safe, protected idyll, one to which the western consciousness is highly susceptible. One of the significant effects of *Watt* is the way in which Beckett manages to enter into this mythical discourse. He is telling stories ('Every word,' he has said elsewhere, 'is a lie')[29], and these stories connect with the same potent material as the myths of 'psuedo-tradition' (albeit in a very displaced fashion), but at the same time they seek 'to avoid the spurious consoling function that [stories] tend to assume'.[30] Brown speaks of Beckett's settings as sites of 'metaphysical absence'. In place of the celebratory, nostalgic, even heroic vision of the past, Beckett shows the past to be irretrievable, mysterious, dark and largely untraceable. David H. Hesla sees paradise as being both tantalisingly proffered to Watt and then whisked away, like an illusion of solid ground pulled out from under his feet: 'Mr Knott's establishment holds out the promise of being a paradise where man's desires are fulfilled, where existence is not estranged from essence, and where life has meaning, it is in fact none of these'.[31] This 'meaning' is very similar to Bowen's 'reason for living' (p. 199).

Watt is not an 'innocent' or 'transparent' narrative in the way in which a realist narrative or an historical discourse often purport to be. It is a mediated narrative: Watt sees, Watt tells, and then Sam retells, and the problems involved in the tortuous journey from the event to the telling of it, to the subsequent retelling of it as it appears in the narrative we read, are repeatedly foregrounded. For instance we are told:

It is so difficult, with a long story like the story that Watt told, even when one is most careful to note down all at the time, in one's little notebook, not to leave out some things that were told, and not to foist in other things that were never told, never never told at all (pp. 124-25).

In the movement from the earlier 'Quin' to the published *Watt* Beckett seems to have exorcised many of the references that suggest the Big House genre, and this tends to increase the mystery of the text and to prevent the too easy identification with either this genre or the 'reality' of the Irish Big House. A strong focus is on the problematics of narrative, the difficulties of communication, of mediation, and of knowledge. One of the most significant differences between *Watt* and 'Quin' is in the way Beckett has shifted the emphasis, and the focaliser, from master to servant, from the powerful to the powerless. With 'Quin' the narrative enters at once into Quin's world, his Big House, with Quin as the central figure. In this way the narrative was originally constructed with a centre surrounded by its circumference. Knott, the parallel figure in *Watt*, is introduced much later in the narrative, and although he is a central figure in as much as the house, servants and garden all belong to him and revolve around him, in terms of the narrative presentation he is a shadowy, marginalised figure, impossible to know in that he is impossible to pin down in language. He is a centre that has become detached from its circumference, displaced to one side. Events in *Watt* in which Knott plays no part involve Quin centrally in the original version. Intriguingly the key encounter (if this is the correct term) of Watt and the piano tuners (pp. 67-69) belongs to Quin ('Quin' pp. 2-5). There is only one piano tuner (first named Hicks, then Green) and the conversation between the piano tuners in *Watt* (p. 69) takes place between the piano tuner and Quin, lasting considerably longer; significantly Quin does not spend any time puzzling over the event in the way Watt does. The birth of the Nixons' child which is related in the opening frame of *Watt* (pp. 10-13) is Quin's birth ('Quin' pp. 13-14); Mr. Hackett (also known as Hunchy) visits Quinn at his house ('Quin' pp. 15-17); the walk in the garden which can be found in the Addenda of *Watt* (pp. 252-54) attributed to Arthur, is Quin's walk ('Quin' pp. 6-7). Obviously, by moving all these events away from the master, Beckett has shifted the focus of the narrative radically. The first Big House narrative, Maria Edgeworth's *Castle Rackrent* (1800) is narrated by a servant, Thady Quirk, and much of the interest of the text stems from the narrative voice and focalisation, which are endlessly problematic in their own right. Beckett has distanced the narrator even further from the master of the house, from the authority figure. He has removed any sense of authority from the text as the reader receives it. Sam, who tells most of the narrative, has been told it by Watt in reversed form; Sam puts it front to back again for the reader. There is no master of language or of knowledge in *Watt* and Watt's quest for meaning is shown as an impossible dream.

Another element that is prominent in 'Quin' and far less stable or substantial in *Watt* is the house itself. Here is how it is introduced in 'Quin':

The House

The house was a regular hollow solid, consisting of six equal sides or faces, counting the roof and the foundations, the angles being all right, therefore equal. [Bowen, tells us that the Big Houses are 'nearly always compact square' (p. 196).]

It was made of granite, wrest from the neighbouring mountains.

The front door was in the middle of the rear, and in the middle of one of the sides there was a side door.

There was a ground floor, a first floor and a second floor. And access to the roof was provided by a sky-light in its midst, for those who wished to go on the roof.

Six large pairs of large flat windows, in all twelve large flat windows, broke the otherwise unbroken large flat front of this box-like house, and were distributed as follows: on the ground floor two pairs, on the first floor two pairs, and two pairs on the second floor ('Quin', pp. 42-81).

This kind of detailed description continues for a long time. The rooms and their contents are described at great length. This plenitude and solidity is absent from the descriptions of Knott's house. Knott's house is a Big House defamiliarised, made strange. It is not the peaceful, safe haven in which anxieties and profound unease can be put to rest: profound unease is what Watt, and thus the reader, experience. Beckett is not providing consolation but is challenging and undermining the bases of the myth-making itself. The reader's point of view is not that of the insider; the reader enters this world with Watt, the outsider, and questions and interrogates and attempts to make sense of the world just as he does. The focus has shifted in *Watt* to Watt's problems in naming his surroundings and his enquiry into 'what they might be induced to mean, with the help of a little patience, a little ingenuity' (p. 72). He has moved into a strange and mysterious other world in which events and things cannot be 'induced to mean' anything:

For Watt now found himself in the midst of things which, if they consented to be named, did so as it were with reluctance. And the state in which Watt found himself resisted formulation in a way no state had ever done, in which Watt had ever found himself, and Watt had found himself in a great many states, in his day (p. 78).

This world or 'state' resists naming; it lacks stability, as in the case of the stairs, for instance, 'the stairs that were never the same and of which even the number of steps seemed to vary, from day to day, and from night to morning' (p. 80); 'the stairs, the stairs that never seemed the same stairs, from one night to another, and now were steep, and now shallow, and now long, and now short, and now broad, and now narrow, and now dangerous, and now safe' (p. 113).

86

In moving the narrative world away from the realism of Quin's house, Beckett is moving the mythical other world of the Big House away from its ability to console and comfort. The mythical aspect is still present, but in a curious way that baffles interpretation and is emptied of meaning; Watt is described as in 'need of semantic succour' (p. 79); he is unable to interpret this world, Knott's house, in ways which make any sense. Beckett is preventing Watt, and the reader too, from 'wrapping [things] up safe in words' (p. 80). The myth, the consoling fiction, is undermined.

The reader is left facing a world which resists interpretation and can no longer be induced to mean anything. The circumference has moved away from the centre; the tale has moved away from a voice of authority. It is a tale without a centre, with the Big House, Knott's house, like an insubstantial, ghostly presence. The circumlocutory narrative goes round and round and round interminably with nothing at its centre: 'nothingness/in words enclose[d]' (p. 247). The telling becomes lost in its own telling. It is a tale that tells of the failure of language to communicate or master the story it tells, and, despite the radical displacement, this does fit in particularly well with the failure to connect and the loss of mastery surrounding the Big House and all it has been used to represent.

Acknowledgements

I would like to thank Jérôme Lindon of Les Editions de minuit, Beckett's executor, for permission to publish the above passages from the early, unpublished drafts of *Watt*, and the Harry Ransom Humanities Research Center at the University of Texas at Austen, who authorised me to work with their collection of Samuel Beckett papers.

NOTES

1. Jacqueline Hoefer, '*Watt*', *Perspective*, II (1959), pp. 166-82. Reprinted in *Samuel Beckett: A Collection of Critical Essays*, eds. Martin Esslin, Englewood Cliffs, N J, 1965, pp. 62-76. David H. Hesla, 'The Shape of Chaos: A Reading of Beckett's *Watt*', *Critique*, 6 (1963), pp. 85-105. Eugene Webb, *Samuel Beckett: A Study of his Novels*, London, 1970.
2. Webb, *Samuel Beckett*, p. 57.
3. Ann M. Trivisonno, 'Meaning and Function of the Quest in Beckett's *Watt*', *Critique*, 12 (1969), pp. 28-38.
4. Eric P. Levy, *Beckett and the Voice of the Species: A Study of the Prose Fiction*, Dublin, 1980. H Porter Abbott, *The Fiction of Samuel Beckett: Form and Effect*, Berkeley and Los Angeles, 1973. Steven Connor, *Samuel Beckett: Repetition, Theory and Text*, Oxford, 1988.

5. John Chalker, 'The Satirical Shape of *Watt*', in Katharine Worth, ed., *Beckett the Shape Changer*, Boston, 1979, pp. 19-37.

6. See J.C.C. Mays, 'Young Beckett's Irish Roots', *Irish University Review*, 14:1 (Spring 1984), pp. 18-33, for an interesting and convincing discussion of why 'Beckett's incorporation into the Irish tradition is recent', an 'indifference [that] had a willed quality about it, a dimension of deliberate refusal which helped to keep minds shut until the latest moment. Ignorance was compounded by defensiveness, and people didn't think much about Beckett because the word was that he didn't think much of them' (p. 19).

7. Eoin O'Brien, *The Beckett Country: Samuel Beckett's Ireland*, Dublin and London, 1986.

8. Ibid, pp. 3, 50.

9. A further problem that I have with the rather too direct manner in which O'Brien equates Knott's house with the 'real' models he suggests concerns the way he confuses Arsene's narrative about Mary the maid and her inexhaustible appetite with Knott's house, whereas it is clear that Knott has no maids, only men servants. The list of rooms: 'the coal-hole, the conservatory, the American Bar, the oratory, the cellar, the attic, the dairy and ... the servants' WC' (p. 53) which O'Brien connects with Boss Croker's house are all a part of the establishment where Mary works (or more exactly eats), not Knott's house.

10. James Knowlson, *Damned to Fame*, London, 1996, p. 3.

11. J.P. Harrington, *The Irish Beckett*, New York, 1991. An interesting and more recent consideration of *Watt* as Big House fiction is Ellen Wolff, 'Watt ... Knott ... Anglo-Ireland: Samuel Beckett's *Watt*', *Journal of Beckett Studies*, 5 (1996), pp. 107-141.

12. Samuel Beckett, Watt, Composite T and Tccms/inc with A revisions and A note S. No date, at the Harry Ransom Humanities Center at the University of Texas at Austin.

13. Terence Brown, 'Beckett and Yeats', a paper delivered at the conference: 'Beckett, London and Other Matters', Goldsmiths College, University of London, 29 March 1996.

14. Unpublished letter from Terence Brown to Julie Campbell, 29 June 1996.

15. '*Watt* was begun in Paris 1942, then continued evenings mostly in Roussillon and finished 1945 in Dublin & Paris'. Letter from Samuel Beckett to Gottfried Büttner, April 12 1978, in Gottfried Büttner, trans. Joseph P Dolan, *Samuel Beckett's Novel Watt*, Philadelphia, 1984, p. 5. Ruby Cohn has pointed out that Beckett has evidently made a mistake about the dating of the manuscript of *Watt*; he began in 1941, not 1942.

The actual dates on this material at the Harry Ransom Humanities Center show that Beckett first began *Watt* on 11 February 1941 in Paris, and the latest date recorded is 18 February 1945, Paris. There are no dates on the typescript.

16. Elizabeth Bowen, 'The Big House', reprinted in *Collected Impressions*, New York, 1950, pp. 195-200. All further references will be included parenthetically in the text.

17. Samuel Beckett, *Watt*, London, 1963, pp. 126-8. All further references will be included parenthetically in the text.

18. Guy Felhmann, 'An Historical Survey', Jacqueline Genet, ed., in *The Big House in Ireland: Reality and Representation*, Dingle, 1991, p. 15.

19. Samuel Beckett, Watt, AmsS with A revisions and A emendations. 1940-45. Notebook 4 (169) at the Harry Ransom Humanities Center at the University of Texas at Austin.

20. I am grateful to Barry Sloan for these useful points.

21. John M. Synge, 'A Landlord's Garden in County Wicklow', in Alan Price, ed., *Collected Works*, Vol. 2, Washington, D.C., 1982, pp. 230-1.

22. John M. Synge, 'A Landlord's Garden in County Wicklow', quoted in Declan Kiberd, 'The Perils of Nostalgia: A Critique of the Revival', in Peter Connolly, ed., *Literature and the Changing Ireland*, Gerrards Cross, 1982, p. 20.

23. Ibid, p. 20.

24. Beckett, Watt, Composite T and Tccms/inc with A revisions and A note S. All further references will be included parenthetically in the text.

25. Terence Brown, 'Beckett and Yeats'.

26. W.J. McCormack, *Ascendancy and Tradition in Anglo-Irish Literary History from 1789 to 1939*, Oxford, 1985, p. 13.

27. Felhmann, 'An Historical Survey', p. 16.

28. Brian Friel, *Translations*, London, 1981, p. 65.

29. Büttner, *'Samuel Beckett's Novel Watt'*, p. 27.

30. Thomas J. Cousineau, *'Watt*: Language as Interdiction and consolation', S.E. Gontarski, ed., in *The Beckett Studies Reader*, Florida, 1993, p. 67.

31. David H. Hesla, *The Shape of Chaos: An Interpretation of the Art of Samuel Beckett*, Minneapolis, 1971, p. 69.

10

A Man in the House:
Mary Lavin and the narrative of the spinster

Sarah Briggs

Hélène Cixous's work on gender-based economies was first published in 1975, near the end of Mary Lavin's writing career, but her theories are foreshadowed by Lavin's depictions of men and women. In *The Newly Born Woman* (1975)[1] Cixous identifies a series of social, sexual and psychological economies in which women are constructed as generous, altruistic earth-mothers who give - of themselves, their time, their bodies - even where there is no possibility of return. Men are more thrifty, giving only when there is likelihood of profit, and generally husbanding their resources. Using Cixous to read Lavin's stories exposes the way in which her characters operate within similar 'economies' which are discovered as being a part of everyday life in mid-twentieth century Ireland. Yet Lavin does more than merely record this situation. Lavin's stories reveal how very damaging to women obedience to such economies can be.

Feminine economies function in much of Lavin's work as she focuses on small, domestic details which divide women in the lower-middle and working classes. Marriage is one of the most important factors in these women's lives, and what happens to women inside and outside the married state is one of Lavin's major literary preoccupations. A brief survey of her stories reveals these concerns at work. Annie, in 'At Sallygap' (1941),[2] is a bitter, sexually unsatisfied and therefore nagging wife who makes her husband's life a burden to him; Bedelia in 'Frail Vessel' (1955)[3] is also unhappy, for, although reasonably content at first in her sensible, work-a-day marriage, she becomes desperately jealous of her younger sister who marries, 'irresponsibly', for love. Rita is a hugely determined widow hunting for a mate and almost trapping one in mild, repressed Mathew Simmins, the protagonist of 'Love is for Lovers' (1942).[4] In 'The Nun's Mother' (1944),[5] the sexually suited, happily married eponymous heroine agonises over the intimacies of marriage which mean so much to her, but which her daughter will never experience. In all these stories it is marriage which defines the female characters and the importance of marriage as a social instrument in deciding the status of women is stressed. Women who do not marry have, accordingly, low status. As Julie Ann Stevens comments in the *Irish Journal of Feminist Studies*, 'Lavin's work has concentrated on Irish women who must survive the conflicts of being female within the Irish state. Being female in Ireland often means social isolation for the spinster or the widow.'[6]

The trajectory from 'The Long Ago' (1944)[7] to 'Heart of Gold' (1964),[8] epitomises the developments in Lavin's work on the social positioning of the spinster. In these stories, Lavin details the complicity of all women in accepting and maintaining a status quo based on marriage. In the first story the wife has more prestige than the widow but both have the social power to oppress the spinster, while their own power is conditional on, and subordinate to, that of their menfolk or the memory of them. This construction is rigorously interrogated in the second story, 'Heart of Gold', where Lavin subverts the structure that she recorded twenty years earlier, showing that some women may well be better off as spinsters than as widows or wives. In Lavin's stories, spinsters cannot be accommodated in material economies which demand that women's bodies harvest babies and engage in domestic labour for men; neither, in the concomitant social and psychic economies, can spinsters live within the demands of feminine passivity and selflessness. This is not only because, as Marina Warner argues, 'there is no place in the conceptual architecture of Christian society for a single woman who is neither a virgin nor a whore';[9] there is also a particularly Irish slant to this social dislocation, and it is worth looking at the background to this, and how it operates, before examining Lavin's narrative of its consequences.

Ireland is perennially depicted as a woman in art, literature and song.[10] The image is so well embedded in the folklore and myth of Ireland that, even though critics are increasingly debating the possible ramifications of the use of such imagery, much of it still goes unquestioned. The *Field Day Anthology of Irish Writing* (1991) provides an early poem, 'Do Mhac i Dhomhnuill' ('In Praise of Conn, Son of O Domhnaill'), by Tadhg Dall O hUiginn (1550-91),[11] in which O hUiginn systematically allegorises Ireland as a woman. The editor's comment that the poet 'employs the *familiar theme* of the *land and sovereignty of Ireland conceived as a woman* who becomes radiant and beautiful when married to her rightful king. As a result of this propitious union, the earth is restored to full fertility and the people prosper'[12] [my italics]. There is no editorial comment about the use of this 'familiar theme' and its influence upon later generations of Irish writers. It is no accident that the use of female imagery to represent Ireland has continued into the twentieth century. W B Yeats deliberately used myths in his attempt to foster a sense of national identity and cultural pride: Yeats's play *Cathleen Ní Houlihan* (1902),[13] where Ireland is portrayed as an old woman restored to nubility by the prospect of violent struggle for Irish freedom, is very similar in theme to O hUiginn's poem. A Norman Jeffares has commented that Yeats 'formed the idea of recreating a specifically Irish literature which would give dignity to Ireland's idea of itself, by making Irish readers aware of their heritage of Gaelic civilisation, by encouraging a new literature not dominated by political rhetoric but distinctively heroic in its return to past traditions'.[14] Celtic myth, heavily reliant upon allegory and illustrated by female iconography, can thus be seen as being an important formative element in the establishment of a sense of Irish national identity. Richard Kearney has explained how this functions in modern Irish culture, acting as a tool of integration and justification in ideological terms.[15] This is not a simple case of a male/female divide. Female writers make use of images of 'woman as Ireland' too. The second sentence in Edna O'Brien's *Mother Ireland* (1976), in which she traces her own path to maturity through the lanes of small-town Ireland, reads: 'Ireland has always been a woman, a womb, a cave, a cow, a Rosaleen, a sow, a bride, a harlot and, of course, the gaunt Hag of Beare'.[16] O'Brien does not take issue with this, or query the construction - she simply states the position and thereby helps to affirm the association.

Literary attempts to present Ireland as anything but a 'decent' woman, let alone as O'Brien's 'harlot', have sometimes caused riotous protest in Ireland. David Cairns and Shaun Richards argue that the personification of Ireland as 'Woman' and 'Mother' has always demanded that the 'purity of that image [is] maintained on all levels',[17] citing J.M. Synge's plays *In The Shadow of the Glen* (1903), and *The Playboy of the Western World* (1907) as meeting with public anger because Synge showed Irish women as sensual and sexually repressed. They add that Synge's 'theory of regeneration for Ireland' lay 'in the acknowledgement, and even celebration, of female desire, a revolutionary concept which starkly revealed the contradictions and limitations ... in the nationalist camp' and observe that it was this theory which elicited 'the furore surrounding Synge's work, a reaction caused by the fact that he dramatised the explicit belief that the revolution required, if not desired, by Ireland, was of the sensual - and frequently female - individual'.[18] That this was the only reason the plays proved contentious is debatable, but if Synge's work is 'revolutionary', it is also reactionary as it still conforms to the tradition of women representing Ireland: female rebellion equating with the rebellion required by the country. Although many critics fail to debate the identification *per se*, modern critics of the use of female imagery have examined some of the consequences of the literary employment of images of women. Margaret MacCurtain, for example, has singled out Lavin in her claim that 'it is Mary Lavin in her short stories who breaks the ritualistic spell that freezes Irish women in the sorrowful rôle of bereft widowhood created by Synge [and others]'.[19] Irish women writers have also debated the point - in an interview in 1993 the poet Eavan Boland said that 'images of women made icons by the male tradition need to be very carefully scrutinised for the assumptions within them', asking the question 'what happens ... to the living image when it becomes passive and objectified?'.[20]

There can be no doubt that the entrenched historical image of women representing Ireland has a large part to play in the social isolation of the Irish spinster, as all this leaves the unmarried, adult Irish woman in an invidious position, on two counts. First, the material economy demands that women should play their part in the exchange between the sexes, specifically by producing children. In order to do this respectably, they must be married. Second, if women represent the land then the nationalist romantic narrative conceptualises women as the prize that strong men deserve to win and to hold. Such a narrative places women as commodities. This is not to say they are invariably depicted as objects, to be bought and sold, as prostitutes, though they can be. More often, women become possessions which a man may have a quasi right to own - possessions which, like the land of Ireland itself, can be fought over and colonised. But spinsters have no rôle in such commerce and exchange, and this construction is bolstered by the church. Nuns are the only 'legitimate' spinsters, and they, while they do not marry as such, still go through a form of marriage with Christ when they cease to be postulants. Nuns therefore inhabit a male-ordered place in an economic structure run by male clergy, and so play a part in the male economy.

There is a limited number of positions a man can adopt towards a woman who is also his country. If he is to treat her badly he can betray her, the gendered accusation levelled at traitors, or he can leave her (emigrate). If he is to treat her well the two main positions he can assume are either to be her son or to dedicate himself to her in marriage. For a young woman immersed in such an ideology, a woman who is also familiar with the workings of the material economy which supports it, the logical conclusion may be that before an Irish girl can be regarded as a woman she must marry (and it is after the wedding-with-Christ ceremony that nuns gain their maturity).

Lavin's interrogation of women's positions in society has frequently been ignored. The usual critical response to her work is to be indulgent towards its evocation of a vanishing pastoral existence with Lavin being described as a '*typical* chronicler of the farms and small towns in the 1930s and 1940s'[21] [my italics]. Such a reading removes it in effect, if not in intention, from the field of serious literary criticism, regarding it instead as romantic matter 'focusing particularly on love and on the lives of women'.[22] Lavin's work is, however, more radical in its critique of established notions of female cultural and national identity than many critics have allowed. Lavin has written directly about women who work the land and are described in terms of the land.[23] More subtly, she exposes the position of working and middle-class women burdened with the load of 'nation'.

On the face of it, there is little difference between the three main characters in 'The Long Ago'.[24] Ella, Dolly and Hallie are three women who were girls together in the small town in which they were born and in which they still live. They are similar in class, education and economic situation, and differ only in that when the story opens one is a wife, one is a widow and one is a spinster. That the main difference between them is one of social status to do with matrimony is made plain by Dolly, the widow. When she is annoyed with Hallie, the spinster, she reflects that 'there was a big difference between a married woman and a spinster, and even a widow was not the same as a woman who had never had a man in the house at all!' (p. 123). Hallie has not married, because she was jilted. Her man married his boss's daughter with the community's full approval for his good sense and good fortune. Hallie's solace is that both Ella and Dolly are aware that she did once have a man in her life, and her thoughts and conversation are concentrated upon those times (the long ago) when she had the high status of being a romantic figure, wanted by a man. When Ella is widowed, and therefore suddenly bereft of the distinction of being a married woman, it is to Hallie that she first turns. Flinging herself into Hallie's arms she demands her understanding and empathy, crying 'How will I live without him?', but Hallie cannot respond to the appeal. Her answer is to retreat to the past, the last time the women shared a common set of experiences, saying: 'While you were all upstairs ... I was sitting here thinking how lovely it would be when you, Dolly and I would be together again like we used to be. Like long ago' (p. 131). Unfortunately for Hallie, the time when all three women were single is so long ago that it has no relevance for Ella or Dolly and, indeed, seems to them to be a denial of their superior status, achieved since. Ella, therefore, turns, screaming, from Hallie's arms to the arms of those women who have experienced what she is experiencing; first to her mother and then to Dolly. The gap between an old maid and women who have 'had a man in the house' is too great to be bridged. Dolly takes over, pushing Hallie to one side:

dropping down on her knees she put her arms around Ella, and whispered something into her ear. Ella stopped screaming at once. Hallie stared at them.

She hadn't heard what Dolly whispered but her eyes fastened on the hands of her friends, that were tightly clasped. And on their hands she saw their wedding rings.

She knew then what Dolly had said (p. 131).

94

Frank O'Connor's comment on this story is a typical, and influential, example of the critical community's attitude to Lavin's work. In an article he wrote in 1960 O'Connor says that in her portrayal of Hallie's spurned offer of comfort, Lavin 'projects an atrocious scene, a scene that for me at least weakens the whole effect of a beautiful story'. He then translates the 'values' (his word) of the story into male terms, comparing the 'old maid' (his words) to 'the good-natured idler who in comforting his successful friends for their reverses presumes too much and slights the years of labour and achievement'. He also says that in male terms 'the reproof would have been quieter and more crushing'.[25] O'Connor makes no allowance for the different set of social values which affect Lavin's female characters and none for the dramatic irony with which she uncovers these issues. Roused abruptly from her dream of re-union, Hallie, suddenly and completely and for the first time, knows herself to be irrevocably excluded from sistership with her two best friends simply by virtue of her low caste, and the dramatic repudiation of her offer of comfort is entirely consistent within the context of the story. Ella and Dolly have always understood Hallie. They know her background and they have formed a bond over the years which occasional exasperation with her has not severed. If Ella and Dolly's reaction to Hallie is so strong as to be 'atrocious' then so is the extent of the damage done to Hallie's sense of self, and so too is the social system which can completely reject a woman just because she is unmarried. It is difficult to imagine a more 'crushing reproof' than that suffered by Hallie. There is no romantic narrative left for her; she has been unable to grow up and leave her youth behind her as it is only as a wife and mother, and less so as a widow, that she could function properly as an adult. Her only avenue of escape has been to retreat to the past and try to re-live it, and this has now been blocked. O'Connor, without apology, explanation or apparent irony, equates the 'old maid' with the 'idler', and the married woman with the 'successful' business man. In other words, the married women are doing something and earning something - labouring, even if domestically, and producing (and re-producing) as part of an economy. The spinster is not. She is unemployed, idle, and culpably so: the inference is that she should have married someone, anyone, rather than just mourned a lost love. O'Connor is thereby unconsciously reinforcing the very structures Lavin is exposing, and exposing his own lack of self-consciousness about his own material and economic judgements - his own 'masculine economy' (one of return for expenditure, or profit, as Cixous would call it).

Cixous's masculine and feminine economies operate throughout this story. Since Dominie's widow, Blossom, has married again, Hallie has tended her dead lover's grave assiduously, giving without thought of return, remaining faithful to his memory and so performing to perfection the self-appointed rôle of grieving widow. She even buys the next-door plot to Dominie's in the cemetery for her own eventual resting place, although she says she would not have done so had Blossom stayed a widow. Hallie, however, was not married to Dominie and her fidelity is misplaced, as is made clear by the reaction of the local community - 'people felt that she was going altogether too far' (p. 119). There is a general feeling that Blossom's position is in danger of being usurped by Hallie's presumption and Hallie has no right to behave as she does. The irony of the situation, though, is plain to Ella and to Dolly, as they know that Blossom will be buried with Dominie no matter how many times she should remarry, as local custom decrees. The material economy at work here declares that, once a woman has officially staked her claim on a man, by marrying him, it remains staked - 'a wife is buried with her first husband' (p. 119). They can only hope that no one tells Hallie who, in her childlike way, has not understood this. Hallie's low status, as a spinster, does not entitle her to a public show of her emotions, emotions which are wasted when spent on another woman's man. She is generous, and therefore technically womanly, but she has got it wrong - she is generous in inappropriate ways. Hallie has a faded face and faded hair and her 'thin body', says the narrator, has 'dried up without giving out any of its sweetness' (p. 121). Hallie should have given that sweetness to a husband, not kept it selfishly to herself, unharvested and showing no return. The social necessity for appropriate emotional response is made clear when Ella's husband dies. A distant relation bursts into tears on hearing of his imminent death and is told to 'Hush!' - 'not to silence her, but to direct her grief into more suitable channels' (p. 129). The fact that these channels exist and are clearly defined in the culture Lavin is writing about underlies Hallie's childlike misunderstanding of social, economic and gender economies.

In 'The Long Ago' Lavin uncovers the social structure which defines women in the small community she examines. The point made is that women are classified, socially, in terms of their relationship with men and that that union is more important than any other. Without it there can be no empathy and no equality of understanding, even though so much else in the women's lives may be shared. Those women who do not participate in the adult world of marriage and motherhood remain set apart by a lack of maturity in their understanding of the material world. The women in this story do not question the hierarchy and those with a higher status act in collusion with it, in order to protect their own position. The final lines of the story, as Ella and Dolly whisper together, their ringed hands clasped, sum the position up.

In 'Heart of Gold',[26] Lavin returned to her consideration of the place of the spinster, this time pushing the disadvantages - and advantages - of this position further. The protagonist is Lucy, a woman who, unusually in Irish literature, is an independent, contented and respected spinster who has inherited the family home from her mother. She marries later in life, when the lover of her youth is widowed, in a secret and hurried ceremony after a swift courtship. When the couple call on Lucy's married sisters to break the news, before catching a train for Dublin, Lucy is disturbed by their comments. Instead of excitement, admiration for her daring and a sense of unity being communicated they say such things as: 'Well, it's your own business, Lucy - I hope you know what you are doing - I hope you'll be happy - You must make the best of it now' (pp. 95-6). Lucy dismisses their reaction as one of annoyance with her for ceasing to be useful to them in her rôle of spinster aunt, but she is definitely shaken. As Lucy takes her seat upon the train that is to take her and her husband to Dublin, where Sam lives, the subtle questioning of the concept of marriage as a 'good thing', implicit in the comments of Lucy's sisters, comes to the fore. Lucy whispers 'Oh, Sam, did we do right?' (p. 95).

As the journey continues and Sam, reminded of his previous wedding trip with his first bride, Mona, begins to talk about their life together, it dawns upon Lucy that she has made an enormous and hideous mistake. The more Sam talks the more he reveals about his first marriage and his own character, and the worse Lucy feels. She escapes as far as the train corridor to get away from the anecdotes about Mona, from the prospect of being 'boxed up' (p. 99) in Mona's house and from Sam's calm assumptions about what is essential to his and Lucy's future happiness. In the following passage Lavin allows the reader to gauge the full extent of Lucy's realisation and subsequent despair. Lavin's inversion of our expectations is surprising. A close reading of this passage reveals an unexpected renegotiation of the amenities of spinsterhood. Lucy's emotions are laid bare as she tries to remove Mona's worn and grime-embedded wedding rings from her own fingers:

they were a tight fit and her fingers swelled when she tugged at them, but she went on trying to drag them off until the skin broke and began to bleed ... Anyway if she were to bare the bone, what difference would it make? For that matter, what difference would it make if she did get the rings off? If she threw them out the window, it would not alter her situation. It would have been more to the purpose to have thrown herself out.

Insidiously, when it came again, this thought was less alien. A strange excitement made a vein in her throat throb, and at the same time it seemed that the train was gathering speed crazily, like a train derailed. The rattling carriages careered after each other, but every now and then they veered slightly, as if they would unlock their couplings and fly asunder. If at that moment she were to press the door handle, she knew exactly what would happen ... Snatched from her feet, freed from all volition, she, too, would be violently caught up and sucked into that rushing current. Like a bit of paper, she'd be blown away. She went nearer to the door ...

But in her heart she knew it was too late. She was committed to being real at last.

Sam had committed her. (pp. 100-1)

Middle-aged Lucy has entered the 'real', grown up world of women for the first time in her life. Sam has made her 'real' by marrying her. Only in marriage can the true economic worth of women be realised, and this worth, and the sequential commodification of women, is clear throughout this story.

Lucy's rings, economically recycled by Sam, symbolise her admission into this adult, 'real' world. Rings are important signifiers in both the stories discussed here. Lucy's ring 'handcuff[s]' (p. 100) her to Sam, while for Hallie her friends' wedding rings symbolise her exclusion from their higher caste. Wedding rings are the public display of the private commodification of women. Mona is first discovered in the local shop, on display as the goods are, playing with a card used for 'taking the measure of a girl's ring finger' (p. 87). Sam is, he explains to Lucy, obliged to become engaged to Mona once he has entered the shop and has been seen publicly discussing rings with her, but his efforts to excuse himself distort the common-sense boundaries of consumption and commerce. After all, just because something, or someone, is arranged as a product, and interest is expressed in that product by a prospective purchaser, one is not obliged to buy. And if one does make a mistaken purchase one can still, under certain conditions, return, refuse or exchange the goods at a later date; and at this time it is only engagement which is being discussed, so there is no question of divorce. Sam, however, convinces himself that his motivation in becoming engaged to Mona is to avoid being 'dishonourable' (p. 87). In fact he is motivated less by concepts of honour than by his own needs and wants. He, from his cultural base, constructs women as desirable commodities much sought after; a man needs a wife even as a woman needs a husband, but he needs her for his comfort while she needs him for respectable status. Expressions such as a woman trying to 'catch' a man become materially and economically literalised here, and women 'lay claim' to men in the same way. The currency with which women trade is their looks; these do not tend to last once they are married (Mona 'looked very badly towards the end' [p. 97]), but by then they have served their purpose so that does not matter. Lucy, however, while she remains unmarried, still good-looking and available, is a 'romantic figure, tantalising, unpredictable' (p. 88), and therefore a dangerous woman, one who can't be left loose and unclaimed. Once Sam has snapped her up she can be safely restrained - 'boxed up in Mona's house' - and so put away like the consumer goods she represents. The story ends, shortly after the passage quoted above, with male pride in having finally got the goods.

Lavin plays with the language of passion in this passage; the phrase 'freed from all volition, she, too, would be violently caught up and sucked into that rushing current' is appropriate to Lucy's wedding day with the wedding night approaching and Lavin invokes an inverse sexual fantasy with these words. The language could be, and, in the context of the story, should be, leading towards the ecstasy of orgasm, not the despair of death. Lucy's sexual fantasy is unlikely to become reality. Sam has woken his one-time lover with a 'quick kiss' - 'so quick it wouldn't disturb a mouse' (p. 92) - and he cannot match the passionate, transporting motion described in the train's rush. Sam's desire is to have what the narrator implies every man wants from his woman: lunch on time and kindness and his buttons sewn on when they fall off (and we know his first wife was a 'good worker' [p. 97]). Again the masculine economy described by Lavin is one of profit, of thrift and not spending without return: the quick, insignificant kiss, the economical honeymoon in Sam's 'cosy' house, the recycling of Mona's wedding and engagement rings. All this is offered in direct contrast to the feminine economy which Lavin presents as ungrudging and generous-hearted; an economy which serves, and which is endorsed by, men. This feminine economy is represented by Mona, a generous woman who tried hard to play her part in this economic structure, but failed as she produced no children. Hard physical labour and 'four or five miscarriages' (p. 98) presumably contributed to her early grave, leaving a space for Lucy to embrace her duty and her previously unfulfilled rôle as wife and, possibly, mother. The young Lucy's real fear of maternity and childbirth is made plain early on in the story, when she is talking, without properly communicating, with Sam:

'matrimony doesn't appeal to me,' she said, 'much less maternity.' For a minute she thought she had uncovered her fears of childbirth, but she hadn't really disclosed anything and so he didn't believe her (p. 86).

This is significant in terms of a feminine economy. The narrator tells us that 'she thought ... he didn't believe her', but whatever Lucy may have thought, it is immediately after this passage that Sam becomes engaged to Mona. If Lucy is refusing to play her part in the economic exchange between men and women then there is little point in Sam wasting time courting her.

Lucy, in the train fantasy, is experiencing a 'violent, dark revolt of being' - one of the phrases Julia Kristeva uses when describing the 'abject'.[27] If, as Kristeva suggests, 'all abjection is in fact recognition of the want on which any being, meaning, language or desire is founded' then Kristeva's theories are relevant to Lucy's desire to marry and become a wife, respectable and respected for the very fact of being so. Her despair upon finding herself trapped in a hopeless situation, married to a man with whom she shares nothing, leads to her internal revolt, made plain by her sensation of rising panic, the spilling of her blood and her fantasy of suicide. It leads her also to another sense of abjection, which concerns the eradication of stable categories and meanings - the inside becoming part of the outside as the whole is broken down into a mass of undifferentiated elements. Lucy experiences such an eradication as she leaves all she has known behind her and sets out for a new life with Sam. Although she thought she knew Sam, she realises that he is a stranger to her, and the carefully constructed memories she had of him shatter and are dashed away. Everything she thought she knew is now open for fresh interpretation, including the fact that marriage is the 'right' thing for her, or for any woman, and Lucy is very frightened by this. Lavin exposes Lucy's vulnerability as she explores the new categories and meanings of her new life, and paces the confines of her 'box'. As Lucy fantasises about being 'violently caught up and sucked into that rushing current', in the train passage, she knows that to be actually caught up in such a current and thus return to the outside would mean certain death. There is eroticism in this knowledge; 'a strange excitement made a vein in her throat throb' and there is violence, the violence of the 'crazy' speed of the train, the carriages 'coupled' but veering 'as if they would fly asunder'. There is also a suggestion of auto-eroticism as Lucy works herself up to an increasing pitch of ever more intense focus upon her inner and physical self. It is only away from Sam that Lucy can become excited, and only alone - essentially a solipsistic and masturbatory exercise and one which, again, indicates an inability or reluctance on Lucy's part to engage in an exchange or economy which involves men. The dissolving boundaries of her own body are symbolised in the shedding of her blood as a result of her own desperation to escape her fate.

Lavin has constrained Lucy in several 'boxes' in this story, not just the 'box' of Mona's house. Before Sam's advent she is free, unrestricted, but as soon as they are married Lucy begins to feel imprisoned. Everything she has known before has made her feel part of her own local landscape but now everything changes. The familiar fields among which she has lived disappear when seen from inside the moving train - they are flung back 'as if flung out of existence' (p. 96). In future, Lucy's world will be a cityscape,[28] and this will add a further set of restrictions to her 'boxed' life. Mona's rings restrict the flow of blood to Lucy's fingers - they are too tight, but cannot be removed even though 'she went on trying to drag them off until the skin broke and began to bleed'. Marriage has confused the perimeters with which Lucy has been familiar, and marriage, in a society which does not allow divorce, has placed her in a position from which there is no escape other than the death of one or both of the partners.

In fact, all that has happened to Lucy is that she has achieved her heart's desire and married her childhood sweetheart. It is a strange inversion of the accepted social code that the prospect of living with 'a man in the house' should be enough to make her fantasise about suicide. Lucy is rightly suspicious of her sisters' cool reception of her marriage - all she has ever known leads her to believe that marriage is the ultimate aim of all women and the proper way to live. Lavin does not demonise Sam. His is the 'heart of gold' of the title, but the irony which characterises so much of Lavin's work is much to the fore here. In his composed remembrances of Mona, his unruffled possession of Lucy and his desire to set her to work looking after him, Sam is not unreasonable; this is how her sisters live, how Mona lived, how, indeed, the community from which Lucy comes expects wives to live, but to Lucy, who knows all that, such 'reality' is intolerable.

Lavin is writing about marriage as entrapment - the sort of entrapment that Joyce wrote about in *Dubliners*, although his was firmly linked to the city of Dublin while Lavin is dealing with small rural towns. Language plays its part in this entrapment; Lavin's characters are trapped by their inability to express themselves even as Joyce's were - a strategy which can function as a trap for the reader, too (as it did for O'Connor). Women can, of course, escape the cultural conditions in which they live, but in order to do this they need to be very strong; strong enough to fight against the cultural influences, including religion, in which they have been immersed since birth. Such a fight is difficult, if not impossible, in the absence of models - real and imagined - who have successfully done so.

Even while the quality and conditions of life in Ireland continue to change, the system Lavin grapples with remains deep-rooted, having evolved from centuries of cultural construction of women as Ireland, a construction which isolates those women who are not wives and mothers, and Lavin invites the contemporary reader to examine the basis to a social structure which effectively damages women, not just by demanding that they marry, but by refusing to value any alternative to marriage except religious seclusion. Lavin is an important chronicler of and commentator on mid-twentieth century Irish social and gender issues. Her virtual exclusion from academic study and serious critical debate leaves the area of Irish studies incomplete.

NOTES

1.   Hélène Cixous, *La Jeune Née* (1975), translated as Hélène Cixous and Catherine Clément, *The Newly Born Woman*, Minnesota, 1976.

2.   'At Sallygap' was first published in *Atlantic Monthly*, 168, October 1941, pp. 464-476, then in numerous collections, the most recent being *The Stories of Mary Lavin*, Vol.II, London, 1974.

3.   'Frail Vessel' was first published in *Irish Writing*, 30, March 1955, pp. 16-34, and then reprinted in many collections, the most recent being *The Stories of Mary Lavin* (2 vols.), Vol. I, London, 1964.

4.   'Love is for Lovers' was first published in *Harper's Bazaar*, 76, January 1942, and then reprinted in many collections, the most recent being *The Secret Self Short Stories by Women*, ed. Hermione Lee, London, 1985, pp. 93-116.

5.   'The Nun's Mother' was first published in *The Long Ago and Other Stories*, London, 1944, then in *At Sallygap and Other Stories*, Boston, 1947, and *The Stories of Mary Lavin*, Vol. II.

6.   Julie Ann Stevens, 'Mary Lavin (1912-1996). A Tribute', in *Irish Journal of Feminist Studies*, 2, 1996, pp. 25-34.

7.   'The Long Ago' was first published in *The Long Ago and Other Stories*, London, 1944, and then in *Collected Stories*, Boston, 1971 and *The Stories of Mary Lavin*, Vol. II.

8.   'Heart of Gold' was first published in the *New Yorker*, 40, June 27 1964, pp. 29-38 and then collected in *The Stories of Mary Lavin*, Vol. III, London, 1985.

9.   Marina Warner, *Alone of All Her Sex: The Myth and Cult of the Virgin Mary*, New York, 1976, p. 235.

10.   For a discussion of the use of female imagery in Irish writing and song see Toni O'Brien Johnson and David Cairns, *Gender in Irish Writing*, Oxford, 1991. And see also almost any cartoon depicting Ireland's relationship with England in the nineteenth century - in particular the *Weekly Freeman* in the 1880s.

11.   Seamus Deane, ed., *The Field Day Anthology of Irish Writing*, Derry, 1991, p. 51.

12.   Ibid., p. 51.

13.   Anne-Marie Fyfe dismisses Yeats's depiction of the old woman made young as a male fantasy, rejecting the metaphorical notion of Irish freedom as a 'form of hormone replacement therapy'. Her article is entitled 'Women and Mother Ireland' in Sarah Sceats and Gail Cunning-

ham, eds., *Image and Power: Women in Fiction in the Twentieth Century*, London, 1996, p. 186.

14. A Norman Jeffares, in his Introduction to *W B Yeats: Selected Poetry*, London, 1990, p. xv.

15. Richard Kearney, *Transitions: Narratives in Modern Irish Culture*, Manchester, 1988.

16. Edna O'Brien, *Mother Ireland*, London, 1976, p. 11.

17. David Cairns and Shaun Richards, *Writing Ireland: Colonialism, nationalism and culture*, Manchester, 1988, p. 77.

18. Ibid., p. 77.

19. Margaret MacCurtain, 'Towards an Appraisal of the Religious Image of Women' in *The Crane Bag*, 4:1 (1980), p. 29.

20. 'An Underground Poet: Eavan Boland talks to Neil Sammells', *Irish Studies Review*, 1:4 Autumn 1993, pp. 12-3.

21. Fyfe, 'Women and Mother Ireland' in *Image and Power*, p. 189.

22. Ibid., p. 189.

23. In 'Asigh', first published in 1972, the female protagonist is for sale as her father's field of grass is for sale; the conversation between the farmer and the buyer is understood to relate both to the girl and the grass, and the attributes of the one relate to the other.

24. All quotations from 'The Long Ago' are from *The Stories of Mary Lavin*, Vol. II. Page references are given in parenthesis in the text. Lavin revised many of her stories when they were republished in different collections over the years - this is one of the ones she reworked.

25. Frank O'Connor, 'The Girl at the Gaol Gate', *Review of English Literature*, April, 1960, pp. 30-1.

26. All quotations from 'Heart of Gold' are from *The Stories of Mary Lavin*, Vol. III. Page references are given in parenthesis in the text.

27. Julia Kristeva, *Powers of Horror, An essay on abjection*, New York, 1982.

28. The tension between an urban and a rural existence is a familiar theme in Lavin's work, touched on here but made much more of in many of her stories and featuring particularly in her novel, *Mary O'Grady*, London, 1950.

11

Blessed Assurance or Struggling with Salvation?
Religion and Autobiographical Writing from Ulster

Barry Sloan

There can be few Irish writers, Catholic or Protestant, whose work has remained untouched by the influence of religion, irrespective of whether or not they were believers in their adult lives. Its presence is reflected in numerous ways in the content, language, imagery, preoccupations and ideology of much Irish writing, including autobiographies which are the focus here. Furthermore, the examples chosen are by writers from Ulster Protestant backgrounds, partly because there are many more examples of such autobiography than may be commonly realised; and partly because the dilemma of Protestant writers and their religious background is much less often observed than that of their Catholic counterparts, and yet is equally significant, albeit for different reasons. To many outsiders and casual observers Ulster Protestantism seems monolithic in structure and uniformly unsympathetic or indifferent towards literary or artistic enterprises of any kind. Its apparent illiberalism, austerity, and disputatiousness make it an unattractive, if not incomprehensible phenomenon associated with raised voices, semi-biblical language and confrontational marches which ostensibly uphold religious liberty against the very-present threat of Catholicism. This sketch approaches parody, yet it includes elements of truth, and is not far removed from some people's perception of reality. What then, is the predicament of the creative individual raised within such a forceful and assertive religious culture? The fact is that, just as Ulster Protestantism is much more complex and multi-faceted than the stereotype allows, so too it has prompted varied responses from those who have emerged from it and have written autobiographically about their experience. Even a simple, and far from complete, roll-call of names such as George Birmingham, Forrest Reid, John Boyd, Thomas Carnduff, Robert Harbinson, Robert Greacen and Louis MacNeice quickly suggests the prominence of autobiographical writing by writers from Ulster Protestant backgrounds, and for those with even a little knowledge of these individuals, may also create an expectation of diversity which will not be disappointed. It is also worth adding that several of these writers turned to autobiography on more than one occasion.

Linda H. Peterson has argued that English autobiography 'derives from a Protestant habit of religious introspection' that 'has placed in the foreground the act of self-interpretation: the autobiographer's interpretation of himself and his experience'.[1] Within an Ulster context Protestant influences have remained particularly strong, even if they have become increasingly secularised. Thus the emphasis on the individual's relationship with and accountability to God, and the primary importance of personal conscience in spiritual matters are necessarily modified in the case of the agnostic or unbeliever, but a sturdy belief in liberty of conscience remains and is generally acknowledged as a Protestant inheritance. This is, of course, one of the definitive ways in which Protestants, especially those from dissenting or non-conformist denominations, claim a freedom which, they say, is denied to Catholics. However, it is also true that this same affirmation of the individual's liberty of conscience has led to repeated splits and factionalism within churches, so that in effect, if Protestantism in Ulster has often thrived upon conformity to certain rigid religious and moral codes, linked to an overbearing notion of respectability which reinforces them, it has always been equally characterised by highly principled rebellion against these same codes, either in whole or in part. For some writers who have found this culture inhospitable to their creativity and hostile to their imaginative freedom, Protestantism has become an obstacle to be circumvented, ignored or replaced by an alternative framework of value and belief as a matter both of conscience and of artistic necessity; but for others, it has provided many of the central experiences in their development and in their representation of themselves. These alternatives may be illustrated initially by reference to the autobiographies of Forrest Reid and Robert Harbinson, two men whose lives and work could hardly be more different in every respect.

The youngest of twelve children, Reid came from a Belfast trading family of reduced means, but was educated privately, then went to the Belfast Royal Academical Institution, and, after a few years working in a tea merchants, in Cambridge, he returned to his native city for the rest of his life. Harbinson, whose real name is Robin Bryans, was born into a very poor Belfast family and was raised by his mother following his father's premature death from injuries suffered in an horrific accident while he was working as a window cleaner. His formal education was minimal, and was interrupted by wartime evacuation from Belfast to County Fermanagh, but he has travelled extensively, lived abroad and written a number of books about these experiences. Reid's background was Presbyterian, and a relative on his father's side was James Seaton Reid whose monumental nineteenth-century history of Irish Presbyterianism is still an indispensable work on the subject. As a child, Harbinson's family were notionally members of the Church of Ireland, and received financial assistance from the parish, but in his teens he became increasingly involved with a variety of Gospel Hall Baptist churches. Private, solitary, and eccentric, Reid was a repressed homosexual whose novels repeatedly centre on boyhood experiences, innocence and its loss, and the evocation of an ideal world of youthful joy. He enjoyed croquet and jigsaws, was deeply fond of animals, and was an expert on the book illustrators of the 1860s. Harbinson confidently projects himself as assertive, gregarious, street-wise and loud. Physically large in early adolescence, and therefore often taken as older, he was defiant towards adults and authority, sexually curious, and intrigued by the rhetorical and emotional excesses of evangelicalism.

In his first volume of autobiography, *Apostate* (1926), Reid dealt with his early years, and in the second, *Private Road* (1940) he reviewed his adult life. Harbinson published four autobiographical works in quick succession between 1960 and 1964, and two further volumes in 1992, although these stand apart from the earlier books. In *Apostate* Reid suggests that his antipathy towards Protestantism dated from an early age. Dispirited by the emphasis on sin - 'an idea', he claims, 'that to me had always proved a stumbling block, because I have never been able to feel sinful' - by the doctrine of the Atonement, which he described as 'offensive and humiliating', and by the representation of Christ in the Gospels which he found unappealing, he presents himself recreating and subverting the religious stories his nursemaid read him as a small child.[2] For the adult Reid, these tales of pilgrimage to reach heaven were instead evocative of the quest for the recovery of a non-Christian, prelapsarian world of perpetual youth, innocence and beauty. 'The scene was there before me', he wrote, 'strangely familiar, as if I were retracing my own footmarks in the sand' (p. 27). He began his first volume of autobiography by declaring that 'The primary impulse of the artist springs, I fancy, from discontent, and his art is a kind of crying for Elysium', or a 'longing for an Eden from which each one of us is exiled' (p. 4). Clearly a connection is suggested here between Reid's appropriation of the religious stories of his youth and his adult view of the motivation behind all art - or at least behind his own art. Equally clearly, Reid, who found nothing transcendent in the Protestantism in which he was reared, sought to use art for transcendent ends; and although elsewhere, in *Private Road*, he questions its adequacy in this respect, herein lies at least part of the apostasy to which the title of his autobiography refers.

If the stories of his childhood were important, so too was Reid's relationship with Emma Holmes, the nursemaid who read them to him, and his memory of her and of her sudden and unexplained removal from the household - presumably because of the family's financial difficulties - both left indelible impressions on him. Emma was a strict English Wesleyan Methodist - in fact the very sort of person one might assume Reid would remember negatively. Yet it was not so. 'Doubtless her creed was narrow, and probably it was gloomy', he writes, yet she was 'the only deeply religious person I have met with whom I have been able to feel quite happy and at my ease' (p. 18). The explanation offered for this is that Emma 'herself was so emphatically *not* narrow and *not* gloomy that it mattered very little what she supposed herself to believe' (p. 18) and this way of interpreting the situation very conveniently enables Reid to circumvent his antipathy to her faith. He quite simply discounts any connection between Emma's beliefs and her values, dismissively implying that she could not have known what she believed. For Reid this is proved by the fact that Emma felt it was even more important to be happy than to be good - an attitude which struck him as incompatible with any form of Protestantism known to him, and which endeared her to him. No doubt the bewilderment and pain he felt at Emma's abrupt departure contributed to his idealisation of her too, coloured his early-formed conviction that goodness, beauty and happiness are fleeting and fragile, and added to his own sense of isolation and difference from other people which remained with him throughout his life. In *Private Road* Reid, writing now in the third person, reviewed his own earlier representation of himself in *Apostate*, and claimed that in his boyhood he led a double life, 'one of the external life of games, collections and the rest of it; the other a private life haunted by visions of beauty and longing for an ideal companion who would bring him the happiness he had only known in the imagination'.[3] This idealism he describes as a religious sense, but he is quick to dissociate it from any conventional beliefs: 'I believe in religion, in so far as it is the symbol of an ideal', he says;

> But no farther, for I also believe that the letter killeth. Man has made God - many gods indeed - in his own image - I have made one myself.... All are human, but that does not necessarily mean that none is divine. And again I am speaking in human terms, for our conception of divinity is of a perfected humanity existing out of space, out of time, and above all out of the body with its animal needs and desires (pp. 15-6).

Reid's view, therefore, is not of an active, involved God, nor of a transcendent reality that can be known and encountered in any of the terms familiarly used in religious discourse. It is a very diminished, animistic understanding of God compared with the God of Protestantism, or of Christianity more generally; but in its insistence on the value and relevance of the individual's conception of God, it reflects the influence of his background.

For Forrest Reid, therefore, the Ulster Protestantism of his upbringing offered neither assurance nor salvation, but was rather an important contributory element to his sense of estrangement, an influence which he sought to replace with a more congenial private mythology rooted in different cultural values that would be true to his own dictates of feeling, desire and conscience. In contrast to Reid's revulsion from the austerities of Presbyterianism, the young Robert Harbinson of *No Surrender* was seduced by the drama and excitement of gospel hall religion: 'doctrine did not concern us and we youngsters liked the Plymouth Brethren, because on Monday evenings a rousing children's service was held in their hall. Hundreds went, where we could yell in chorus as hard as lungs would go, "I am H-A-P-P-Y" and "I am S-A-V-E-D"'.[4] For the Belfast poor of his boyhood, church-related activities were almost the only alternative source of entertainment to self-devised games and escapades. Furthermore, they were free, there was often food, and there were numerous opportunities to winkle odd pence from earnest adults who were anxious to encourage the salvation of the young. This is important because throughout his 1960s autobiographies Harbinson presents himself as a religious consumer, his involvement with various sects serving as a means of taking advantage of other people, and increasingly also of exercising power. By the fourth volume, it is his involvement in religion which has enabled him to leave Northern Ireland, go to the Barry Religious College in Wales (also attended by Ian Paisley), and begin a bizarre series of entanglements with religious eccentrics, practitioners of the black arts, and members of the British aristocracy, who often turn out to be the same people. His own relationship to Protestantism is difficult to define precisely because it is so volatile and at times opportunist, but it is a permanently influential factor throughout the years covered by the four books, and largely determines the story of his life as he tells it. He is, by turns, the victim of evangelical indoctrination and its exponent, revelling in the respect shown to him as a preacher of the Word and giver of his testimony. 'Born again' not once, but twice, with different religious sects, he relays the occasions with a sense of drama which is balanced perilously between high seriousness and pure farce. Swept along at intervals on waves of religious enthusiasm, missionary enterprise and church activities, at other points he is brought up short by the reductive thinking, narrowminded values and internal bullying and factionalism within the sects.

Given his attraction to evangelical Protestantism and unquestioning familiarity with Orange celebrations, Harbinson's attitude towards Catholics is notable. His childhood conviction that 'Mickeys existed only in parts of Belfast and nowhere else except the Free State and Rome itself' (p. 132) was challenged when he discovered his friend Eoin's religion, and when Eoin's sister, who had entered a convent, gave him a holy medal. Torn between fear of the consequences if he took 'the piece of popery into our good Orange household' (p. 183) and unwillingness to insult the giver, he concealed it outdoors, but was also prompted to contrast the image of maternal gentleness on the medal with the unyielding militancy of the heroes depicted in Protestant iconography:

> Fine though Billy king on his charger might be, or however handsome the periwigs and lace portrayed on the Orange banners, the savage element in them was cold comfort. But Mary, so near to our own kind of life, I could well imagine bending over the tinker's fire, warming a sup of milk for the 'wee Jaysus' (p. 184).

This experience, followed by the lessons in neighbourly living which he learned in Fermanagh, and to which he returned in the long celebratory poem, *Songs Out of Oriel* (1974), deeply affected Harbinson, who never succumbs to mere bigotry or fear of Catholic domination.

The volumes cover the period from his early boyhood up to 1949, when Harbinson was twenty-one, and although he repeatedly reminds the reader of his youth, it is easy to forget that such action-filled accounts span a relatively short though formative part of his life. Whereas Forrest Reid presents his early years as largely a solitary affair during which the withdrawal from company that characterised his adulthood began, Harbinson shows himself as naturally possessed of an appetite for whatever life has to offer, and a raw and fearless responsiveness to people and experience of all kinds. He seldom suggests that life is a source of intellectual or spiritual difficulty or distress to him, and however great his physical privations on occasion, his ability to survive is never in doubt. Protestantism in its various forms is all around him, the element in which he moves - at school, in the Orange Order, in the churches and mission halls which, he says, were as familiar as pubs and pawn shops, and at home where even his colourfully non-religious mother had a copy of the Lord's Prayer mounted on silver paper, framed texts, and unused Bibles and hymn books. Thus Harbinson's autobiographies of boyhood and adolescence are essentially accounts of his growth and development within this culture. As John Keyes noted, they are distinguished by their successful combination of two tones which are 'both separate and coherent: those of the boy Robin Bryans and of the writer Harbinson'. He continues: 'Harbinson preserves an almost clinical detachment; as the subject, he is so involved in his own development that the contradictions of adolescence are accepted without reservation.'[5] Those contradictions are most evident in the tensions and unease between Harbinson's evangelicalism and his eagerness to use it as the means of enabling him to extend his own adventures and realise his romantic fantasy of serving as a missionary overseas. His fourth volume is titled *The Protégé*, referring to the view taken of him by his evangelical sponsors, but the irony of this cannot escape the reader any more than it does the adult author of this tale of youth, because the young man who had been so shaped by his experiences within Protestantism, and who had offered himself as its witness, reveals greater doubts and insecurities than ever, even though he still declares that 'the Christian faith hung about me like an old cloak'.[6]

Although the cases of Reid and Harbinson may seem as extreme as they are opposite, their experience also turns out to be strikingly representative in certain key respects, as examples from other autobiographies make clear. Thus Forrest Reid's dismay in *Apostate* at the tedium of Sundays in his childhood when 'Everything seemed to have a natural life ... except people ... who thought that this was wrong and that was wrong, and did what they didn't enjoy doing' (p. 148), was immediately recognisable to John Boyd and Robert Greacen, both of whom mention in their autobiographies the impact that Reid's book made upon them as young readers. 'I felt as if the book had been especially written for me', comments Boyd, which is all the more remarkable given the differences between Reid's middle-class upbringing and his own working-class origins.[7]

This oppressiveness of Sundays and the judgemental and sin-obsessed theology which overshadowed them and intruded into many aspects of life, encouraging suspicion of anything that might overstimulate the senses or encourage idolatrous tendencies is a recurrent source of comment. George Birmingham - otherwise James Owen Hannay, an ordained Church of Ireland clergyman - observed wryly that 'We see sin as it appeared to men like Bunyan. We do not attach any meaning to the saying that to understand all is to forgive all';[8] and Robert Harbinson alludes to the 'regular thesaurus of arson' (p. 51) common in the gospel halls of his boyhood which terrified children into attendance where they would hear awesome warnings of perdition and punishment. Likewise, in *The Strings are False* (1965), Louis MacNeice locates the origins of some of the nightmares that plagued him in childhood and haunted the poems of his maturity in the menacing and guilt-inducing religion of his 'mother's help', Miss MacCready, and in the 'stony, joyless anti-time' of church services.[9]

One particularly graphic account of the impact of parental religion upon an adolescent is given by the painter Paul Henry. He recorded how, having exchanged a friendly look and a few words with a girl after evening service, his mother confronted him with the question: '"Paul, do you want to ruin your young life for the pleasure of a moment?"'; and having failed to get a satisfactory answer from her son, she poured out 'the torrent of her righteous wrath, of her love for me and her care for my future, of her hatred for what she would have termed my "looseness"', all substantiated by carefully chosen warning texts from scripture.[10] The episode must be understood in the context of the family's religion: Henry's father, like his grandfather, was a Presbyterian minister, but left the church on an issue of conscience over baptism. He subsequently became the pastor of an impoverished Baptist congregation in Belfast, only to break from them, again on grounds of conscience. Later he formed his own mission in the neighbourhood of Sandy Row, pursuing his vocation with courage and passion, and motivated, as his son wrote, by 'his very strong sense of religion and his desire to behave as he thought the early Christians would behave'.[11] But although Henry's second volume of autobiography shows admiration for his father's singlemindedness, desire for integrity, and readiness to work among the poorest and roughest people, he could never overlook the authoritarian, guilt-inducing and freedom-denying theology he preached and imposed upon the lives of his children. Denied the chance to visit the circus or military displays, obliged to listen to General Booth or Moody and Sankey, debarred from smoking, drinking and thinking - 'three unpardonable sins' - and unable even to mention sex, he soon became convinced that 'until I had my liberty, complete liberty to do as I liked and think as I liked, my life would be barren and useless'.[12]

Neither John Boyd nor Robert Greacen was exposed to such intense religious demands, but they were constantly made aware of the Protestantism of their background, and were often puzzled by aspects of it. From an early age Boyd was perplexed by his grandfather's enthusiasm for parading with the Orangemen in July and listening to the pronouncements of clergymen and politicians in 'the field' when he normally had no interest in either. Greacen was equally bemused by apparent self-contradictions in Presbyterianism: the fact that living uprightly seemed more important than being 'saved'; the problem of what constituted 'necessary' work on Sundays; the tension between anxiety over money and the professed belief that God will provide; and the dilemma between his mother's endemic anti-Catholicism and her admission that some Catholics were good and some Protestants bad. As boys, Boyd and Greacen were sent to Protestant Sunday schools where they both enjoyed the company, but were largely unmoved by the religious instruction, Boyd even admitting that it 'accelerated my unbelief'.[13] Their parents' attitude to church going was relaxed: Boyd's father went to a Congregational church in Belfast, but Greacen's parents, like Harbinson's mother, were not church-goers, and he acknowledges that he was sent to Sunday school partly to get him out of the adults' way for a time. In the end, Boyd's move to atheistic socialism was accomplished without lasting bitterness or rancour towards the Protestantism of his upbringing, while Greacen, the one-time 'self-righteous young Presbyterian and would-be sensualist' defined his passage from childhood influences to his own adult perspective in the poem, 'Church and Covenant'. 'I chose a slacker way,/ An anxious tolerance'.[14]

Despite this religious acquiescence, however, Greacen displays an uncompromisingly Protestant belief in the supreme value of individual conscience, and announces it in language reminiscent of a pulpit exhortation. Nor is he any less forceful in declaring his commitment to expressing his opinions openly, irrespective of the reaction they may provoke, or in his refusal to submit to 'mediocrities in authority'.

The connection between Protestantism and a particular view of history in the north of Ireland appears as another potent influence in the lives of most of these autobiographers. Robert Harbinson recounts how he acquired a notion of Irish political history which was inextricably conflated with particular religious fixations. The schools, he declares, 'dinned into us over and over again the Protestant story', and pupils were required to learn a book titled *How We Differ from Rome*. He even claims to have believed for a time that Edward Carson was one of the twenty-four elders mentioned in the book of *Revelation* sent to defend Ulster Protestants against the designs of the Pope.[15] However, in Robert Greacen's experience, 'the Protestant version of history' was passed on by word of mouth from one generation to the next: 'The "quality", who had education and leisure, knew the details and the dates, but ordinary folks like ourselves carried the facts - or alleged facts - of history in our very bones and in our hearts.'[16]

These 'facts' were reaffirmed annually in the ritualistic events of 11-12 July, which were almost unique as approved opportunities for enjoyment in the Protestant community. 'Protestants did not celebrate anything except the Twelfth of July', wrote Greacen. 'Many of them were teetotallers and non-smokers and frowned on entertainment of any kind.'[17] Gathered round the Eleventh Night bonfire, however,

> The crackle and the flames inflamed excitement, and gave some of us Prods a deep sense of belonging. God's Chosen People - not the Jews, but ourselves - would leap and skip and caper round the blaze and, when the great fire had been reduced to a few smoking embers, we would creep sadly away to snatch a few hours' sleep before the start of the truly serious business of the following day.[18]

This account draws attention to the complex node of feeling and thought surrounding an occasion which is both an act of affirmation and also a fleeting compensation for deep insecurities. If its suggestion of the participants' primitive wish to lose themselves briefly in the fireside revelry and party-making, and of a degree of licence that has no place in strict Protestantism, is surprising, this is counterbalanced by the discipline, formal dress and focus on remembering that are the essence of the processions on the day after.

Whether viewed separately or together, these autobiographies all confirm the impact of the specifically Protestant elements in their writers' backgrounds. Each had to negotiate a way of managing this influence upon his personal ambitions as an artist, thereby asserting his own right to dissent. For Paul Henry, this meant flight from his home environment was the necessary prerequisite to his achievement as a painter. In contrast, Forrest Reid remained in Belfast, but rejected its religious and commercial culture and largely withdrew from its society. Ironically, this dissent did not truly liberate him because his novels endlessly pursue a regressive, nostalgic state of permanent childhood in surroundings which combine features of rural Ulster and ancient Greece. Eamonn Hughes has shrewdly linked the ahistoricism of Reid's fiction with his intense desire to avoid the instabilities and betrayals of contemporary Irish politics in the same way as he longed to wish away the insecurities of personal relationships.[19]

John Boyd's estrangement from Protestantism and Unionism led him in the opposite direction to political engagement. His autobiography includes an amusing account of a vain attempt to arouse Reid's interest in politics, but it also shows his own acceptance of socialism as the only credible way of enabling his society to overcome its divisions and develop. Perhaps because he has never had a strong personal involvement in the Protestant church or the organisations associated with it, Boyd was able to write that he 'found it no hardship to stay in Belfast'; and in his plays he has shown evenhanded detachment from the contesting factions, although works such as *The Farm* and *Facing North* pay particular attention to the situation of Protestants in a changing and uncertain political and social environment.[20] Finally, the autobiographies of Robert Greacen and Robert Harbinson, both of whom have lived much of their adult lives away from their native province, reflect little real hostility to the Protestant culture of their youth. Greacen shows himself rapidly beginning to outgrow its constraints without feeling ensnared by it, while it is the very lifeblood of Harbinson's books. His turbulent relationships with religious individuals and various evangelical sects are inseparable from his growth to maturity. Yet although Harbinson's books are perhaps more obviously dependent on his personal engagement with Ulster Protestantism than the autobiographies of Henry, Reid, Boyd or Greacen, each of them demonstrates his awareness of its relevance as a determinant not only of the religious, social, economic and political priorities and values around him, but of his own creativity as well.

NOTES

1.   Linda H. Peterson, 'Gender and Autobiographical Form: the Case of Spiritual Autobiography', in James Olney, ed., *Studies in Autobiography*, Oxford, 1988, p. 213.

2. Forrest Reid, *Apostate*, London, 1926, pp. 130-1. All further references will be included parenthetically in the text.

3. Forrest Reid, *Private Road*, London, 1940, p. 16. All further references will be included parenthetically in the text.

4. Robert Harbinson, *No Surrender*, Belfast, 1987, p. 55. All further references will be included parenthetically in the text.

5. John Keyes, 'God's Protégé', *Fortnight*, May, 1994, p. 45.

6. Robert Harbinson, *The Protégé*, London, 1963, p. 178.

7. John Boyd, *Out of My Class*, Belfast, 1985, p. 81 and Robert Greacen, *Even Without Irene*, Belfast, 1995, p. 128.

8. George A Birmingham, *An Irishman Looks at his World*, London, 1919, p. 86.

9. Louis MacNeice, 'Experiences with Images', in Alan Heuser, ed., *Selected Prose of Louis MacNeice*, Oxford, 1990, p. 61.

10. Paul Henry, *An Irish Portrait*, London, 1951, p. 7.

11. Paul Henry, *Further Reminiscences*, Belfast, 1973, pp. 30-1.

12. Henry, *An Irish Portrait*, p. 6.

13. Boyd, *Out of My Class*, p. 74.

14. Greacen, *Even Without Irene*, p. 27.

15. Harbinson, *No Surrender*, pp. 121-2.

16. Greacen, *Even Without Irene*, p. 38.

17. Ibid., p. 108.

18. Ibid., p. 40.

19. Eamonn Hughes, 'Ulsters of the Senses', in *Lost Fields*, a supplement to *Fortnight*, May, 1992, p. 11.

20. John Boyd, *The Middle of My Journey*, Belfast, 1990, p. 197.

12

Tact and Tactics: A Case for Matrifocality in John McGahern's *Amongst Women*

Siobhán Holland

It is a critical commonplace that John McGahern's novels deal with Irish patriarchy. Three of his five novels - *The Barracks* (1963), *The Dark* (1965) and *Amongst Women* (1990) - feature fathers who are similar in their aggressive resistance of both external authority and insubordination. Reegan, Mahoney and Moran respectively, have all been read as products, and emblems, of patriarchal society in twentieth-century Ireland and as McGahern's novels repeat this image of the rural Irish father in the nineteen-fifties and sixties, that repetition seems to gain the insistence of truth.[1] The style of the prose in McGahern's most recent novel, *Amongst Women*, has left the novel particularly open to claims for its objectivity. Fintan O'Toole has described it as 'this single beautiful narrative that has no interest in contradicting itself, that commands and expects to command the trust of the reader, and that yet is never ever false to this place, that is completely convincing as a story of modern Ireland'.[2] In *Amongst Women* though, as in McGahern's other novels, patriarchy fails to emerge as an absolute and immutable truth. I want to install my argument in the spaces between the patterned repetitions of patriarchal authority in *Amongst Women* to demonstrate that patriarchy is not an ontological fact but is instead a carefully assembled discursive construct which can be opened up for discussion and deconstruction. I will also re-evaluate the usefulness of the 'mammy' stereotype for feminist readings of Irish novels, as I use Moran's belief in the power of the maternal role to open up gaps and absences in his attempt to situate his own power as prediscursive. Parodic or manipulative uses of the 'mammy' figure are potentially beset by the dangers of non-subversive repetition, but the stereotype can also usefully interrupt fathers' attempts to secure their own authority as natural.

Whereas the families and the readers of the father figures in the novels mentioned above see the domestic space as the site of patriarchal tyranny, the father figures themselves read the domestic space as signalling the frustration of their authority. Each of these men regarded their participation in the War of Independence as a fight for personal authority. The war seemed to promise them autonomy but instead made them subject to a new patriarchal order which demanded their support. Reegan and Moran rebel against institutionalised patriarchy; Reegan resigns from the position of police sergeant in the *Gardai* and Moran is forced out of the army so that, like Mahoney in *The Dark*, they have to exercise their power only in the home and on the farm. As Michael Moran, the patriarch in *Amongst Women*, explains to his daughters, he sees the domestic role as a sign of disenfranchisement rather than power.

'The war was the cold, the wet, standing to your neck in a drain for a whole night with bloodhounds on your trail, not knowing how you could manage the next step toward the end of a long march ... What did we get for it? A country, if you'd believe them. Some of our own johnnies in the top jobs instead of a few Englishmen. More than half of my own family work in England. What was it all for? The whole thing was a cod.'[3]

Moran's earlier attempts to gain authority through participation in guerrilla warfare are repeated in the home where he has to employ the military strategies he learned in the War of Independence in order to assert the primacy of his position. Moran needs to do this in order to win patrifocality, the emotional focus on the father figure. The stereotyped image of the Irish mother has such great citational force (Judith Butler's term for the cumulative effects of validatory repetition), that it is not usually co-opted for subversive purposes by Irish feminists.[4] But matriarchy becomes an unhelpful obstacle to the Irish patriarch who accepts the authority of the mother as an ontological fact, or, in Moran's words as an 'old story' (p. 156) which has powerful citational force. Of course, Irish matriarchy is a powerful cultural myth, but in *Amongst Women*, where Moran accepts the domestic authority of the mother figure as natural, his attempts to claim authority as indisputably his own become more transparently constructed: his prediscursive rights to power are no longer above or beyond discussion.

The authoritative discourses which promote Irish patriarchy, and might be expected to support Moran's claim to focality in the home, actually undermine his claim because they endorse the imaginative power of the mother. Although the State ratifies patriarchy outside the home, it collaborates in the idealisation of the domestic maternal role and helps to give citational force to matrifocality. The home which is centred around the mother is made essential to the project of the Irish State. De Valera clarified the importance of the maternal role in Article Forty One of *Bunreacht na hÉireann*, the Irish Constitution, which became law in 1937:

41 1.1 The State recognises the Family as the natural, primary and fundamental unit group of Society, and as a moral institution possessing inalienable and imprescriptible rights, antecedent and superior to all positive law.

116

41 2.1 In particular, the State recognises that by her life within the home, woman gives to the State a support without which the common good cannot be achieved.[5]

This idealisation and iconisation of women offers them no practical authority in the home and restricts their rights to exercise that power beyond the domestic space. De Valera had rejected a constitutional amendment that would have acknowledged the work a woman provided 'for the home' as separable from the home itself. Because her labour is not allowed to have value in other spheres, a woman is restricted to gaining status through 'her life within the home'. The Constitution does though ensure that if the home is patriarchal by the force of law it is also matrifocal, that is to say, the maternal role provides the symbolic focus of the home. This clearly complicates the apparently simple patriarchal hierarchy of the Irish home and problematises attempts by father figures to give citational force to the focality of their own position.

In *Amongst Women* the maternal role is, for the most part, not essentialised because Moran's wife, Rose Brady, is the stepmother of all of his children. Rose recognises the relative power offered by the performance of the maternal role and tries to attract Moran in a clear bid to maximise her authority in the position which offers her the greatest possible social status. After her marriage, she plans to defend and advance her position by capitalising on the idealised and limited role she is co-opted to perform in Moran's patrifocal family and the vocabulary of military manoeuvre used below - the language of pursuit, vulnerability and defence - situates her decision to marry as both a strategic intervention into the hierarchy of the Moran family and part of a bid for status and power.

> Out of the many false starts her life had made she felt they were witnessing the pure beginning that she would seize and make true. No longer, exposed and vulnerable, would she have to chase and harry after happiness. From a given and confident position she would now be able to move outwards
> (p. 3).

As wife and stepmother, Rose works assiduously to conceal the constructedness of her maternal performance. Although she is a conspicuously late addition to the family, Rose disguises the performativity of her mothering duties in order to promote her status, particularly through the use of tact which she employs to advance her own position without alerting the more powerful Moran to her designs. The narrator links tact to a type of power he signals as conventionally masculine when he echoes, several times, the loaded claim that 'Rose's tact was ... masterful' (p. 34). Her tact is concealed but maintains a covert threat to the gendered power structure of the home. The definition of 'tact' in the *Oxford English Dictionary*, helps to signal Rose's occupation of the maternal role as part of a covert attempt to win some of the authority Moran claims as his own. 'Tact' is described as

> [A] ready and delicate sense of what is fitting and proper in dealing with others, so as to avoid giving offence, or win good will; skill or judgement in dealing with men or negotiating difficult or delicate situations; the faculty of saying or doing the right thing at the right time.[6]

During her time as housekeeper for the Rosenbloom family in Glasgow, Rose was learning to manipulate socially conventional behaviour to help her win personal status. Significantly, this involved her in the refusal to indicate that social conventions were being manipulated at all. This concealment plays an important part in her subsequent manipulation of the maternal role but, at first, tact appears to be the first victim in her pursuit of Moran. We are introduced to her tactful skills just as she rejects them:

> Her true instinct was always to work behind the usual social frameworks: family, connections, position, conventions, those established forms that can be used like weapons when they are mastered. Behind them she could work with a charm and singleness of attention that became so smooth as to be chilling, except for the friendliness of her large grey eyes. The Rosenblooms had long known that they could take her with them anywhere in society. These skills she could not use with Moran. Her interest was too great. She had too little time. There was too much of the outlaw about him that held its own fascination. Painfully, and in the open she had to make all the running (pp. 24-5).

Rose's abandonment of tactful behaviour is tactical, controlled and brief. Like Josephine in McGahern's previous novel, *The Pornographer* (1979) and Judith in Brian Moore's *The Lonely Passion of Judith Hearne* (1955), she finds that the time she has left in which she might find a husband is limited by her advancing age. More successfully than these other women, she dissimulates her interest in marriage and so dissociates herself from the unsaleable image of the manipulative or desperate woman. Even while she makes overt her interest in Moran, Rose exploits conventional assumptions about femininity to signal her strategies as largely guileless. The stereotypical friendliness of her 'large grey eyes' appears to undermine the possibility that she shares the capacity to chill with McGahern's war veterans, Moran and Reegan. She even disguises the urgency of her desire to marry from her mother when she uses 'that little laugh and smiled the charming smile that hid the pure will' (p. 26).

Rose makes her strategic skills visible for only a short time but even during this period she uses her knowledge of conventional assumptions about femininity 'like weapons' to promote her self-advancement. Having gained access to Moran's family, Rose again exploits her knowledge of 'established forms' to advance her attack and reverts to concealed forms of the offensive. Tactically speaking, she has to win over Moran's 'troops' (p. 31) if she is to marry and she secures their approval by diverting the attention due to her as an outsider towards the children who are used to all attention focusing on their father. The ambiguity over who feels enclosed in attention after Rose's meeting with the Morans seems significant. Rose benefits from the attention she gives away as much as do the children when her kindness prompts them to speak to Moran in her defence:

> As she said goodnight to them in turn she managed by some technique of charm or pure personality to convey to each of them that they were important to her in their own light. They left her enclosed in a warm glow of attention and to Moran's repeated questions over the next days were able to say genuinely how much they liked her. In fact, the response was so uniform and repetitious that it started to irritate him before long (p. 33).

Her selfless behaviour seems to dissociate her from any accusations of self-interest. Rose's femininity is only discussed and plotted outside the arena of verbal interaction and she advances her status precisely because she does not seem to be performing her motherliness. Even the narrator here seems unsure whether or not Rose's performance can have been constructed for her own advantage when he debates whether she is maternal by some self-conscious and learned 'technique of charm' or whether instead her behaviour is the product of 'pure' - and by implication, innate and unpremeditated - personality. Nobody can trace Rose's influence in the conciliation between her family and the Moran children, and, as a result, nobody can accuse her of having tried to make her passage into the Moran family easier. Through tactfulness - the careful negotiation of the usual social frameworks - Rose advances her position more safely than through the use of overtly tactical techniques. Through the concealment of performativity, Rose plays with the social conventions of ideal femininity to her own advantage:

> No one was ever able to see quite how it had all been managed. Rose's tact was so masterful that she resembled certain people who are so deeply rad that they can play with all ideas without ever listing books (p. 34).

Tact emerges here as a self-conscious and relatively subversive activity, but of course, tact involves the strategic validation of the conventions of dominant discourses. As such, it remains a politically precarious method of self-advancement. Tact depends on the speaker's careful imitation of acquiescent behaviour and on the assiduous construction of a performance which does not appear to subvert dominant matrices of power at any point. Indeed, tact should never be visible above the level of attribution. This highlights the possibility that tactful behaviour is nothing more than an illusion which helps the tactful subject to justify her own acquiescent behaviour and tact is arguably more likely to contribute to the construction of the dominant order than to its subversion. For example, if Rose demonstrates 'the faculty of saying or doing the right thing at the right time' in the Moran household, she effectively participates in the construction of patrifocal patriarchy, as Antoinette Quinn argues.[7] The tactful subject increases her status only if she helps to focalise authority away from herself, and so tact manifests non-subversively as co-operation.

A close examination of Rose's first two speech acts in the novel helps to highlight the limited possibilities tactful behaviour provides for the redistribution of power in the patrifocal family. Rose's tactful use of language necessarily involves a careful rearticulation of vocabulary which endorses patriarchal order. In her first speech act, Rose seeks to win Moran's goodwill for Monaghan Day in order to please his daughters. Any ill-feeling would threaten the myth of Moran family unity, and dispel any connection between that unity and the presence of the mother figure. Rose secures Moran's co-operation by deploying speech acts which register her contributions as supportive rather than authoritative. She conceals the level of organisation involved in the day so that Moran can retain his sense of automatic authority and she arranges for the girls to see a visible improvement in Moran's appearance as a supposed result of their visit. When she supersedes their plans in order to bring about the type of reunion they are hoping for, she allows the women to retain their own sense of achievement by refusing to reveal that she has overruled their wishes: 'In spite of their wish to make the visit a surprise, Rose had told Moran they were arriving' (p. 3). Rose reassures Moran rather than ordering his co-operation, and asks indirect questions rather than making suggestions so that he 'chooses' or allows himself to co-operate. Moran registers his retained free will in his 'who cares' response and Rose wins no direct praise but the presence of the mother seems to act like a talisman against dispute:

'They must think I'm on the way out.'

'The opposite' she reassured 'But they think you should be getting far better.'

'How can they all manage to get away together like that?'

'It must have fallen that way. Isn't it worth getting dressed up for once?'

'Who cares now anyhow?' he said automatically but changed into his brown suit.

His face was flushed with excitement when they came (p. 3).

Rose's second attributed speech acted is designed to distract Moran from the critical tone he has taken in his discussion of his old friend, McQuaid, but this time Rose's attempt to affect Moran's behaviour is problematised by her failure to significantly disguise her criticism as supportive and subordinate. Although she modifies the content of the speech act by using a gentle tone of voice to imply submissiveness, and tries to forestall Moran's criticism of McQuaid (she cites clichés which provide conventional formulas for the closure of all discussions of the dead), Rose's attempt to influence Moran is not fully concealed and prompts Moran to vigorously assert his independence:

'They've come all this way to see you and is that all the welcome they get,' Rose chided gently.

'Who cares about poor McQuaid, God rest him, he's long gone.'

'Who cares about anything now anyhow?' he demanded.

'We care. We care very much, we love you.'

'God help your wits them. Pay no attention to me ... '

He went silent and dark and withdrew into himself, the two thumbs rotating about one another as he sat in the car chair by the fire (p. 4).

Rose's success in influencing Moran's behaviour is proportionate to her apparently selfless conformity to the stereotype of the ideal Irish wife. Tact, far more than the act of caring which Moran frequently demands, is oriented on the status of the self as well as the well-being of the Other but the necessary concealment of self-interest makes tact a limited strategy for the disruption of patriarchy. The tactful subject only increases her status if she helps to focalise authority away from herself, so her behaviour mimics the effects of and threatens to collapse into, co-operation. To maximise her status as a childless woman Rose has to appear to implicate herself in the construction of patriarchy and to a great extent she does help to enhance Moran's authority. Rose deploys the maternal role to maximise her authority in the patriarchal home but she fails to overturn the power of the patriarch and indeed collaborates in the institution of his authority.

Paradoxically, it is Rose's failure to expose her attempt to gain power as well as the efficacy with which she repeats the performance of the idealised maternal role which interrupts Moran's attempt to establish his own authority as prediscursive and indisputable. Rose's generally successful dissimulation of the performativity of her motherliness offers to destabilise Moran's claims to natural authority in the text, not least because Moran seems to accept the myth of Irish matriarchy as having more than citational force. In *Amongst Women*, Moran tries to lease the power of the mother figure to bolster the unity of the patrifocal, patriarchal family when he decides to marry Rose Brady. Of course, Moran's decision to marry is partly a reaction to his loss of control over men after his argument with his old colleague, McQuaid. Through marriage, Moran is looking to assert control over an easier constituency - Luke Moran argues that 'only women could live with Daddy' (p. 133). But Moran also implies that the presence of a mother figure will increase the stability of the family he wants to control. Rose will provide the 'centripetal attraction'[8] Quinn attributes to the Moran family unit, because, although Moran envisages the family as patriarchal and patrifocal, he reluctantly endorses the idea that a mother figure will increase the stability of the family he wants to control:

> After years he had lost his oldest and best friend but in a way he had always despised friendship; families were what mattered, more particularly that larger version of himself - *his* family; and while seated in that same scheming fury he saw each individual member slipping out of his reach. Yes, they would eventually all go. He would be alone. That he could not stand. He saw with bitter lucidity that he would marry Rose Brady now. As with so many things, no sooner had he taken the idea to himself than he began to resent it passionately (p. 22).

As a stepmother, Rose's performance in the roles of wife and mother should be self-evidently performative, but her assiduous attempt to conceal the fictionality of her maternal performance, complicates Moran's attempts to control this citation of the matrifocal ideal. Moran himself inadvertently helps to give the stepmother all of the status accorded to the maternal role when, in order to convince his daughter, Maggie, that his remarriage is a good idea, he cites and gives currency to clichés which reinforce the romantic view of the matrifocal family. He succeeds in winning his own way, but even as he self-consciously performs the role of law-giving patriarch, he helps to idealise the functions Rose will fulfil:

> 'There's something very important that concerns all the family that I want to discuss seriously.' He felt garbed in the robes of responsibility and consequence as he spoke. 'What would you think if I were to bring someone new into the family ... If I was to fill your mother's place - the Lord have mercy on her soul - with someone new' ... 'A woman would be able to help you in ways that I can't,' he said. 'There's only so much a man can do on his own, ... I wouldn't even think of it for a minute if it wasn't the best for everybody. After all these years it'll be a real house and home again. It'll be a place that will always be there for you to come back to' (p. 27).

When Moran gives Rose his name and brings her to his home she should be made clearly subject to him in the domestic hierarchy. But the patriarchal discourses of Church and State which enforce Moran's control over Rose seem ineffective once Moran returns to the house with his new wife:

> All seemed a kind of mockery. It was as if nothing at all had happened. He was tired of wrestling with it, brooding about it, sometimes looking at his bride's back with violent puzzlement; but now, surrounded by this covert

attention, he was glad to let it go: he would take tea like a lord with his family (p. 46).

In order to reassure himself about his superiority, Moran uses figurative language to describe his authority, language borrowed from an English, and therefore more easily patriarchal, register. Rose's seamless assumption of the maternal role does not prevent Moran from exercising control while he has the strength to do so, but it does mark the contestation of Moran's authority. Rose has given Moran something to wrestle with:

'I don't know about anybody else but I'd love a nice hot cup of tea,' Rose said as soon as they were all in the house. At once she set a tone that would not easily be wrested from her. Moran watched in silence (p. 45).

Rose's presence and her failure to subvert the maternal role help to expose the ways in which Irish patriarchy is constructed. Moran responds to Rose's tact by using the tactics he learned as the leader of a flying column in the War of Independence. Tactics has a different etymological root to tact and stresses not concealment but the deployment of learned strategies in combat with the enemy.[9] In his combat with Rose, Moran is forced to overt the strategies which succeeded only because of their secrecy in his military manoeuvres.

I want to focus on Moran's first attempt in the novel to shift the family's focus towards himself in order to demonstrate that his attempt is complicated and undermined by the State's ambivalence towards domestic patriarchy. Moran's daughters have travelled to see him to celebrate the anniversary of McQuaid's visits, Monaghan Day, in the hope that memories of old times will help to start their father back to health. On the morning after the commemorations, the women are eating breakfast in the kitchen and Moran is absent. Although the kitchen provides the focus for the women's socio-economic contributions to the upkeep of Moran's home, they have invested it further as a centre for comfort and communication, 'chatting' while they are 'idling in the luxury of a long breakfast' (p. 6). They are interrupted when Moran fires a 'single shot gun blast' (p. 7) from inside the house to kill a jackdaw in the garden. The unity and sense of wholeness they have established in his absence is only emphasised as they move to respond to the gunshot, 'quickly as one person to the room' (p. 7). Moran's shot comes from the front room, the area of the house where outsiders can witness a formalised performance of family life, one which displaces the role of the focal and femininised kitchen. However, Moran's attempt to use the room as a base from which to mobilise the patriarchal authority which operates outside the home remains problematic. He shoots into the land he owns, away from the house, in order to secure his authority within it: 'He was standing at the open window in his pyjamas, the shotgun in his hand' (p. 7). His attempt to capitalise on his military experience

123

is parodied because his pyjamas, which signify his convalescence, not only mock a military uniform but also signal his restriction to the interior of the house where the women exercise custodial control over him. When Rose intervenes, she closes the window to protect Moran from the patriarchal world outside and restores him to the feminised space of the kitchen. The presence of the gun in the kitchen marks the continued threat of Moran's violence. Just the idea that he might use it is enough to frighten his son, Michael, into running away from home later in the text. As the novel progresses, moving back chronologically to the days of Moran's physical strength, that threat gives Moran's authority the support it lacks from institutionalised patriarchy. But in the opening pages of the novel it has already been made clear that Moran's violence stems partly from an attempt to win power away from the maternal role and to displace the mother from the focal position in the family endorsed by popular and Constitutional discourses. The violence signified by the presence of Moran's gun is always being contested by other, less obvious types of force in the text. Here, Rose defuses the aggression of the shooting incident by marginalising the signs of violence within the domestic space and refusing to allow the incident to take precedence over familiar, domestic routines:

> He allowed Rose to take the gun away but not before he had removed the empty shell. He dressed and had breakfast with them at the table. The gun was returned to its usual place in the corner of the room and no more mention was made of the dead jackday.
>
> 'Tired again,' he said simply after an hour and went back to his room (p. 7).

Moran's use of the Rosary to bolster his claim to power is paradigmatic of the complications involved in his attempt to co-opt the maternal figure into the service of the patrifocal family. Moran follows Father Peyton's advice in using the Rosary to keep his family together and in doing so - in assuming the role of the character, 'amongst women' - he displaces Our Lady as the focus of the prayer and the devotion it articulates. Antoinette Quinn notes that 'As in many Irish homes the Rosary in the Moran household is a public prayer that reinforces a hierarchical social structure'.[10] Moran uses the Rosary to assert his primacy and stabilise the patrifocal family, and the structure of the prayer endorses that aim in that the order of prayers in the Rosary prioritises the 'Our Father' over the 'Hail Mary'. However, the initial focus on the father in the hierarchy of the prayer does not deflect from the fact that ten 'Hail Marys' are recited for every one 'Our Father.' The Mother of God remains the emotional, if not the practical, focus of the prayers and Moran has to exert force to keep the attention on the patriarch. As he explains to Sheila's boyfriend Mark, he has re-nuanced Father Peyton's motto to ensure that through the recitation of the Rosary, the father's will will be done: 'They say the family that prays together stays together even if they're scattered if there's a will to do so. The will is the important thing' (p. 137). Once Moran can no longer control the deployment of the prayer to promote its focus on him, its association with blessed and adored mothers is re-established. Rose replaces Moran as the Moran amongst women, and her name - Rose - helps to suggest that the re-focalisation of Rosary on a mother figure, restores an appropriate and validated matrifocal chain of citation both in the prayer and in the family. When Rose initiates the Rosary as Moran lies on his deathbed, Moran tries to reject it for the first time. The Rosary helps to construct and idealise a matrifocal family now that he has lost the will to control its deployment:

> ... it grew clear that Moran was trying to speak. [Maggie] stopped and the room was still. The low whisper was unmistakable: *Shut up!* They looked at one another in fear and confusion but Rose nodded vigorously to Maggie to ignore the whispered command and to continue. She managed to struggle back into the rhythm of the prayers when Mona cried out 'Daddy's gone!' (p. 180)

Amongst Women does not provide a sympathetic portrayal of patriarchy in the home and Rose is not a powerful matriarch, but as the novel constantly implies, the construction of the family is a contested, discursive process in which the parent figures employ discourses with citational force to situate their own roles as secure and natural. Moran's attempt to endorse patrifocal patriarchy as the natural form of the family is complicated and exposed because of the primacy of Irish and Catholic discourses which idealise the position of the mother. The Irish feminist project has in many ways been disrupted by the citational force of those popular and official Constitutional discourses which idealise and iconise Irish women but as I have demonstrated, we can, at least in relation to *Amongst Women*, appropriate these discourses in order to radically destabilise the claims of domestic patriarchy to ontology and permanence.

NOTES

1. See Antoinette Quinn, 'A Prayer for my Daughter: Patriarchy in *Amongst Women*', *Canadian Journal of Irish Studies*, 17:1 (1991), pp. 77-90, and Denis Sampson, *Outstaring Nature's Eye: The Fiction of John McGahern*, Washington, 1993.
2. Fintan O'Toole, 'Both Completely Irish and Universal', *Irish Times* Weekend section, 15 September 1990, p. 5.
3. John McGahern, *Amongst Women*, London, 1990, p. 5. All further references will be included parenthetically in the text.

4.	See Judith Butler, *Gender Trouble: Feminism and the Subversion of Identity*, London and New York, 1990.
5.	*Bunreacht na hÉireann (Constitution of Ireland)*, Dublin, 1938, pp. 86-8.
6.	*The Oxford English Dictionary* (2nd. ed.) Vol. XVII, Oxford, 1989, p. 533.
7.	Quinn, 'A Prayer for My Daughter', p. 84.
8.	Quinn, ibid., p. 88.
9.	*The Oxford English Dictionary*, p. 534. The definition of 'tactical' as 'of or relating to arrangement esp. the arrangement of procedure with a view to ends' (2a), helps confirm that Moran's use of tactics makes the construction of his authority overt.
10.	Quinn, 'A Prayer for My Daughter', p. 86.

13

'Chronicle of a Death Foretold': J G Farrell's *Troubles* and the Unravelling of the Union

Gerwin Strobl

Troubles, J.G. Farrell's great novel of Ireland on the eve of Partition, begins in the burnt-out shell of a Victorian hotel. Imagery and narrative structure thus combine, from the outset, to emphasise a mood of imaginative retrospection: of assembling - almost in the manner of an archaeologist - the clues to a long-gone past. And in so doing the novel implies a finality about that past as fierce as the fire that consumed the old Majestic Hotel. *Troubles* covers the period of 1919-1921: in other words, the years of what the blurb on the standard paperback edition calls 'Ireland's struggle for independence'. It is worth lingering for a moment over that phrase, just as the narrator, at the beginning of the book, lingers in contemplation of the Majestic's ruins; and it is instructive to compare the two. Both effectively predetermine the reader's vision of the past. From the blurb's perspective, the events leading to the destruction of the old hotel are seen as the birth pangs of a new nation state. The implied image of a phoenix rising from the ashes, like the view of Irish history underlying it, is designed to reassure. Most existing readings of *Troubles* also warm themselves at the flame of Nationalist historiography.[1] Reassurance, however, is one thing Farrell's novels conspicuously fail to dispense. There is certainly no sign of it in *Troubles*. Amid the ruins of the Majestic Hotel a bleaker view of events suggests itself: for every triumph involves of necessity someone else's defeat. And against that outcome of twisted metal and molten glass, the year 1921 marks not a beginning but a catastrophic end.

Thus, before we have even met any of the hotel's erstwhile inhabitants, many as decrepit as the surroundings, and most long since dead, a mood of relentless pessimism has been established. *Troubles* is not about birth - national or otherwise - but overwhelmingly about death. The first paragraphs provide in fact a perfect summary of the novel. As the Majestic slowly declined and, we read, 'whole wings and corners of it ... [had become] dead and decaying, there would still be a throbbing cell of life on this floor or that ... Slowly, though, as the years went by and the blood-pressure dropped, one by one they died away'.[2] And if death finally comes in the guise of sudden conflagration, well 'the place was in such a state of disrepair, it hardly mattered' (p. 11). Nor is there any suggestion of subsequent regeneration. Decades later, the site of the old hotel has remained noticeably barren: 'For some reason - the poor quality of the soil or the proximity of the sea - vegetation has only made a token attempt to possess ... [the ruins]' (p. 11). All of this, of course, would be mere flourishes in a Gothic tale were it not for the highly specific historical setting. As the narrative slips back from an indeterminate present to the summer of 1919, the synopsis of the Majestic's fate takes on wider significance. The hotel itself is clearly more than just a location or even a way of life. In its crenelated appearance and 'shabby magnificence', it stands for the old Union between Britain and Ireland before Lloyd-George took a knife to it. The image of a blackguard in Downing Street plotting treason against the King and loyal Irish patriots is important. It may be at variance with general perception; but it represents the view of events to which the inhabitants of the Majestic themselves subscribe. This is not without consequences: it creates a permanent tension between the characters' perceptions and expectations and the reader's knowledge of their ultimate fate. This tension, in turn, drives Farrell's account of the Troubles and confers upon it a sense of overwhelming fatefulness.

History, as the *cliché* has it, is written by the winning side. Farrell, however, was not greatly interested in winners. As a private man, his political sympathies lay with the disenfranchised, and economic injustice could, famously, drive him to public rage.[3] Something of that anger also shines through in his work, though it is usually transmuted into irony. All of which would suggest little natural sympathy for Anglo-Ireland. Indeed *Troubles*, too, with its pointed glances at the squalor and near-starvation beyond the Majestic's terraces and tennis courts provides more than just a nod at history's nameless foot soldiers.[4] Yet - paradoxically perhaps - this sympathy for the underdog is also at the root of his interest in the old Protestant Ascendancy. After all, it is de Valera's version of history that has triumphed, not Sir Edward Carson's. To the novelist in Farrell, therefore, the muted voice of a vanished Anglo-Ireland was of greater interest than the Nationalists' familiar tropes. Other factors probably came into it too. Farrell, for all his cool, ironic prose, was clearly susceptible to the romanticism of lost causes. Old-style high-Tory Unionists were, like the Cavaliers in Sellar and Yateman, 'Wrong but Wromantic'. There is more than a suggestion of the enchanted castle about the Majestic; and in the figure of the Major, it even comes complete with a gentle parfit knight. But the ironist is quick to reassert himself: for the resident damsels-in-distress are - like the Union - elderly, ailing, and plainly destined not to be happy ever after. Another attraction Anglo-Ireland must have held for Farrell lay in its inherent moral and political dilemmas. It might highlight the tension between the individual's moral

128

susceptibilities and the imperatives of power. This is a recurring theme in all of Farrell's mature fiction. He was consistently more interested in teasing out the tortured humanity in the oppressor - particularly the reluctant oppressor - than to celebrate the patient heroism of the oppressed. Interestingly, though, in the case of Ireland this does not really seem to have worked. There is an ongoing moral dialogue between the Major and his host about the ethics of Unionism: but it is undercut by both men's transparent lack of power. Unlike the imperialists in Farrell's later Indian and East-Asian novels, the denizens of the Majestic are mere pawns in someone else's game; no less so in fact than the faceless crowd in the fields. They are on the fringe of events in another respect too: for they are not even genuine members of the Ascendancy. Edward Spencer, who owns the Majestic, is Anglo-Indian, not Anglo-Irish; and the hotel's patrons are without exception English visitors, who have somehow ended up staying on. This does have advantages: it emphasises the quasi-colonial nature of British rule. (At the end of the book, when the exodus from the Majestic begins, it seems quite logical that the departing guests should be heading for 'Egypt, India and other places [...] where the natives were better behaved' (p. 423). But it obviously limits the extent of the novel's engagement with Ireland's old ruling caste. It is almost as if Farrell's imaginative powers had failed him in the effort of portraying a likeable Unionist. (Certainly, the only bona fide *Irish* Protestant in the novel, a character called Boy O'Neill, is a stereotypical thug with an Ulster accent.)

The vagueness of Farrell's portrayal of Irish politics has not gone unremarked. The American critic Margaret Scanlan, for instance, notes, disapprovingly, the absence of a 'worthy spokesman of the cause of Pearse and Maud Gonne'.[5] There is some truth in this - even if, as Scanlan herself acknowledges, the character of old Dr Ryan comes close to fitting the bill; but her comment is revealing not so much for what it says as for what it fails to say. It is surely indicative of where our collective sympathies lie, that no one seems to have noticed the absence, in a novel written from an openly British perspective, of a Unionist who is even remotely credible. Edward Spencer is a problematic representative of the Ascendancy at the best of times; but his effectiveness as a political spokesman is further undercut by a gnawing suspicion that the man is unhinged; and the zeal of the various old ladies in berating suspected Irish impertinence is mitigated by their obvious vulnerability. It may be argued that that is exactly Farrell's point: Unionism is no longer rationally defensible, and its exponents should inspire pity more than anger. It might also be said that the ironic impulse in his work is too strong for it to be able to take politics - any politics - seriously. No one who has read *Troubles* is likely to forget the earnest rendition in a public house of 'God Save the King' by a party from the Majestic intent on 'showing the flag'. And it is true that this kind of treatment is not reserved for upholders of the Union. A reference to a society for the promotion of the Irish language, for instance, prompts cries of 'How delightful! How original!' from an English visitor, followed by the apposite memory that, as an undergraduate at Oxford, he had belonged to a society 'which specialized in trying to make contact with poltergeists in haunted houses' (p. 118). Yet the fact remains that Nationalism - though relegated to the margins of the novel - is portrayed as an effective ideological force, whereas conscious political Unionism invariably degenerates into farce. Since Farrell is otherwise a consummate manipulator of his readers' opinions this reluctance to examine Unionism in its own terms is significant. It cannot have been due to political distaste alone: he was perfectly happy in his subsequent novels to get into the skin of the coloniser east of Suez. The likeliest explanation, then, is that he did indeed perceive a gap between the central tenets of old Unionism and present opinion so wide it had become unbridgeable. If his potential readers should be unwilling to engage emotionally with the former Ascendancy, his novel would lose much of its impact. The way out of the imaginative impasse, of course, lay precisely in a careful choice of central characters. Membership of that august circle must be limited to visiting Britons, who are less controversial than their Protestant Irish cousins. Besides, Britons are by definition amiable eccentrics, and playing up their endearing foibles will make them appear even more harmless. The denizens of the Majestic, the reader is meant to conclude, cannot be held to account for the appalling conditions in Ireland because they have not been there long enough to make much impact either way. In any case, since they are all, in Malcolm Binns's phrase, also 'characters in the secondary sense of the noun', their grasp of reality is too limited to make them fully responsible for their actions.[6] Edward Spencer's crackpot scientific experiments practically excuse his disastrous approach to landownership, and the old ladies are no more than a chattering chorus unaware of the tragedy in which they are appearing. But perhaps the most important sleight-of-hand in Farrell's narrative strategy of keeping his readers onboard, lies in the pronounced sense of fatefulness noted earlier, which brings us back, yet again, to the blackened shell of the Majestic in the opening paragraphs. In *Troubles* Unionism becomes acceptable precisely because it is so plainly doomed. Its death has been foretold, and the manner of its passing made known at the outset. The interest thus shifts to the victim's inner life during the final days. In a sense, the image of the Majestic in ruins becomes the yardstick against which everything else is measured. The antics of the hotel's inhabitants and their more outrageous pronouncements rather lose their sting when they are followed by a suggestive glance at the decaying fabric of the place. Hints at the impending collapse therefore go beyond matters of pure detail: they have a structural function in the narrative, and provide obvious links with developments outside the hotel. The eventual appearance in the Majestic's grounds of IRA posters threatening violence against 'spies and traitors' thus seems merely part of a general pattern.

Troubles, as will have become apparent, works both on a level of narrative realism and on a transparently symbolic or metaphorical one. Actual newspaper reports of the period jostle gaily with the Majestic's Gothic excrescences. The description of the hotel's decay is realistic enough: the flaking ceilings, the scattered tiles, the wash stand giving way under the Major's unsuspecting arm, none of these would offend the Gradgrinds of narratology; but when the letter M detaches itself from the hotel's cast iron name, reducing the place to AJESTIC and prompting the owner to hope that none of the remaining letters will fall off, things have evidently moved beyond strict realism. Likewise, the assertion of a structural engineer, called in by an anxious Major, that the Majestic is as solid as Dublin castle moves us squarely into the symbolic; and in so doing, of course, makes explicit the equation between hotel and Union, and their shared doom.

If the pointers to eventual disaster form part of the novel's structure, they are also present in the very blueprint of the Majestic. Built in dangerous isolation on a small spit of land, it risks being cut off altogether by a spring tide. Moreover, it has its back literally and metaphorically turned on Ireland: its wings opening out to the sea to embrace the distant shores of Britain. Clearly this is also a fair description of its patrons. And, like the Anglo-Irish, the Majestic is also alarmingly isolated from the Mother Country: more and more so, in fact. With its glory fading, the number of visitors from England has steadily declined; and the yachts which used to come over have long since stopped coming. Nor have the defiant attempts to remain English against the odds been crowned with much success. The grass for the tennis courts, for instance, which had been brought over specially from England, has regrettably 'gone native' and become wild and unkempt. The courts themselves have had to be abandoned one after the other: sacrificed to rioting vegetation or suffering the final indignity of being turned into a potato patch. In the grounds of the Majestic, horticultural realism and political metaphor go hand in hand. In a similar vein, a squash court is converted into a pig sty - in fine symmetry with the hotel itself, whose Prince Consort Wing, becomes a temporary base for a number of distinctly unsavoury Black and Tans. The offending grass on the tennis courts is in fact part of a wider phenomenon. Vegetation becomes a central metaphor in the hotel's decline. As the Majestic's masonry crumbles, plants flourish and encroach on it from every direction. The Palm Court, once redolent of the Empire's sunnier reaches and scene in former years of elegant tea parties, turns into a nightmarish jungle. 'The greenish gloom had deepened into intolerable darkness' and after some half-hearted attempts to stem 'the advancing green tide', the English owners of the place decided to abandon it (p. 152). Beyond, orchards run riot, English privet hedges lose all recognisable shape, and unwelcome native grass and moss appear everywhere. Contemplating 'the advancing green tide', Margaret Scanlan speaks of an 'outrageously obvious symbol'.[7] This is in fact one of the secrets of Farrell's success in *Troubles*. Much of the book's symbolism is 'outrageously obvious'. But at the same time it is unforced. It grows, as it were, naturally out of Farrell's descriptions. Take another famous example: the Majestic's large colony of cats. These seem innocent enough at first and well within the confines of realist fiction. The spectacular increase in their number over the years, though certainly ominous, still seems convincing, what with all those mice around. But then 'outrageous symbolism' rears its head, for many of the cats are of marmalade hue and sport poisonous green eyes. At this stage in Farrell's history, it comes as no surprise to learn that they are also ferocious fighters, ready to sink their claws into man or beast. In short, they are as unstoppable as the green tide. Inevitably, the first room of the Majestic they overrun completely is the Imperial Bar. The stench they produce is too much for delicate English noses, and eventually even the intrepid Major has to admit defeat. Next, they drive out Edward Spencer's faithful dogs. With names such as Rover, Haig or, more exotically, Foch, it is clear which side of the imperial equation they are meant to represent. But things do not stop there. Farrell's key symbols are like Russian dolls, each containing another - almost *ad infinitum*. Take the matter of the cats' monstrous fertility. They simply outbreed all competing species. The dogs are no match for them; nor, on another level, are the human inhabitants of the Majestic. For these are to a remarkable degree sexually and biologically barren. Most of the old ladies are spinsters. The Major seems doomed to turn into a reluctant bachelor. Angela, his so-called fiancée, quietly withdraws and dies. Her father, Edward Spencer, does experience a brief Indian summer with the village siren but proves too old to throw convention to the wind and marry her. Edward's children, who do possess pronounced sexual appetites, are clearly anxious to get out and leave the world of Anglo-Ireland behind them. Against this dispirited band with neither future nor hope of progeny to carry on the fight are ranged 'the vast and ruthless armies of the Pope' (p. 432). And *their* fearful fertility brings us neatly back to the cats, and the dilemma of what to do about them. Eventually, the Major and Edward embark on a half-hearted massacre, which results in bloodstains everywhere but completely fails to solve the problem. The parallel with the contemporaneous activities of the Black and Tans outside the Majestic is too obvious to require comment.

Much of the pleasure of Farrell's novel in fact lies in these kinds of symbols and parallels; in leitmotivs and incidental scenes encapsulating the history of those years or foreshadowing the ultimate fate of the Union. The proprietor of the Majestic, for example, may be a powerfully-built man ready to take on allcomers; but he is also the owner of a broken nose, inflicted - in youthful boxing days - by a fearful Gaelic adversary who managed to fell the lighter Edward (p. 26). The equally obvious symbolism in Edward's failure to meet the prospective Catholic father-in-law of his son Ripon - the two men keep missing each other in the Majestic's warren of corridors and stairwells - has been much remarked upon by reviewers and critics. (The fact that Ripon is, *of course*, expected to convert to Catholicism if he wishes to have a future in the emerging new Ireland seems to have occasioned rather less comment.) The Major's various adventures are, likewise, richly symbolic. If Edward Spencer stands, *faute de mieux*, for the Ascendancy, the Major speaks, or fails to speak, for England.[8] His perpetual indecision, his inability to make up his mind about Ireland (his mood lurching wildly from enthusiasm to disgust and back again) and, above all, his repeated half-hearted attempts to leave, are, like 'the advancing green tide', 'outrageously obvious' in their symbolism. Often, though, the obvious and the subtle are mixed. Early on in the history of the Majestic, for instance, over tea in the Palm Court, the activities of Sinn Féin are discussed. From a Protestant Ulsterwoman this elicits the comment 'Those who live by the sword' (p. 23). So far so unsubtle, and that goes both for the observation itself and the rather obvious way it will be turned against the speaker and her ilk. But the Major meanwhile has spotted sustenance: mustard-and-cress sandwiches. And taking one of these suggestively coloured offerings, he 'cut it in half with a small, scimitar-shaped tea-knife' (p. 23). And, since we are thus on the topic of Partition, a final example: glancing at a paper upon arrival in Ireland, the Major is confronted, in a headline, by the name of de Valera. It merely produces a yawn, whereas an advertisement for a music-hall artiste captures his interest: 'a juggler "of almost unique legerdemain"' (p. 15). The dig at the hero of Nationalism's coming hour is unmistakable, but is it too fanciful to be reminded also (indirectly) of the other protagonist of the period, the Downing Street juggler of unique legerdemain, who at that time was looking at a map of Ireland and, for all we know, may well have been slicing in half a mustard-and-cress sandwich as he did so?

Farrell wrote *Troubles* half a century after these events. By an appalling coincidence the conflict in Ireland re-ignited as he was researching his novel. Inevitably, one scans its pages for suggestive parallels. All the more so, as Farrell repeatedly claimed that his novels were as much about the present as about the past.[9] The similarities are in fact all too obvious. The catalogue of violence, the psychology of violence, and, not least, the rhetoric of violence are distressingly familiar. *Troubles* contains sharp vignettes about both main parties in the conflict. But, unsurprisingly in view of its narrative perspective, it is strongest in its analysis of the British response. No branch of the British state emerges with much credit. Its security forces in Ireland are plainly out of control, the judicial system has all but collapsed, and the press toes the government line. All in all, the picture is one of brutality, leavened on occasion by incompetence. The water supplies of Dublin Castle, runs the rumour at the Majestic, have been poisoned:

and the entire Executive laid low with the exception of a handful of the heaviest drinkers. These latter were desperately trying to conceal the situation while they coped with it. But what could they do? They were in a situation reminiscent of classical tragedy. The very elixir which had saved their lives now had them groping through an impenetrable fog. As one cheerful intoxicated manoeuvre followed another, Sinn Féin prepared to strike a mortal blow at Ireland's heart (p. 197).

It is not hard to see why such rumours should have seemed credible. But least flattering of all are the glimpses of the political protagonists, dealing then as now, in half-truths, if not downright deception. Faced with the collapse of their policies, they rise to dizzy heights of rhetorical bravado ('We have murder by the throat') while secretly parlaying with the enemies of the Crown (p. 279). It comes as a genuine shock in *Troubles* to read that Lloyd-George has invited de Valera to talks; and there is now for us the added shock of recognition: surely that slippery Premier is a cousin to the Prime Minister Major, who stoutly declared that it would 'turn his stomach' to talk to Sinn Féin, even as his emissaries were covertly doing just that.

While such political developments reach the reader through selected newspaper cuttings, the abiding images of the price England pays for hanging on to Ireland are Farrell's own: the spectacle of the good-natured Major's patience finally giving way to a murderous rage equal to Sinn Féin's; the antics of the Black and Tans at the Majestic; and, most memorably of all, the haunting image of a young officer slowly, methodically devouring a red rose. The more one thinks about Farrell's novel the more disturbing its images become, and it must make particularly grim reading for Unionists. For it describes in detail the process they most fear: Britain's gradual disengagement from the very idea of the Union. As the initial enthusiasm for the Protestant cause in Ireland evaporates in the heat of sustained violence, what is left is 'a sediment of contempt and indifference' (p. 244). 'After all', thinks the Major, 'if one lot was as bad as the other why should anyone care? "Let them sort it out for themselves"' (p. 244). The structure of *Troubles*, its narrative perspective and

134

choice of characters are all indirect testimony to that process. To read Farrell's novel is to realise how deeply eroded the emotional foundations of the Union already were in Britain at the start of the present conflict. The image of the Majestic in ruins may, once again, prove prophetic.

NOTES

1.   There are, in truth, not very many. The continuing dearth of critical writing on Farrell is particularly pronounced in the case of *Troubles*. The book is considered in some detail in Ronald Binns's *J G Farrell*, London, 1986, and - rather less so - in Neil McEwan's panoramic *Perspective in British Historical Fiction Today*, London, 1987. References to it of varying length can also be found in the newspaper articles and obituaries that followed Farrell's tragically early death. Inevitably these appreciations tend to concentrate on recurring themes and motifs rather than the specifics of Farrell's vision of Ireland. *Troubles* itself is the focus in only a handful of articles. Some of these largely bypass historiography altogether. For example, Lars Hartveit's 'The Carnivalistic Impulse in J G Farrell's "Troubles"', *English Studies: A Journal of Language and Literature*, 73:5 (1992), pp. 444-57; and Fiona MacPhail's 'Major and Majestic: J.G. Farrell's "Troubles"', in Jacqueline Genet, ed., *The Big House in Ireland: Reality and Representation*, Dingle, 1991, pp. 143-52. Where there is historiographical awareness, it is monochrome: pure green, undisturbed by any hint of orange that might complicate the picture. This is certainly the case in Margaret Scanlan's interpretations of Farrell: Rumours of War: Elizabeth Bowen's 'Last September' and J.G. Farrell's 'Troubles', *Eire-Ireland*, 20:2 (Summer 1985), pp. The only thing Scanlan is prepared to incorporate into her simple Nationalist weave are some additional American flourishes of her own. The same assumptions are also apparent in some of the early reviews, especially - again - the American ones. Frederick Bush, writing in the *Saturday Review*, 25 September 1971, p. 38 is revealing even in his very urbanity: 'Those who want to know Ireland in her earlier agonies will probably forsake Mr Farrell's well-intentioned ... story and return to Yeats's "Easter 1916"'.

2.   J.G. Farrell, *Troubles*, London, 1984, p. 10. All further references will be included parenthetically in the text.

3.   He caused something of a stir at the Booker Prize ceremony in 1973 by pointing out in his acceptance speech that the sponsors' munificence

contrasted strikingly with the very modest wages they payed their third-world employees.

4. For a concise summary of Farrell's interest in 'history from below' see James Vinson, *Contemporary Novelists*, London, 1972, p. 399.

5. Scanlan, 'Rumours of War', p. 85. Scanlan reprises much of her argument in *Traces of Another Time: History and Politics in Postwar British Fiction*, Princeton, 1990; the chapter on Farrell ranges beyond Ireland, but the section on *Troubles* is closely related to her earlier article.

6. Binns, *J G Farrell*, p. 79.

7. Scanlan, 'Rumours of War', p. 82.

8. Even the Major's name, Brendan Archer, mixes portentous symbolism with characteristically impish Farrellian humour. Archer, after all, is not merely a good English name, it also has the appropriate military - and historical - overtones. For if the earliest origins of the embryonic British Empire can be said to lie in the technical superiority of English archery, Farrell's Major represents the generation with which British military dominance ended. It is not for nothing that the Major is haunted by the memory of Flanders. But this shell-shocked Archer is also a Brendan - hardly the most common English name. An authorial reminder, no doubt, of England's own Celtic links. But are we perhaps also intended to be put in mind of the Major's saintly Irish namesake? After all, both return from perilous journeys to tell strange tales of scarcely credible islands.

9. See, for instance, Vinson, *Contemporary Novelists*, p. 400. A point, incidentally, picked up by the more perceptive commentators at the time; as, for instance, in A.N. Wilson's observation, quoted by Binns in *J G Farrell*, p. 28, that Farrell's novels tell you more about the Britain of Harold Wilson than about its days of empire.

14

John Hewitt's disciples and the 'kaleyard provincials'

Sarah Ferris

Despite its considerable volume John Hewitt's work does not enjoy a wide audience. By contrast, the launch of the Hewitt Summer School in 1987 reflected his laureate status among 'sections of Ulster's liberal Protestant intelligentsia'.[1] A recurrent theme in criticism of Hewitt is that he was victimised for his political views and driven into exile. This has transformed him from time-served Council official to principled martyr of an abortive intellectual revolution against a 'culturally amputated' junta.[2] In 1957, Martin Wallace commented that Hewitt's liberal views provoked 'ill-considered opposition to his application for the post of [Belfast Museum and Art Gallery] Director in 1953 ... it also sent him to Coventry'.[3] Nearly thirty years later, Edna Longley suggested that Hewitt's 'open and open ended' regionalism failed because in 1953 he was 'made a political scapegoat for his socialist and literary allegiances'.[4] Martin Mooney gives the broader picture when he observes that Hewitt 'twinned his Regionalism and his socialism to give an account of the role of the writer in society, in opposition to the complacencies of the Unionist establishment and the kaleyard provincials'.[5] By 1992, Ian Duhig had claimed that Hewitt's Protestantism 'nurtured the libertarian socialism he developed ... at the anarchist end of the spectrum, against what he called the anthill or the beehive states', and that his 'progressive non-sectarianism cost him a career on his home ground'.[6] In the Biographical Chronology to *The Collected Poems of John Hewitt* (1991), Hewitt's 'victimisation' is presented as historical fact; it records that in 1953 Hewitt 'applies for the Directorship ... but is denied the post, largely because of his radical and socialist ideals'.[7] To understand how Hewitt's 'victimhood' became a focus for the misrepresentation of his politico-cultural significance, it is necessary to investigate the Belfast City Council's decision not to appoint him Director of the Belfast Museum and Art Gallery, a decision that was in fact taken in September 1952.

Hewitt graduated from Queen's University Belfast in 1930; surprisingly, he took six years to complete, having twice been unable to 'proceed'. While on leave from university, Hewitt contributed to left-wing journals, attended Trade Union and Labour Party conferences and was a regular patron of McLean's

Progressive Bookshop. Significantly, none of this compromised Hewitt's employment prospects; he recalled that, as he 'idly read the morning papers' in Autumn 1930, he saw an advertisement for an art assistant's post at the Museum: 'it struck me that this would be a pleasant job ... So I applied ... The advert said "No canvassing" which, of course, made it obligatory ... So ... I went along to a local councillor ... Eventually I got the job'.[8] Hewitt was short-listed with an Englishman, Wilfred Arthur Seaby; the candidates were approximately matched, except that Seaby had taken intermediate art at London University and 'showed ... critical discrimination'.[9] Hewitt, who had no formal training in the arts, secured his place in the 'beehive state'.

Hewitt proved to be a volatile employee. Kenneth Jamison recalled that 'some people found him difficult, seemingly rude even ... [and] ... disconcertingly monosyllabic'.[10] Hewitt admitted he was a self-absorbed, 'bumptious and difficult person', and that he had attracted Thomas Carnduff's disapproval for his 'brash ideas ... a little dogmatically expressed'.[11] In *Odd Man Out* (1945), F.L. Green caricatured Hewitt as 'Griffin', an officious opportunist whose self-aggrandising interest in 'art' inclined him to applaud or dismiss in 'robust, crisp fashion', and who 'sometimes exalt[s] fools or make[s] little mistakes regarding men of talent'. Notably, Green based his parody on personal knowledge of Hewitt, whose popular association with 'Griffin' in contemporary newspaper articles suggests that his alter ego's inclination for bombast mimicked a personality consummately predisposed to confrontation.

More formal evidence of Hewitt's Griffinesque qualities is logged in the Libraries, Museums and Art Committee Minutes of the Belfast City Council. In 1935, for example, they record the Committee's unease at Hewitt's 'adversely criti[cal]' review of Sir John Lavery who is listed in the Museum's History as a 'distinguished Belfast-born artist' and important benefactor. In an article published in *The New Northman* Hewitt remarked:

> There is an eternal fitness of things, and the people [Lavery] paints get exactly the painting they deserve. The Lonsdale portrait looks as if it had been painted by a coachman. The shoddy, reach-me-down handling, the badly realised crosslegs, the bungled distribution of light, the clipped-off cigar.[12]

Of the exhibition generally, Hewitt observed that, 'not more than fifteen ... of the two hundred and forty works ... [on display] ... should have been allowed to leave the studio'. Unsurprisingly, the Museum, which was rate-supported and had an official policy to promote local artists, disassociated itself from this unprofessional review, disciplined Hewitt and required him to give an unspecified undertaking. Undaunted, in 1951 Hewitt returned to Lavery in 'Painting and sculpture in Ulster', one of a collection of essays published to promote

138

Ulster art during the Festival of Britain. Now Keeper of Art, Hewitt conceded that 'in his approach to portraiture Lavery knew what he was doing', but described him as 'native Irish stock', observed his 'certain peasant honesty of observation', judged his penchant for making earls 'almost regal ... no more than the Irishman's innate desire to please' and determined his 'vigorous gusto for ceremonial colour surely another racial characteristic'.[13] Hewitt's comments are marginally less strident than those in the earlier review; nonetheless, they are blatantly inappropriate and reveal a patronising approach to the person and achievement of an artist whose work comprised the Museum's main contribution to the Festival of Britain. By contrast, in the same essay Hewitt observes of contemporary 'Protestant working-class' street art that it displayed a 'bold sense of pattern carried out with a naïve sincerity ... roundels and insets [that] frequently achieve a surprising quality ... waver[ing] between medieval and Douanier-like conceptions'.[14] Roberta Hewitt's Journal, which is held in the Public Record Office Northern Ireland, records that when Hewitt wrote this article he fully expected to become Museum Director, and it is significant that, shortly before he accepted the post of art director at the Herbert Art Gallery, he re-evaluated Lavery's 'native' qualities. In 'Sir John Lavery : Centenary', which was published in the Belfast Telegraph in February 1956, he described Lavery as 'formal ... very courteous ... of a gentle dignity ... a very good man who had no need or wish for the emphatic gesture'. Interpreted in context, therefore, it might be argued that Hewitt's contrasting perspectives on Lavery and 'Protestant' street art in The Arts in Ulster during the Festival were more calculated to align him to the status quo in Northern Ireland than hinder his promotion prospects.

When the Belfast City Council appointed a new Director of the Belfast Museum and Art Gallery in September 1952, it was not Hewitt but the outside candidate and Englishman, Wilfred Arthur Seaby. Mary O'Malley challenged the decision in Council. Ironically, in view of Hewitt's canvassing for privilege in 1930, O'Malley objected on the grounds that any 'appointments system which depended on pressure ... by council members ... was naturally undemocratic and unjust'. Specifically, O'Malley claimed that a letter 'from a member of the Eire Labour Party' influenced the Committee against Hewitt. Chairman Tougher's casting vote decided Seaby's appointment and his reply is interesting:

> Nothing written in a letter to me made any difference ... I knew a year and a half ago I would not be able to agree to Mr. Hewitt's appointment ... I found it very hard to vote against a Belfastman, but ... I had to decide either to be popular ... or appoint the best man for the job.[15]

While Tougher's remarks admit prejudice incompatible with the integrity of the Chair, their political naïveté undermines the view that there was a co-ordinated

139

'plot' to exclude Hewitt. First, given Hewitt's vigorous lobbying for support, Tougher cannot have known his vote would be required. Second, Tougher locates the emergence of his antipathy in Summer 1951, which is coincident with Hewitt's Griffinesque review of Lavery. Third, Tougher's claim that he was motivated to 'appoint the best man for the job' is compatible with Hewitt's being told that his poor administrative skill was a significant factor in the decision not to promote him. Further, O'Malley's recollection that Hewitt did not interview very well is consistent with his having failed on three previous occasions to proceed beyond interview for senior posts in Liverpool, Norwich and the West Indies.[16] Notably, in the Museum's History there is only a brief reference to Hewitt's Keepership compared to the fulsome account of his successor's energetic innovation. Fourth, it is possible to detect a note of sincerity in Tougher's expressed reluctance to be 'unpopular' and appoint an outsider. In context, local employment had fallen disastrously and the Unionist administration was being harried by a resurgent Labour Party; the *Irish News* headline, 'Museum job given to Englishman instead of Belfast applicant', reflected this pressure and typified unwelcome press scrutiny.[17] Finally, Hewitt often claimed he was Deputy by September 1952 and, indeed, Frank Ormsby's Biographical Chronology to *The Collected Poems of John Hewitt* (1991) also registers Hewitt's progress from 'chief assistant' in 1943 to 'deputy Director and keeper of art' in 1950. Both versions imply Hewitt's career prospects were inexplicably halted in 1953. Problematically, neither is consistent with the Libraries, Museums and Art Committee Minutes which record that Hewitt became Keeper in 1945, and that a total of three Keepers were subordinate to a Deputy and Director by 1950. After the Deputy became ill, in January 1952 the Director proposed Hewitt as his temporary replacement. This is important because it seems unlikely that the Director would not have consulted Hewitt on his willingness to serve; yet in 'From chairmen and committee men' (1968) Hewitt implied that the Director had colluded in a plot to block his promotion. Significantly, the Committee refused to appoint Hewitt as Deputy, but did make him temporary 'Senior Keeper'. This is evidence that, eight months before the Director's retirement, Hewitt knew he had been sponsored to become Deputy but that the Committee had acted to avoid raising his hopes of the Directorship by denying him a temporary elevation to the Deputy's post. Surprisingly, Hewitt's memoir of events omits these details; as suicidal protagonist in 'From chairmen and committee men', he recalls only instinctive unease and some curiosity that the 'silver-haired, naked-faced Director' and his 'silver-haired and naked-faced cronies' spent an evening plotting with Chairman Tougher before the interview.

While it is impossible to reconstruct the internal politics of the Museum in 1952, when it is considered beside the calibre of his Lavery reviews this evidence suggests that long-term friction between Hewitt and Museum policy was not rooted solely in crude Unionist vendettas. Crucially, in her Journal, Roberta Hewitt criticised her husband's insistence on being forthright and not paying much attention to the people on the Town Council, and yet expecting them to give him the job. Accordingly, it is possible to speculate that Hewitt was generally perceived as operating with a professional hubris that was incompatible with his role as public servant, and that he was considered temperamentally unsuited to manage the diverse priorities of a public resource.

By contrast, introducing *Ancestral Voices* in 1987, Tom Clyde claimed Hewitt was 'denied the post of director through backroom manoeuvring and for no reason other than that he was regarded as politically unsuitable'. Clyde maintains that after this Hewitt was traumatised and suffered 'acute depression' which ended an 'extraordinarily fertile ten years' culminating in 'Planter's Gothic'. Clyde continues, 'that very success ... made the blow which he received in 1953 seem even more cruel ... until he left Belfast there was not one major article or large-scale project'.[18] This chronology is wholly misleading. Hewitt bid for the Directorship in September 1952, and his failure did not result in literary paralysis. In 1953, Hewitt's autobiographical extracts appeared serially in *The Bell*'s Spring, Summer and Autumn issues, he became art critic for the *Belfast Telegraph* and *Irish Times* and wrote two seminal essays, 'The course of writing in Ulster' and 'We are marking our place in literature'. With McFadden, Hewitt produced an 'Impression' of the International PEN Conference. In 1954 *The Bloody Brae* was broadcast, and in 1956 Hewitt published *Those Swans Remember*. Hewitt's emotional recovery may have been accelerated when, finally promoted to Deputy in October 1952, he received a salary increase backdated to February. Indeed, recalling the period for John Montague, Hewitt declared, 'my tone grew firmer ... more courageous ... This was the beginning of my freedom ... I was more active than ever in art criticism ... It was perhaps the period of my greatest influence in Belfast, for I now had the advantage of wearing a martyr's tie'.[19] Writing privately to Roy McFadden in 1971, Hewitt confided he felt free to be candid with Montague because, 'the generation-gap keeps us from jostling'. Together with his admitting to having exploited his 'victimisation', these comments expose Hewitt's competitive spirit, and evidence that he held an egocentric view of his artistic and intellectual status further illustrates this crucial aspect of his character. In his letter to Montague, he claimed that in the 1940s he had been, 'the only person to call myself a regionalist and had no disciples ... My critics inadvertently spread my gospel by their unstinted attacks'.

Edna Longley is one of Hewitt's most influential disciples. Discussing his 'new way of thinking about the North' in the 1940s, she links the eclipse of his regionalist 'phase' to his frustrated job prospects:

But in 1953 Hewitt missed an important change to implement his vision when Unionist intrigue denied him the directorship. This was largely due to his communist opinions. In the same year he published The Colony, which translates his cultural meditations into his most sophisticated poetic model of Ulster politics.[20]

Longley's reading of 'The Colony', and her implied connection between it and Hewitt's 'victimisation', is interesting beside a more precise chronology. Although 'The Colony' was first published in 1953, in 'No Rootless Colonist' (1972) Hewitt located the genesis of the poem, 'precise[ly] ... after Christmas 1949', and declared that it, 'allegorised the regional circumstance as that of a Roman colony at the Empire's waning, and in what terms the colonists viewed the situation ... this is the definitive statement of my realisation that I am an Ulsterman'. Hewitt did claim that 'The Colony' had 'some representative validity', but equally he admitted that his work, 'no more than outline[d] the chart of a highly personal journey to a point of self-realisation. I have not offered a routing for another's setting out ... Nor have I discussed the matter of the Two Nations'. Arguably, therefore, Longley's hypothesis stands only if the problems of contemporary 'Ulster politics' are digested and allegorised within identity crises in descendants of Plantation immigrants. Typically, Hewitt presents a paradox, describing 'The Colony' as a recreation of a 'colony's' birth with 'every statement backed by historical fact', and a means to 'admit our load of guilt ... and ... make amends'.[21] Perhaps 'The Colony' enacts a tentative experiment in Jungian analytical psychology, or to use Hewitt's phrase from 'The Bitter Gourd' (1945), 'the lonely ascents of practical mysticism'. John Layard observes:

Analysis conducted on these lines ... recognize[s] symbols of ever less personal nature ... reaching down layer by layer through the stages of cultural evolution ... to primitive beliefs ... returning upward again to make a synthesis of varied experiences.

Layard contends that, once activated, the 'redemptive process ... resolve[s] personal complexes'.[22] Interpreted within this paradigm, 'The Colony' invoked a 'less personal' symbolic reality to invite cultural synthesis. This reading of 'The Colony' is consistent with Longley's emphasis on Hewitt's 'region' as a sort of embryonic 'fifth province', and her interpretation of his poetry as being 'largely inspired by cultural retrieval ... as opposed to the dubious *imperium*'.[23]

Alternatively, in 'The course of writing in Ulster', which was published in the same year as 'The Colony', Hewitt dismissed Gaelic influences in 'Ulster' as being 'outside the experience of the colonists' because they had had 'no obvious effect upon our tradition, except ... in the ears of those who have an affection for the odd dialect word'. A year later, when still in confident hope of 'the succession' to the Directorship, Hewitt identified the 'racial' characteristics of Northern Ireland's 'natives' and picaresque ingenuousness of loyalist 'Folk Art' in 'Painting and sculpture in Ulster'. This evidence subverts Longley's claim that in the 1940s Hewitt had a superlative cultural vision, and that he imagined an Ulster that 'exemplifies, and might capitalise on, the cultural interpenetration of "these islands" [and] the subtler ideology unionist paranoia precluded'.[24] Terence Brown's cautionary note that Hewitt's engagement with, '"the story of our country's past and the rights and wrongs of it" ... was to be from a particular vantage point' is more appropriate.[25] Specifically, if this simplistic and reductive thinking reflects Hewitt's cultural vision in that context, it seems unlikely that he would have been 'victimised' for his progressive, non-sectarian 'nitty gritty' socialist perspective.[26] However, as Hewitt's 'Mosaic' (1972) concedes, 'history is selective' and Plantation narratives are famously disputed. In 1991 the twin publications, *The Collected Poems of John Hewitt* and *The Field Day Anthology*, symbolised a decade of institutionalised dialogues between the New Irelanders of Field Day locked in serried reaction to the colonial experience and academics from, in Longley's phrase, the island's 'beleaguered liberal enclave[s]'.[27] Longley's proscription of Protestant cultures and benign interpretation of Hewitt's claim to 'rights drawn from the soil and sky' are germane to her efforts to seize critical initiative. In her lecture to the John Hewitt International Summer School in 1995, 'Making Celtic waves: John Hewitt and Ossian', Longley attempted to redraw critical battle lines between competing literary histories by exploiting Hewitt's clash with unionism and subsuming the national question within his figurative regional boundaries.[28] Depicting Hewitt as an 'artist beset by bigots', Longley hurled a secular, 'Protestant' poetic model of 'Ulster' politics at the complacencies she perceived in the relationship between Irish socialism and nationalist politics. Hewitt as atheist, socialist and victim of cultural philistines is transformed into a symbolic link to an eighteenth-century intellectual Protestant elite, one without archaic superstitions and stubborn allegiances.

Paradoxically, Longley's Arnoldian interpretation of Hewitt as a 'cultural missioner' relentlessly pursues a sacrificial motif. This feeds from a pervasive theme in her writing that the 'political consciousness' of 'writers from a Protestant background ... illuminates the darkest area'.[29] For Longley, the 'darkest area' is Unionism which 'avoided literature'; she contends that 'Unionists and Protestants have often culturally amputated themselves by claiming kin with extra-territorial, imperial, Anglo or Anglo-American culture'.

143

Longley's discourse elaborates wider critical reluctance to engage with Northern Irish Protestant cultures and languages and is striking beside Joe McMinn's analysis of her 'sustained and obsessive objections to the ideology of Field Day' because it, '"revealed [the] incurably absolutist thought-processes of even sophisticated Nationalists"'.[30] Arguably, Longley takes a contentious starting point; eliding cultural and political analysis she imposes a powerful 'given' on the reality of Protestant cultures, a tendency which is also evident in Declan Kiberd's questioning the relevance of Hewitt's progressive spirit. Kiberd contended this was peripheral because, Hewitt 'felt it enough to be the critic of his own people's rigidity ... Not for him the dazzling dialectics of a Yeats'. Kiberd extends his argument with an ambiguous caveat, which links Hewitt's cautious craftsmanship to his having 'come from the north where he had many brushes with the intransigence of the unionist establishment'. Kiberd's remarks mischievously reassert an earlier, singularly 'unrevised verdict' on the 'barbarous vulgarity and boot-faced sobriety' of the Protestant imagination.[31] With its assumption that the reader will readily identify an obdurate 'unionist establishm- ent' with the Belfast City Council as microcosm of the political state and exemplar for the mores of all its Protestant peoples, Kiberd's reference to Hewitt's 'victimisation' is an intriguing exposé of its bipartisan appeal.

In *Tuppenny Stung* (1995), Michael Longley recalled that his first enterprise as 'temporary Exhibitions Officer' at the Arts Council was *The Planter and the Gael*, a reading tour featuring Hewitt and John Montague.[32] The rubric on the accompanying booklet stated that, 'Montague defines the culture of the Gael ... Hewitt that of the Planter'. In 'No Rootless Colonist' (1972), Hewitt admitted that, whereas previously 'The Colony' was ignored, it was plucked from oblivion for the tour and printed in the booklet. This revealing transformation of Hewitt's public persona from 'exile' to cultural exemplar on a public stage reflects the commitment he shared with Michael Longley to 'resolution through the arts council'.[33] Compare Hewitt's exhortation to the 'alert' in the forties to breathe life into the 'dry bones' with Longley's vision of the arts as a 'path of stepping stones' in a 'civilised' society.[34] Problematically, it might be argued that, like the Irish nationalist commitment to a teleological view of history, Hewitt's exhortation and Longley's vision are inherently undemocratic. An *Irish Times* editorial published in 1972 suggests that, just two years after he had appeared with John Montague in *The Planter and the Gael*, Hewitt had been taken up as representative of the 'Northern majority'. The editor advised Northern Protestants to 'make up their minds to put their roots down here permanently' and quoted from 'The Colony' to hammer home his message: 'in the words of their own poet, John Hewitt, the Northern majority will be able to say, "we would be strangers in the Capitol;/ this is our country also ... / and we

144

shall not be outcast on the world"'.[35] The editor's co-option of Hewitt is ironic because 'The Colony' can be read as an apologia for colonialism rather than as a redemptive recasting of the 'Northern Protestant' mind-set.   An early exposition on the 'immigrant' mind and purpose, 'The Colony' addressed an overwhelmingly proud, patriotic context sure of Caesar's integrity and suspicious of that part of the island outside 'the Roman peace'.   The Roman exemplar is a distancing device breaking ground for subsequent waves of colonists to Ireland's shores.   As in all Hewitt's poetry, rhyme and metre are complementary and stately, ironic intention is muted and controlled so that the Roman allegory becomes submerged in the minutiae of colonial enterprise.   There are rabble-rousers among the generals, tax absconders among the skilled law clerks, profiteers among the debtors and mistresses bedded down with men-at-arms. The barbarism of brutal conquest is refracted through an image of mercenaries 'smoking out the nests / of the barbarian tribesmen, clan by clan'.   With masterly understatement, 'The Colony' captures the paralysis engendered by the threat of dispossession and counter-dispossession, slaughter and counter-slaughter when it observes: 'we had to build in stone for ever after'.

Reviewing *The Collected Poems of John Hewitt* (1991), James McKendrick wondered if Hewitt's 'natives' were in danger of being 'overwhelmed by his open-mindedness', and if 'The Colony' offered 'radical concessions for the Ascendancy of the fifties'.[36]   Like Hewitt's whimsical manipulation of regionalist ideas around Ulster's political idiosyncrasies, the casuistry that informs 'The Colony' indicates that the balance of probability is against overtly original or radical 'concessions' outside theoretical exchanges in Belfast's Progressive Bookshop and Campbell's Cafe during the 1940s.   Commenting on the local scene in 'Belfast is an Irish city', published in *The Bell* in April 1952, Thomas Carnduff complained that 'there is a cultural problem in Ireland deriving from a sectarian problem, and Irish writers are not as conscious as they should be'.   Is it, the erstwhile Corporation binman astutely enquired, 'that they do not see, or that they dodge it?'[37] Gréagóir Ó Dúill addressed Carnduff's enquiry when he asked 'how many lines of poetry of social realism ... Hewitt wrote despite the fact that it was the fashion of his youth and the duty of his ideology'. Seeing a certain inevitability in Hewitt's being ignored by 'Unionists' who then robbed him of his 'career prize', Ó Dúill's indictment of Hewitt's failure to conform to ideological 'duty' is peremptory but instructive.[38]   Hewitt was officially censured by his employers, but for lack of professional integrity, not for being at the 'anarchist end' of the socialist spectrum.   Edna Longley's attempts to link progenitive 'evangelical origins of the Irish Literary Revival' to Hewitt's 'missionary spirit' in his mobilising of 'proletarian writers ... [and educating] ... Ulster Young Farmers about their poetic heritage'[39] flounder before evidence that he was embarrassed to encounter working men 'denounc[ing] Ulster writers for not facing up to political realities', and that he inclined to patronise farmers with homilies like, 'Man does not live by cattle judging alone'.[40] Hewitt was not, as Longley claims, disillusioned by 'theoretical and literary socialists'. Rather, he admitted he found it difficult to talk to the 'literate but not educated ... plumber in Coleraine', and considered factory workers and their families impervious to the 'tangle of aesthetic theory'.[41] As Hewitt's forty years in Council service suggests, his cultural ambitions did not transcend existing civic structures; his pursuit of marriage between 'planners' and 'artists' mimicked precisely Arnold's axiomatic impulse towards 'State' as the 'expression ... of our best self'.[42] Hewitt's myopic vision is striking beside David McDowell's observation that traditionally, 'political Unionism ... dourly left culture to the clever folk in velvet smoking jackets'.[43] McDowell's remark deftly reassigns the complacency Mooney identifies as the sole prerogative of the 'Unionist establishment and the kaleyard provincials', and enhances too McFadden's comment that Hewitt 'endorsed progressive thought and unpopular causes, but ... did not offer dedication'.[44]

The coincidence of the 'Troubles' and launch of the *Honest Ulsterman* in 1968 provided Hewitt with a context and platform to redeploy the myth of his 'victimisation'. *Honest Ulsterman*'s early volumes offer an iconoclastic exposé of the 'Orange Bigot'. Volume One carried Hewitt's 'From the Tibetan' and Derek Mahon's 'Ecclesiastes', twin satires on the 'bleak afflatus' and 'ritual ... chanting' of the bibliophobic 'lamas' of Protestant cultures. Significantly, 'From the Tibetan' lampoons loyalist musical traditions, parading them as crude cousins of the 'Douanier-like conceptions' Hewitt observed in loyalist street art in 1951. In June, 'Lines for a dead Alderman' blatantly petitioned a troubled context. Written as an epitaph for Chairman Tougher in 1953, the revised, retitled and previously unpublished 'Elegy for an enemy' exhumed the 'rascal' who had finally 'had his day'. Simultaneous with the release of *Collected Poems* (1968), August's *Honest Ulsterman* printed 'Alec of the Chimney Corner', in which Alexander Irvine names Hewitt 'torchbearer' for social justice and exhorts him to 'say the unpopular things ... maintain the imperilled values'. Arguably this was an astute moment for a competitive spirit to exploit the priestly blessing, and in September coincidence turned to farce when Hewitt published 'From chairmen and committee men', his dramatic martyrological memoir of persecution and despair.

In the event *Collected Poems* was received with critical indifference and, as Roberta Hewitt's Journal records, like *No Rebel Word* (1948) it was eventually remaindered. Hewitt was bitterly disappointed.[45] Reviewing *Collected Poems*, Douglas Sealy observed, 'no particular brilliance in the handling of words; the rhymes are so unemphatic as to pass almost un-noticed ... Mr Hewitt's verse is not exciting, he makes no attempt to woo his readers by art'. Ironically counterpointing Hewitt's approach to Lavery, Sealy asked, 'is it merely the voice of the Ulster Protestant.... The Puritan dislike of show and distrust of art may be responsible for the plainness of the line?'[46] Despite the poor response to *Collected Poems*, by 1969 Hewitt's image as an 'artist beset by bigots' had gathered a mythological impetus that superseded indifference to his prosaic style. In his review of *Collected Poems*, Seamus Heaney observed that Hewitt was 'evolving into a man without a mask'; saluting 'Funeral Rites', Heaney's remark that he was 'shouldered out of his island on to "The mainland"' symbolised Hewitt's elevation to Protestant martyr.[47] By 1992, Ormsby was hailing Hewitt as an important 'exemplar and influence' and *Collected Poems* as a 'poetic milestone of the 1950s'.[48]

By 1971, Hewitt had begun to wish 'people wouldn't keep on referring even obliquely to my "victimisation"'.[49] Through service on the Arts Council, Hewitt established a productive relationship with Blackstaff press and was being regularly published by them by the mid 1970s. Hewitt appeared to almost simultaneously abandon 'liberal initiatives pioneered under the "Cultural Traditions" umbrella'.[50] Writing in 1976 he said of *The Planter and the Gael* that it was a 'chance coming together' that had 'misled some ... [because] ... John Montague is ... in the transatlantic tradition ... John Hewitt ... is in the English tradition - Crabbe, Wordsworth, Edward Thomas'.[51] Three months after his appointment as writer in residence at Queen's University in January 1977, Hewitt reminisced that going into 'voluntary exile' had been the best thing he had ever done, he had enjoyed being among 'civilised people'.[52] Eight years later, Hewitt declared that the Irish people, 'before my ancestors came here, were a tribe of cattle-rustlers, fighting each other and burning churches and what not'.[53] Having been vice-president of the Irish Academy of Letters and received honorary doctorates at Queen's and Coleraine Universities, in 1983 Hewitt somewhat controversially accepted the freedom of the city by which he had previously declared himself spurned. Ironically, in 1985 after fruitfully exploiting his 'victimisation' for more than thirty years, he denounced Yeats's mythology as 'bogus'.[54] Clearly, if examined within a chronological framework, Hewitt's radicalism evinced a 'dangerous' edge only when sharpened by personal bitterness. What is surprising, however, is the widespread failure by his 'disciples' to apply this framework scrupulously when analysing both his place in Northern Irish writing and his relationship to the 'kaleyard provincials'.

147

NOTES

1. M.A.G.Ó. Tuathaigh, 'A limited regionalism', in M. Crozier, ed., *Cultural Traditions in Northern Ireland, Varieties of Britishness*, Belfast, 1990, pp. 170-6, 170.
2. Edna Longley, 'Writing, revisionism & grass-seed : literary mythologies in Ireland', in Gerald Dawe and Edna Longley, eds., *Across a Roaring Hill : the Protestant imagination in modern Ireland*, Belfast, 1985, pp. 11-21, 19.
3. Martin Wallace, 'A poet and his past', *Belfast Telegraph*, 15 March 1957.
4. Edna Longley, 'Progressive Bookmen', *Irish Review*, 1 (1986), pp. 50-7, 56.
5. Martin Mooney, 'A native mode: language and regionalism in the poetry of John Hewitt', *Irish Review*, 3 (1988), pp. 67-74, 69.
6. Ian Duhig, 'Pictures carried with singing', *Irish Review*, (Spring-Summer 1992), pp. 165-70, 166, 168.
7. Biographical Chronology, F Ormsby, ed., *The Collected Poems of John Hewitt*, Belfast, 1991, p. xxxvi.
8. John Hewitt quoted in Neil Johnston, 'John Hewitt', *Belfast Telegraph*, 13 April 1983, p. 10.
9. 'Appointment of Museum Assistant', Libraries, Museums & Art Committee Minutes, Belfast City Council, 17 October 1930.
10. Kenneth Jamison, 'A personal reminiscence by Kenneth Jamison, Director of the Arts Council of Northern Ireland', in Sheila Flanagan, ed., *A Poet's Pictures*, Antrim, 1987, pp. 7-11, 8.
11. John Hewitt, *I Found Myself Alone*, Landseer Films, Arts Council of Northern Ireland, Belfast, 1978. John Hewitt, 'The Carnduff Lecture', AMs, 29 November 1960, John Hewitt Collection, University of Ulster at Coleraine.
12. John Hewitt, 'The Ulster Academy of Arts Exhibition 24 October - 1 December', *The New Northman*, (Autumn 1934), pp. 8-9.
13. John Hewitt, 'Painting and sculpture in Ulster' in, Sam Hanna Bell, ed., *The Arts in Ulster : A Symposium*, London, 1951, pp. 71-98, 82.
14. Ibid., p. 93.
15. Mary O'Malley and Percy Tougher quoted in, Anon., 'Privilege query over museum post', *The Northern Whig and Belfast Post*, 2 October 1952.
16. John Hewitt, 'Griffin', Extract from an unpublished autobiography, 'A North Light', (c1961), TMs, John Hewitt Collection, University of Ulster at Coleraine. Notably, Mary O'Malley was new to this committee; in

148

Never shake hands with the Devil, Dublin, 1990, pp. 64-5, O'Malley recalled, 'it struck me in the course of the meeting that there was considerable prejudice against Hewitt' but conceded, 'I had to admit that Hewitt had not made such a good showing at the interview, and did not have army service. This factor could be a deciding one'.

17.   *Irish News*, 2 October 1952. Other examples are, 'Belfast Museum Director', sub-headed 'Casting vote for Englishman', *Belfast News-Letter*, 27 September 1952, and 'Englishman proposed as Museum Chief', sub-headed 'Casting vote in "tie" ousts Belfast candidate', *The Northern Whig*, 27 September 1952. Local employment had fallen by 6%. See Andrew Boyd, *The Two Irelands*, Fabian Research Series 269, London, 1968.

18.   Tom Clyde, Introduction, Tom Clyde, ed., *Ancestral Voices: The Selected Prose of John Hewitt*, Belfast, 1987, p. ix.

19.   John Hewitt to John Montague, TLU, Spring 1964, John Hewitt Collection, University of Ulster at Coleraine.

20.   Edna Longley, *The Living Stream*, Newcastle Upon Tyne, 1994, p. 126.

21.   John Hewitt, 'No Rootless Colonist', Tom Clyde, ed., *Ancestral Voices: The Selected Prose of John Hewitt*, Belfast, 1987, p. 154-6.

22.   John Layard, Introduction, *The Lady of the Hare : being a study in the healing power of dreams*, London, 1941. For further discussion on Hewitt and Jung, see Roy McFadden, 'No dusty pioneer', *Threshold*, 38 (Winter 1986-87), pp. 6-12, 9, and Terence Brown, 'John Hewitt : an Ulster of the mind' in Gerald Dawe and John Wilson Foster, eds., *The Poet's Place*, Belfast, 1991, pp. 299-311.

23.   Edna Longley, 'Including the North', *Texts and Contexts*, 3 (1988), pp. 17-24, 21.

24.   Edna Longley, 'John Hewitt, 1907-1987', *Fortnight*, 254 (September 1987), pp. 22-3, 22.

25.   Terence Brown, 'John Hewitt : an Ulster poet', *Topic 24 : A Journal of the Liberal Arts*, Washington (Fall, 1972), pp. 60-8, 61. Brown quotes from John Hewitt, 'The family next door', *Threshold*, 23 (Summer 1970), pp. 17-8.

26.   Edna Longley, *The Living Stream*, Newcastle-Upon-Tyne, 1994, p. 118.

27.   Ibid, p. 15.

28.   Edna Longley, 'Making Celtic Waves: John Hewitt and Ossian'. Unpublished Conference Paper, *Celts & Saxons*, Eighth John Hewitt International Summer School, 24-30 July 1995, Co. Antrim.

29.   Edna Longley, 'Progressive Bookmen', *Irish Review*, 1 (1986), pp. 59.

30. Joe McMinn, 'In defence of Field Day : talking among the ruins', *Fortnight*, 224 (September 1985), pp. 19-20, 19. McMinn quotes from Edna Longley, 'More martyrs to abstraction', *Fortnight*, 206 (July-August 1984), p. 18.

31. Declan Kiberd, 'The Winding Stair', in *Inventing Ireland*, London, 1995, pp. 438-53, 452. In Declan Kiberd, *Anglo-Irish Attitudes*, Field Day Pamphlet, 6, (1984), p. 22, Kiberd compliments F.S.L. Lyons's documentation of 'that curious blend of resolution and hysteria, of barbarous vulgarity and boot-faced sobriety which lies beneath the emotions of Ulster Protestantism'.

32. Michael Longley, *Tuppenny Stung*, Belfast, 1994, pp. 45, 49.

33. Felix, 'The Planter and the Gael', *Fortnight*, 6 (December 1970), p. 10.

34. Michael Longley, 'Poetry' in *Causeway : The Arts in Ulster*, Belfast, 1971, pp. 95-117, passim.

35. Editorial, 'Not outcast on the world', *Irish Times*, 25 March 1972. The editor addressed the aftermath of Direct Rule in Northern Ireland.

36. James McKendrick, rev., 'Stoats and hedgehogs: *Collected Poems of John Hewitt* - ed., Frank Ormsby', *Independent*, 23 April 1992, p. 23.

37. Thomas Carnduff, 'Belfast is an Irish city', *The Bell*, 18:1, (April 1952), p. 6.

38. Gréagóir Ó Dúill, 'No rootless colonists : Samuel Ferguson and John Hewitt', in Gerald Dawe and John Wilson Foster, *The Poet's Place*, Belfast, 1991, pp. 105-17, 106.

39. Edna Longley, *The Living Stream*, Newcastle-Upon-Tyne, 1994, p. 126.

40. In John Hewitt and Roy McFadden, 'International-PEN in Dublin', *The Bell*, 18:12 (Autumn 1953), pp. 73-81, 77, Hewitt recalls a 'slightly embarrassing start' for a PEN trip to Belfast when 'young men came round handing out stencilled sheets denouncing Ulster writers for not facing up to political realities'. John Hewitt, 'Poetry and you', *The Ulster Young Farmer*, 2:8 (May 1948), pp. 21-2.

41. John Hewitt quoted in John Evans, 'Profile of John Hewitt : "now poetry is what I'm about"', *Coventry Evening Telegraph*, 29 August 1968, p. 6, and in Anon., 'Proposals for Coventry Art Collection', *Coventry Evening Telegraph*, 1 November 1957.

42. Matthew Arnold, *Culture and Anarchy*, London, 1893, p. 159.

43. David McDowell, 'Historical gerrymandering : The abuse of the past' in, Ian Adamson, David Hume and David McDowell, *Cuchulain, The Lost Legend*, Belfast, 1995, pp. 19-36, 21.

44. Roy McFadden, 'No dusty pioneer' in Gerald Dawe and John Wilson Foster, eds., *The Poet's Place*, Belfast, 1991, pp. 169-80, 180. This is an edited version of the essay published in *Threshold* cited above.

45. John Hewitt to Michael Longley, ALS, 8 February 1969, Hewitt Correspondence, Public Record Office Northern Ireland.

46. Douglas Sealy, 'An individual flavour', *Dublin Magazine*, 8 (Spring/Summer 1969), pp. 19-24.

47. Seamus Heaney, 'The poetry of John Hewitt', *Threshold*, 22 (Summer 1969), pp. 73-7, 77.

48. Frank Ormsby, Introduction, *A Rage for Order : Poetry of the Northern Ireland Troubles*, Belfast, 1992.

49. John Hewitt quoted in Kenneth Jamison, 'A personal reminiscence by Kenneth Jamison, Director of the Arts Council of Northern Ireland', in Sheila Flanagan, ed., *A Poet's Pictures*, Antrim, 1987, pp. 7-11, 8.

50. Richard English, '"Cultural Traditions" and political ambiguity', *Irish Review*, 15 (1994), pp. 97-106, passim.

51. John Hewitt to Miss Craig, ALS, 17 April 1976, Hewitt Correspondence, Public Record Office Northern Ireland.

52. John Hewitt quoted in Niall Kiely, 'John Hewitt : Northern poet of planter stock', *Irish Times*, 23 April 1977, p. 6.

53. John Hewitt quoted in Ketzel Levine, 'A tree of identities, a tradition of dissent', *Fortnight*, 213 (February 1985), pp. 16-7.

54. John Hewitt quoted in, 'so much older then ... younger than that now: an interview with John Hewitt', *North*, 4 (Winter 1985), pp. 13-6, 15.

15

The Psychotic Tradition:
Insanity and Fantasy in the Contemporary Irish Novel

Gerry Smyth

The Irish novel, like Irish identity itself, is a discourse founded on the paradoxical concept of the border - those imagined but absolutely necessary lines that are used to differentiate between voices, genres, subjects, histories and geographies. It is precisely because of this peculiar formal character, moreover, that the novel has been one of the primary locations for the rehearsal of the imaginary borders that have impinged on the evolution of the Irish cultural imagination throughout its modern history. Novelistic discourse is organised around the multiple borders between different kinds of writing - narrative, romance, historiography, (auto)biography, journalism, polemic, dialogue, and so on. The 'voice-zones' orchestrated by the novelist, as Bakhtin has shown, stand in complex but distinct relation to the kinds of society from which they emerge.[1] And as both Northern Ireland and the Republic continue to evolve into highly complex modern societies, the novel, with its built-in capacity to register change, conflict and contradiction, offers the ideal means for narrating the nation - even if (or perhaps precisely because) the existence of the nation is itself at issue.

The links between novel and nation are all the more interesting because in recent times the border has become an increasingly significant and useful concept for the analysis of fiction produced in colonial and post-colonial societies. The border is the grey area where established narratives of identity and authenticity come under pressure, where the concepts differentiating self from other, presence from absence, coloniser from colonised, are tested. The border, in fact, is the place where the very principles of opposition and of difference, so important to the colonial enterprise, are blurred, turned around and sent back to the subject. In a classic post-structuralist trope (from which much post-colonial theory is derived), the border is absolutely necessary yet contains within itself its own impossibility, the impossibility of absolute difference which the border was invented to formalise: *Here* is where *this* stops and where *this* begins.[2]

I should like to examine the impact upon recent novelistic practice of two particular border motifs that may be seen to recur throughout the canon of Irish fiction: the borders between sanity and insanity, and between reality and fantasy.

It seems clear that since the inception of the tradition in the eighteenth century, the Irish novel demonstrated a recurring scepticism with regard to a colonially controlled reality, and a concomitant investment in any trope or form which exposed the partiality and bad faith of realism. From *Gulliver's Travels* (1726) onwards, Irish writing revealed a deep fascination with themes of insanity, horror, dreams, fantasy, nightmare - any instance in which received versions of 'normality' or 'reality' were skewed. The standard post-colonialist line regarding the subaltern's need to combat a reality organised around the disabling myth of authentic, essential identity is of course relevant here, as is the general stress on anti-mimetic cultural practices. However, I wish to elaborate on this orthodoxy by focusing upon a specific Irish dimension to the uses and representation of fantasy and madness in artistic discourse, before going on to examine a number of more recent examples.

There are four major sources for the recurrence of madness and fantasy as themes in Irish fiction. The first concerns madness as an actual clinical condition rather than an artistic strategy, and the socio-psychological damage wrought by colonialism as a politico-cultural system. The work of Frantz Fanon and Ashis Nandy has been influential in this respect. Next, there are the experimental possibilities afforded by an invented or rediscovered Gaelic tradition of non-realist narrative based on legend, myth and magic. Thirdly, madness and fantasy were important themes for the Anglo-Irish Protestant imagination and the gothic variations which emerged from its attendant racial, religious and gender discourses. And finally, there is the general affinity between writing (Irish or otherwise) and madness as two of the 'silenced' discourses of history. The history of Western thought demonstrates a systematic process of discursive stratification in which madness stands to sanity as writing stands to the spoken word, as perhaps criticism stands to literature, literature to philosophy and philosophy to science.[3] Taken together and in a wide range of possible combinations and degrees, these four sources provide a discursive matrix in which it would in fact have been highly unlikely for madness and fantasy not to appear in some form or other in Irish cultural history. The ubiquity of these motifs throughout the history of the Irish novel, moreover, is capable of being inflected to a wide range of ideological positions, of which two are worthy of remark here. In the first place, the radical emancipatory potential of anti-mimetic strategies has already been mentioned. In this respect, Joyce remains the most typical Irish novelist in his development of fantasy and madness as tactics within a wide-ranging strategy of aesthetic decolonisation, a strategy all the more radical (though not necessarily effective) for remaining unfocused and largely unformulated. But the nexus of Irishness and what came to be seen as the race's general antipathy towards the 'real' had a more insidious politico-cultural provenance. In large part responsible for this myth was the French anthropologist and historian Ernest Renan who, in the mid-nineteenth century, had written about the Celtic race in terms which categorically linked biology and culture:

> [The Celtic Race] ... has worn itself out in taking dreams for realities, and in pursuing its splendid visions ... The characteristic failing of the Breton peoples ... is due to this invincible need of illusion ... the vision of the invisible world ... It is thus that little peoples dowered with imagination revenge themselves on their conquerors.[4]

In the hands of English 'organic' intellectuals like Matthew Arnold, this pathological preference for dreams over reality was fed into a model of the political relations that should exist between the Celtic margins and the English centre. Renan's idea of the imaginative revenge of the Irish on their English conquerors also runs through Arnold's work, as if racial access to the realm of the imagination was some sort of compensation arranged by Nature for the politically dispossessed Celts. Leaving the English to get on with the messy business of organising the market place, the Irish should learn to embrace the visionary realms for which they were naturally endowed.

Thus, the aesthetic strategy of anti-mimeticism as manifested in discourses of madness and fantasy is caught up in a complex discursive economy in which it simultaneously resists and reinforces colonial ideology. On the one hand, the pursuit of the alternative realities and alternative histories to be found in dreams and madness proves a constant attraction for any discourse of decolonisation. Colonial reality, and its attendant discourse of realism, constitutes a problem for the colonised community and for the decolonising writer. In this context, madness and dreams are enabling devices that can be used to constitute the unique characteristics upon which a narrative of Irish difference can emerge, a way of out-manoeuvring a history and a reality which do you no favours: the realm, in fact, in which alternative national realities have their genesis. On the other hand, the Irish artist's traditional reluctance to countenance the organisation of the world along materialist, positivist lines might appear to those with an investment in that world to be a form of madness, a perverse refusal to accept the world as it 'really' is. The colonial subject's movement from reality to the dream world confirms all the coloniser's suspicions regarding their utter, albeit curiously attractive, difference, while once again confirming the notion of a fatal link between biology and cultural destiny. Much contemporary Irish fiction may still be located, albeit more and more problematically, within the terms of this inheritance. Consider the opening paragraph from Patrick Quigley's *Borderland* (1994):

> It is many years since the fire, but I still dream of coming awake to the beating of giant wings in the darkness. I am four years old again and the world is a vast place where anything can happen. A luminous bird lands on the thatched roof of our farmhouse. It lays glowing eggs which burst into life among the dried rushes. The red chicks fly beneath the roof, spreading streamers of flame, changing night into day. Helpless in my bed I watch for the burning ceiling to fall.[5]

Borderland tells a story, familiar to anyone with an interest in contemporary Irish fiction, about a young boy negotiating the rocky road towards emotional and political consciousness in the Ireland of recent times. From a critical-theoretical standpoint, however, the novel is also interesting in its self-conscious invocation of the concept of the 'border', suggesting not only the actual border between the Republic and the North where the action is set, but the borders between different versions of the real. In this passage, the hero Shane dreams, paradoxically, that he is waking up - dreams, in other words, that he is leaving the realm of fantasy for the realm of reality, only to go on to describe that reality in the fantastical, dreamlike language of the child he once was but presumably, as narrator, no longer is. This theme, moreover, introduced at such an early stage in the novel, recurs throughout and is finally and paradoxically revealed as the truth, the reality underlying the illusory world of sectarian violence and doomed love that Shane experiences. The novel ends:

> My human identity was a transitory thing, but that didn't matter at all; life extended far beyond the limits of an individual being. At the same time I was aware of the precious miracle of my life, though I knew that some day I would lose my skin of separateness and merge with the flow of dream and memory. I looked in wonder at the fields and sky. My eyes went up to the great mound, the Fort standing guard between this world and the others which lay so close at hand (p. 254).

So, the title of the novel refers not only to the imagined borders created by humans to differentiate counties, states and political identities, but also to the borders between different apprehensions of the world. This theme, moreover, finds a narrative resonance in the restrained but insistent thread of madness running through the text. Shane's job as an orderly in the local mental asylum is in many ways the quintessential Irish career choice, preparing him both for the (disabling) madness of sectarian violence and the (liberating) madness which acknowledges the presence of other realities besides the physical one mediated by his senses.

As a narrative, *Borderland* constitutes a hybrid drawing on discourses of Celticism, New Ageism and Platonism, and is typical of the strain of contemporary Irish fiction which is self-consciously concerned with the relations between reality and representation. But the dream as a motif crops up in more unexpected places in modern Irish fiction. In Roddy Doyle's *The Woman Who Walked Into Doors* (1996) Paula Spencer tells the story of her marriage to the brutal Charlo, and she tries to explain what attracted her to him, the seventeen years of abuse and how despite her alcoholism she manages to cope since his death in a botched kidnap attempt. It is all fairly gritty material of the kind that made the television series *Family* so controversial. Yet, in the middle of all the beatings and the descriptions of squalid working-class life, there is a small passage in which Paula considers her dreams, how they work and what they might offer her by way of compensation for the highly unsatisfactory reality in which she finds herself:

> I could never go. I thought about it; I dreamed about it all the time. I made it up. I sat for hours, going from one step to the next. New house, a job, new hair and clothes. The kids in a new school in black school uniforms with a maroon stripe on their V-necked jumpers. A job in an office. I believed it as I sat there. I believed it all day ... I ran away in my dreams, the ones I could handle and control. I didn't have real dreams, night dreams. I just went black. I didn't want the real ones. I drank myself into the blackness. I could never run away in the real dreams. I didn't let them in. Sometimes, though, they got through. I fought myself awake. I could never move; I couldn't breathe. I ran away to twenty years ago. I ran away to another country.[6]

Paula only wants the dreams that she can control, those which her waking self can direct. Her escape is of the Hollywood kind in which the fantasies of escape are actually the result of highly managed, highly intentional acts. She fantasises about being able to direct her own fantasies - the camera angles, the lighting, the casting. Her real dreams, on the other hand, will not let her forget, or repress, her predicament, even if they might dress that predicament up in the outlandish disguises of the dreamworld. She prefers the blackness and the blankness offered by the bottle. All the colour she requires can be found in the fantasies of escape which punctuate her day. In a classic Freudian opposition, she prefers fantasies to dreams.[7] Fantasies allow her to survive; dreams do not. It is also very interesting, of course, that in these fantasies Paula wishes to get as far away as possible 'from anything Irish' and escape into a world ordered along Hollywood lines and the affluent middle-class life found in an American sitcom such as *The Cosbys*. If for some the Irish nation itself remains a dream come true, for others that dream has turned into nightmare; escape can be found not in a return to reality, not in the false pleasures of the dream, but in that halfway house, that borderland between dream and reality which is the fantasy.

We find a different fix on the dream motif in Kathleen Ferguson's *The Maid's Tale* (1994). This is the story of Brigid Keen who has spent her life as a housekeeper in the service of a Catholic priest in Derry, the appropriately named Father Mann, from the 1950s till the 1980s when he is struck down with Alzheimer's Disease. Brigid's father has killed her mother in a fit of rage and is in the local mental hospital, so Brigid is raised in a convent and is recruited, or more accurately press-ganged, into service by the local clergy into what is life-long slavery. The novel is thus the story of one who has been systematically marginalised from the official national narrative, a voice from the cracks of modern Irish history. To combat the silence, the boredom, the physical frustrations and emotional starvation of life in the House she shares with Father Mann, Brigid begins to dream:

> The House made me a dreamer ... I seemed to sleep during the day and come awake at night, like a vampire. The only problem was the dreams had a bad tendency to get out of hand. I mind a real black period when every time my head hit the pillow, I'd see my father - or who I took to be my father - for I hadn't seen the man at the time. He never had the same face twice but I knew him to be my father never-the-same. Pictures, like snapshots, of my mother's grave plagued me about this time too. I had no peace with them. Of late I'd been wandering around in the same dreams, night in, night out. My mind was starving for new faces, new places, new notions of who or what I might be - if only in a dream. I'd picked the old dreams to the bones.[8]

Here, the dream is evoked as compensation, but turns out to be no compensation at all. Brigid has 'picked the old dreams to the bones', but dreams have their basis in reality, and it is not until the end of the novel, when she turns her back on the Catholic Church which, as she says in the opening lines of the novel, was her family for over fifty years, that Brigid can shake off the familial ties and start to lay the basis for an alternative, enabling dream. This is because while Brigid is busy dreaming the old dreams, reality is slipping away from her, and she finds herself condemned to silence, to emotional and physical frustration. She dreams to survive, but surviving isn't enough after a while. She has to act in the world, to become part of the reality which will form the basis for new dreams. The work of John Banville offers a particularly interesting example of the recurrence of madness as a theme in Irish fiction, precisely because of his (and his critics') refusal of any narrowly conceived national tradition in favour of a much broader cultural inheritance. It is clear that an analysis of Banville's work in terms of a critical matrix formulated in nationalist or post-colonialist terms is obviously at odds with the current orthodoxy regarding this most international of Irish writers, for the author has always been keen to insist upon a universal - or at least a European - canvas for his preciously crafted narratives. It is the arbitrariness and the contradictions of the dominant discourses of time and space as determined by Western science and Western modes of thought that concern him:

> I must say I've never felt part of any movement or tradition, any culture even ... I feel a part of my culture. But it's purely a personal culture gleaned from bits and pieces of European culture of four thousand years. It's purely something I have manufactured. I don't think any writer ever felt part of a culture.[9]

What I would like to suggest here is that despite this reticence Banville can in fact be understood to tap into specific discourses which have their provenance in Ireland's unique cultural and political history, and that his exploration in his first novel, *Birchwood* (1973) and the later novels of familial madness, supernatural terror, political violence and existential nihilism represents in part a peculiarly Irish philosophico-artistic inheritance. With an irony worthy of Banville's own artistic vision, the Irish author casts off his (national) inheritance only to re-encounter it again at the heart of a European rationalist tradition he has embraced as an alternative to the constricting vision enforced upon his homeland by its colonial history. But the tradition of fantasy and madness which informs Irish cultural history cannot be so easily discarded, and this is something he recognises and deliberately exploits at an early stage of his career. In fact, *Birchwood* explores in particularly interesting ways the complex cultural traffic between what are still perceived to be a cultural centre (a broad European tradition) and its margins, and thus might provide a significant rejoinder to current orthodoxies of post-colonial theory which has tended to imagine the flow of cultural exchange between coloniser and colonised to be solely one way - that is, from the former to the latter.

Without labouring the issue of the precise genealogy of particular textual instances, formal or conceptual, I should like to analyse the interplay between 'universal' and 'national' representations of madness in *Birchwood*. The story is apparently set in Ireland during the nineteenth century, and we encounter the narrator Gabriel Godkin reflecting upon the decline and fall of what would appear to be his Protestant Ascendancy family. Although such specifics seem deliberately beside the point, one thing of which we can be sure of is that this is a mad world. Gabriel describes his bark-chewing grandfather, his toad-like Granny Godkin who spontaneously combusts, his louche, alcoholic father hiding a dark secret, and his mother who descends into paranoid imbecility. Gabriel frequently suspects his own sanity, especially when he learns that he is the result of an incestuous union between his father and his Aunt Martha. Likewise, the structures of life in the countryside around Birchwood, the ancestral home of the

Godkins, are breaking down. Famine and rebellion stalk the land, men roam around dressed as women, the moral and natural orders are out of kilter. The divine 'Godkins' (related to God) are overcome by the local 'Lawless' family, who in turn succumb to seemingly random violence as things fall completely apart towards the end of the story for a variety of personal and political reasons. It is entirely fitting that Gabriel should take up with a circus when he runs away from home in search of his imaginary twin sister, because the circus offers him a license to indulge that and other fantasies - a realm to dream, the only sane place to be in a mad world. Like all Banville's subsequent fiction, *Birchwood* is an immensely rich and evocative discourse in which meaning works on a number of levels to suggest the conventionality and arbitrariness of all systems of meaning. Names in the novel, for example, function as allegorical signifiers.[10] 'Gabriel' and his twin 'Michael' recall the archangels guarding the kingdom of heaven, in this case the decrepit pile that is the family home of Birchwood. The Catholic 'Lawless' family and the Protestant 'Godkins' manoeuvre for possession of the land, like Jason Quirk and the family Rackrent in the prototype of the Big House Novel which Banville is ironically sampling. Other names resonate in an intertextual *mélange*: the elusive Prospero from Shakespeare's *The Tempest*; Rainbird, a character from one of Banville's earlier short stories; Silas from Sheridan Le Fanu's Gothic chiller *Uncle Silas*; and so on. Likewise the various plotlines: the fall of a once-great estate, familial struggles for inheritance, the coming to knowledge of the innocent, the youngster running away to join a circus, the search for a long-lost sister - all these belong to a collective store of archetypal Western stories which Banville samples and invests with ironic overtones. In a metaphor that recurs in Banville's fiction until it becomes the explicit theme of *Ghosts* (1993), the story of Gabriel the character is *haunted* by other stories, something to which Gabriel the narrator alludes:

> Once, when I was very young, I had this strange experience. I was standing, I remember, by the french windows in the library looking out into a garden full of butterflies and summer, as gardens always seem to be when we are very young. I thought to open the windows and walk out there, into the sunlight, but with my fingers on the handle I hesitated, for no reason, and for an instant only, and then I went out. But I was followed by a terrifying notion that there was ahead of me, as far as the duration of that momentary hesitation, a phantom of myself who mimicked my every movement precisely, but in another world, another time.[11]

This 'other' Gabriel haunts the narrator throughout the story in the form of Johann Livelb, the alias he adopts on joining the circus (a name which is also an anagram of 'John Banville'), in the form of his imaginary twin sister Rose, and in the form of his real twin brother Michael. The very familiarity of these

159

uncanny presences reflects back on Gabriel's sense of identity, a constant reminder of the arbitrary nature of the notions, such as time, space, authenticity and originality, used to ground the self in the West. Gabriel's narrative begins: 'I am, therefore I think. That seems inescapable' (p. 11). It ends thus: 'Intimations abound, but they are felt only, and words fail to transfix them. Anyway, some secrets are not to disclosed under pain of who knows what retribution, and whereof I cannot speak, thereof I must be silent' (p. 175). The novel thus charts the movement from a sort of perverted Cartesian universe in which, as Richard Kearney writes, 'being' (I am) predates 'consciousness' (I think), to a Wittgensteinian one, in which identity and presence give way to silence and absence.[12] This novel, indeed one might say Banville's entire corpus, is fixated with this dual impulse: the present is haunted by the past, in the same way that presence is haunted by absence.

Gabriel is also the 'Godkin', the little god who is organising the story, and this turns out to be as exciting and ambiguous an adventure as any of the ones he describes in the story of Birchwood. The flow of the narrative is constantly interrupted by Gabriel's interjections from the moment of narration, and he seems intent on reminding the reader of the inherent fictionality of all writing. In a typical postmodernist device (although it is based primarily on the structure of Joyce's *A Portrait of the Artist as a Young Man*), the *narrative* begins just as the *story* is ending, while the end of the *story* represents the moment at which the *narrative* can begin to be written. This paradoxical relationship between story and narrative is central to the text, for what Gabriel discovers both as a character and as a narrator is a fundamental hiatus between language and experience, between human beliefs about the past and the ability of language to describe these beliefs: 'We imagine that we remember things as they were, while in fact all we carry into the future are fragments which reconstruct a wholly illusory past' (p. 12). This statement, cast here in a universalist context, also functions as part of a much more local narrative. When read from an Irish perspective it is reminiscent of more than one contemporary cultural critic and perhaps even some of the more theorised historical revisionists. The whole issue of Irish history and the way it has been used to construct seamless stories which in turn feed into seamless identities is being questioned here. Banville's appeal as an *Irish* novelist lies in these moments when universalist and local narratives intertwine, when the reader suddenly becomes aware of another set of possibilities, another set of correspondences, which have been shadowing the 'real' narrative and whose appearance throws that narrative and all its effects into question. In moments such as these the specific and the general, the local and the universal, get caught up in an undecidable exchange of priorities. Moreover, it is precisely because of the 'wholly illusory' nature of our experience of the world that the novel becomes such a fruitful metaphor for the human, and the Irish, adventure. The novel, like experience itself, is both part of a pattern, a continuity, and a singular event; every novel bears a structural similarity to every other novel, and yet every novel is unique, a testament to the precise moment of its conception and execution. This paradox of 'fixity within continuity' (p. 128), of our ineluctable reliance upon the past even as we are cut free within the present, represents for Banville the tragedy and the absurd insanity of the human, but also the Irish, predicament. The novel as a form is uniquely endowed to illustrate this predicament. With regard to characters from his past, Gabriel confesses:

> I began to write, as a means of finding them again, and thought that at last I had discovered a form which would contain and order all my losses. I was wrong. There is no form, no order, only echoes and coincidences, sleight of hand, dark laughter. I accept it (p. 174).

Novelistic discourse offers a suggestive (and seemingly necessary) myth of form and order that is constantly challenged by its own materiality, by the hiatus between writing and experience, between the moment of narration and the world of the narrative. In the face of this, Banville appears to suggest, one can only laugh darkly, indulge one's fantasies regarding origins and destiny and ultimately accept the unacceptable: - a strategy for survival which recalls the words of Beckett's 'unnamable': 'I don't know, I'll never know, in the silence you don't know, you must go on, I can't go on, I'll go on.'[13]

Emphasising the Irish dimension to his work might seem a petty revenge on Banville for daring to be so eclectic in his artistic imagination, but such a critique is not intended. Rather, I would maintain that in exploring the interplay between different discourses and different traditions of fantasy and madness *Birchwood* is part of a larger, truly critical and truly post-colonial, perspective which is enabling modern Ireland to move beyond received notions of a history and a culture formulated on the basis of exchange between equally authentic though unequally empowered identities. In this, Banville reveals his national inheritance, for throughout its history the Irish novel has demonstrated an ability to sample other forms and influences, to improvise and evolve in the light of changing circumstances. This ability, moreover, makes the Irish novel typical of, rather than marginal to, a wider European tradition. For if the 'novel' asks questions of what it is to be 'Irish', then the word 'Irish' has always challenged any normative notion of what a cultural form such as the 'novel' is or can achieve. As David Lloyd has written:

> We are only just beginning to forge the theoretical terms in which the atypicality of the Irish novel can be analysed but ... it may be that we are approaching a 'less coherent but in many ways more interesting' theory of

the novel. The same may perhaps be said, in more general terms, of emerging theories of Ireland's putatively 'post-colonial' culture.[14]

In 1979 Banville himself said:

There is the simple fact that Irish fiction at the moment is in the doldrums. It's coming to be regarded in the way in which it was in establishment circles during the Victorian era. People regarded fiction, apart from Dickens and so forth, as being rather suspect, rather unhealthy, because it was a dreaming and of course the age of progress didn't like dreaming. The books that sell now, the books that are popular, are packed with so-called facts, autobiography, books of naturalism.[15]

Both in the realms of fiction and civil society, however, the period since 1979 has witnessed a massive rejection of what was perceived as an unsatisfying national reality, a project for which fantasy and madness offer particularly enabling metaphors. Even a brief glance at the fiction produced in Ireland over the past twenty years reveals a steady move away from the situation described here by Banville. Indeed, fantasy and madness now function as a sort of narrative tic in Irish fiction, introduced by novelists from the most 'literary' to the most 'popular' almost as a matter of course. And as one of what Edna Longley calls the 'twin pillars' of the Southern literary edifice (Dermot Bolger is the other) Banville himself has been in no small way instrumental in this development.[16] 'Banvillism', as the above quote makes clear, disdains literary realism and has an investment in the ineluctably marvellous which is Rational Man's other. 'Bolgerism', on the other hand - urban, demotic, anti-hierarchical - went into rapid reaction after being unhelpfully characterised as 'dirty realism' or 'Northside realism' around the turn of the 1990s. Even at its grittiest, however, Northside realism trafficked significantly in the cultural currency of fantasy and insanity. Bolger's own recent novels have become rather self-conscious graftings of a mannered anti-realism onto gruff indictments of post-nationalist Ireland. With only a hint of irony then, we might speculate that the modern Irish novel is, or is on its way to becoming, a psychotic discourse. We could further speculate on whether this is a good thing or a bad thing. Freud believed that 'If phantasies become over-luxuriant and over-powerful, the conditions are laid for the onset of neurosis or psychosis.'[17] The same could be said, I would suggest, of the contemporary Irish novel. If it engages, as it appears to be doing towards the end of the millennium, too much with figures of madness and fantasy - if the distance between the (textual) fantasy and its (contextual) 'real' becomes too great - then the text itself risks psychosis, the narrative breaks down. Not *another* forecast of the imminent demise of the novel! No, merely a speculation as to the focus and direction of future criticism. As the over-reliance on dreams indicates the breakdown of the subject's ability to cope with 'reality', so the analysis of such narrative breakdowns, as articulated in figures of madness and fantasy, might reveal much about the modern Irish context from which such dysfunctional texts are emerging.

NOTES

1. See Mikhail Bakhtin, trans. Caryl Emerson and Michael Holquist, ed. Michael Holquist, *The Dialogic Imagination: Four Essays by M M Bakhtin*, Austin, 1981.

2. See Jacques Derrida, trans. G.C. Spivak, *Of Grammatology* (1967), London, 1976, especially 'Linguistics and Grammatology', pp. 27-73. In the field of postcolonial theory, the border is an important aspect of concepts such as mimicry and hybridity in which Homi Bhabha invests so much of the potential for resistance to colonial power, and which he deploys throughout the essays collected in *The Location of Culture*, London, 1994.

3. I have elaborated on all four sources in my book, *The Novel and the Nation: Studies in the New Irish Fiction*, London, 1997. But see Frantz Fanon, 'Colonial War and Mental Disorders', *The Wretched of the Earth* (1961), Harmondsworth, 1967, pp. 200-50; Vivian Mercier, *The Irish Comic Tradition*, Oxford, 1962; Siobhán Kilfeather, 'Origins of the Irish Female Gothic', *Bullán*, 1:2 (Autumn, 1994), pp. 35-46; and Shoshana Felman, trans. S. Evans and S. Felman, *Writing and Madness: Literature, Philosophy, Psychoanalysis*, Ithaca, New York, 1985.

4. Ernest Renan, from *The Poetry of the Celtic Races* (1859), quoted in Mark Story, ed., *Poetry and Ireland Since 1800: A Sourcebook*, London, 1988, pp. 58-9.

5. Patrick Quigley, *Borderland*, Dingle, 1994, p. 9. All further references will be included parenthetically in the text.

6. Roddy Doyle, *The Woman Who Walked Into Doors*, London, 1996, pp. 210-1. All further references will be included parenthetically in the text.

7. Sigmund Freud, 'Creative writers and day-dreaming' (1908), in J. Strachey, ed., *Standard Edition of the Complete Psychological Works of Sigmund Freud*, Vol. 9, London, 1959, pp. 143-53.

8. Kathleen Ferguson, *The Maid's Tale*, Dublin, 1994, p. 19.

9. 'Novelists on the Novel: Ronan Sheehan talks to John Banville and Francis Stuart', in M.P. Hederman and R. Kearney, eds., *The Crane Bag Book of Irish Studies (1977-1981)*, Dublin, 1982, p. 412.

10. See Joseph McMinn, 'Naming the World: Language and Experience in John Banville's Fiction', *Irish University Review*, 23:2 (Autumn/Winter 1993), pp. 183-96.

11. John Banville, *Birchwood*, London, 1992, pp. 98-9. All further references included parenthetically in the text.

12. Richard Kearney, *Transitions: Narratives in Modern Irish Culture*, Manchester, 1988, p. 92.

13. Samuel Beckett, *The Unnamable*, London, 1973, p. 418.

14. David Lloyd, *Anomalous States: Irish Writing and the Post-Colonial Moment*, Dublin, 1993, p. 155.

15. *The Crane Bag Book of Irish Studies (1977-1981)*, p. 410.

16. Edna Longley, *The Living Stream: Literature and Revisionism in Ireland*, Newcastle Upon Tyne, 1994, p. 64.

17. Freud, 'Creative writers and day-dreaming', p. 147.

16

'Guns and Icons':
Encountering the Troubles

Michael Parker

It was our icons not our guns
You spat on.
(Padraic Fiacc, 'Credo Credo')[1]

One of the limitations of some recent critical writing on Northern Irish poetry, I would suggest, has been its inattentiveness to contemporaneous political events which framed the poets' responses.[2] Too often literary, ideological and moral judgments are passed without regard to the particular contexts in which the poets were composing; where historical and political contextualisation is sometimes attempted, frequently it results in simplifications or highly misleading statements. For example, from Henry Hart's *Seamus Heaney: Poet of Contrary Progressions* (1993) - one of the most scholarly studies of Heaney's poetry to date - one learns that 'the civil rights movement in the sixties' was followed by 'the resurgence of the I.R.A.' which then prompted 'Protestant counterattacks in the early seventies', and that 'England ... entered Northern Ireland in the early seventies to exert a civilising force when Protestants were terrorising Catholics'.[3] While the first statement ignores the fact that loyalist violence and British policy played a major role in the resurgence of republicanism, the second implies that 'England' rather than 'the British Government' is an invasive power, an alien presence in Northern Ireland, and that 'Protestants' - not militant Loyalists - needed 'English' constraint in order to get them to behave in a 'civilised' manner. Later in the book, Hart implies that the British Government's decision to send in troops 'ostensibly to protect Catholics'[4] may in fact have masked darker colonial purposes. What perhaps we are being presented with here is a repetition of Edward Said's version of 'Ireland', which imagines a homogeneous people 'possessing a common history, religion and language' falling prey 'to the dominion of an offshore power'.[5]

What I will be endeavouring to do within this chapter is to place a number of poems from the earlier phases of the 'Troubles' within their historical and political contexts, examining the different strategies writers used to represent the crisis. I do so knowing full well that even though certain indisputable facts can be established - by, for example, sifting through chronologies of the events, or examining contemporary or later interpretations of the various dates and statistics[6] - the narrative one constructs from them will be affected by one's own ideological stance, inflected by one's position in time, in my case the late 1990s. Inevitably one reads Padraic Fiacc's 'Credo Credo', for example, with its references to the destructiveness of soldiers searching for arms ransacking Catholic houses on the Falls in July 1970, with a knowledge of the terrible price that would be paid over the next two and a half decades, by those soldiers, by those who applauded them, by those they appalled.

One of the earliest texts attempting an analysis of the ideological background to the contemporary Northern Ireland Troubles was Conor Cruise O'Brien's *States of Ireland* (1972). Though historians may differ on the merits of his interpretation,[7] O'Brien does provide a useful, accurate chronology with which to examine the literary texts and their contexts, subdividing the conflict between October 1968 and January 1972 into four main phases. The first of these concludes in August 1969, and comprises the early Civil Rights marches, the Burntollet ambush, the 'Battle of the Bogside', and the riots, burnings-out and shootings in Belfast which prompted the deployment of British troops. O'Brien's second phase takes place between June and August 1970, and includes the Ballymurphy riots and the Falls Curfew, during which a deepening hostility developed between the Catholic minority and the British Army. The third phase, 'more intense and more prolonged' than either of the previous two, covers the period up until the introduction of internment without trial in August 1971, which itself 'opened a fourth phase, still more violent than the previous three'.[8] As the 'politics of polarisation'[9] came to prevail in the course of these phases, poets attempted to resist slipping into partisan, sectarian positions. Instead they adopted a range of approaches in their efforts to address an inexpressible horror, or to keep it temporarily at bay by constructing counter-narratives of compassion. There was an anxiety about their writing exacerbating the situation, but the force of events was such that they were unable to maintain a position of lofty neutrality. Derek Mahon constructs and ironises just such a position in 'Last of the Fire Kings', when his artist-narrator talks of

> Perfecting my cold dream
> Of a place out of time
> A palace of porcelain.[10]

Though at times during these critical early phases several major writers chose to represent their responses to the politics and the violence in a somewhat oblique, seemingly distanced manner - I am thinking, for example, of Brian Friel's *The Gentle Island*, Seamus Heaney's *Wintering Out*, and two early Ciaran Carson poems, 'The Maze' and 'Peter'[11] - particular episodes such as the riots in Derry and Belfast in August 1969, the Falls Curfew in 1970, and the murders of the three Scots soldiers in 1971, insisted on making their mark on texts, as writers found themselves unable to escape the 'Pains from a shattered past', 'The dead man on the gate and in the myth'.[12]

At 4.15pm on the afternoon of Thursday, 14 August, 1969, in what was hoped would be 'a limited operation', eighty British soldiers from Prince of Wales Own Regiment were despatched towards Waterloo Place in Derry with the intention of helping 'to restore law and order'.[13] Though the arrival of the troops brought a temporary cessation to hostilities in Derry's Bogside, elsewhere mayhem continued, particularly during the evening of the 14th. In Belfast a new pitch of ferocity was reached, particularly around the Falls and the Shankill, and in 'mixed' areas such as Cupar Street, Dover Street and Percy Street.[14] The most detailed and vivid account of that appalling night is given by the *Sunday Times* Insight Team, but Paddy Devlin's succinct, matter-of-fact summary conveys many of the key 'events':

> The police thought a full scale I.R.A.-inspired uprising was under way and they put Shorland armoured cars, equipped with Browning heavy machine-guns, on to the streets. They fired hundreds of rounds throughout the night, killing two people at Divis Flats in the Lower Falls, including a nine year old boy. The crowds on the Shankill, frightened by the scenes on the Falls over the previous nights, feared for their lives. Crowds were organised early in the night and arms were brought in from rural areas and given out to some of the men. Local people who knew the streets daubed whitewash marks on the doors or windows of Catholic homes. These homes were then emptied of people and burned. As far as I could tell around 650 Catholic families were burned out that night. Five people lost their lives in exchanges of sniper fire. Police in uniform, covered in civilian coats, were recognised amongst loyalist attackers in Dover Street and I myself saw police armoured cars in Conway Street, standing by as mobs broke the windows of hastily abandoned Catholic houses before pouring petrol in to burn them.[15]

Many of these scenes were directly represented or alluded to in literary texts soon after. In 'Elegy for a "Fenian Get"', for example, Padraic Fiacc commemorates the death that night of Patrick Rooney,

> shot dead

By some trigger-happy cowboy cop

Whose automatic fire penetrated

The walls of the tower flat the young father

Hid the child in out of a premonition![16]

The poem's outrage is directed not so much at the juvenile 'trigger-happy cop' responsible for the killing, as at the obscene and vicious bigotry that begat and sanctioned it. Fiacc's elegy ends desolately with nothing learnt from the tragedy, with the next generation of little-minded children loyally intoning the previous generation's cry, 'Burn 'im/Burn 'im. Burn the scum, Burn the vermin!'. Such is the intensity of the poet's feeling that for him allusions to the trial of Christ and to the racist vocabulary deployed by the Nazis against the Jews seem entirely appropriate.

The burnings-out of Catholic homes would feature subsequently in such short stories as Mary Beckett's 'A Belfast Woman' and Anne Devlin's 'Naming the Names',[17] but more immediately within many Northern Irish poetry collections published in the three years following these terrible events. Michael Longley's 'Letters' in *An Exploded View* (1972) speak of 'the burnt-out houses of/ The Catholics we'd scarcely loved',[18] the 'blazing gable's/ Telltale'[19] marks, 'The stereophonic nightmare/ Of the Shankill and the Falls'.[20] With its aptly-snapped final adjective, and its echo of Larkin's line in 'MCMXIV', Derek Mahon's germinally ironic 'Homecoming' at the outset of *Lives* (1972) voices a shared sense of displacement and guilt:

> we cannot start
> at this late date
> with a pure heart,
> or having seen
> the pictures plain
> be ever in-
> nocent again.[21]

Typical of Mahon is the subtle choice of words and rhythms, which can be seen in the final enjambement, which draws attention to that divided adjective, and its Latin origins, *nocere*, 'to hurt'.[22] In another of his poems, the opaque, but aptly-titled 'A Dark Country', a defamiliarised, defamiliarising narrator seems to offer a diagnosis of the province's ills, 'a waste/ Of rage, self-pity bordering on self-hate', but then appears to envisage little hope of remedy:

> With practice you might decipher the whole thing
> Or enough to suffer the relief and the pity.[23]

This sense of the North as a text which ultimately resists interpretation, defies closure, recurs in John Hewitt's 'Conversations in Hungary, August 1969'. Written in late October 1969, it recalls how an eager, abstract discussion ranging from 'book to play/ to language, politics' suddenly acquired painful immediacy when their host interjected

> 'You heard the bulletin?'
> And added, with no pause for our reply:
> 'Riots in Northern Ireland yesterday;
> And they have sent the British Army in.'[24]

Awkwardly, the narrator reaches for narratives, analogies, a rhetoric that will help explain to their foreign hosts 'the savage complications of our past', and to himself why 'tragedy/ close-heeled on hope'.[25] Like several other poems in *An Ulster Reckoning* (1971), it bears witness to the difficulty Hewitt faced trying to find a language to express 'the impact of the terrible days of August 1969'.[26] In another poem, 'The Iron Circle', the speaker admits reluctantly that the conflicting ideologies in the North are not simply the source and cause of the problem; rather they are simultaneously means by which inequities and control are sustained, *and* means through which distinct cultural identities define themselves.

Given the scale of the collapse, the enormity of the violence occurring around him, where 'brandished gun demands a gun's reply;/ hate answers hate', Hewitt's choice of final image - hare-coursing - may well seem woefully inappropriate and inadequate, yet perhaps it effectively exhibits the problem other poets would face. With their lyric ground and private spaces invaded, the difficulty would be to find language, metaphors, which might begin to address, and redress.

The most significant event in O'Brien's second phase of the conflict was the Falls Curfew, an event bitterly recalled in Fiacc's 'Credo Credo'. Following an arms search by the British Army on the afternoon of Friday, 3 July, 1970, at 24 Balkan Street on the Catholic Lower Falls - an area where the Official IRA held sway - intensive rioting broke out. This occurred after the platoon conducting the search were about to depart in their personnel carriers. The soldiers found themselves hemmed in by a gathering crowd at either end of the street. When one vehicle, in attempting to reverse, crushed a man against some railings, stone-throwing began; extra troops, dispatched to extricate their stranded colleagues, met with similar resistance, and so resorted to the use of CS gas. As this then drifted into neighbouring streets in the densely-populated Falls, incensed residents appeared on the scene. Less than an hour and a half after the original operation began, soldiers found themselves the targets of nail-bomb and petrol-bomb attacks. The Army's decisive response at 8.20 that evening was to pour into the area 3,000 troops, backed by helicopters and armoured vehicles.[27] These immediately came under fire from the Official IRA, prompting the British forces to reply in kind and with a new intensity; over 1,500 rounds were fired by the Army, three people were killed and sixty wounded. At 10pm., in a determination to establish complete authority over the Falls and to avoid more bloodshed, the British GOC, Freeland, imposed a curfew, that would stay in force for thirty-five hours, until 9.00am., Sunday morning, 5 July. The length of the curfew enabled Freeland's men to conduct meticulous house-to-house searches, which netted a total of fifty-two revolvers, twenty-eight rifles, fourteen shotguns, 100

169

incendiary devices, 250 pounds of gelignite, 21,000 rounds of ammunition, and eight two-way radio sets.[28]   As a consequence of these searches, which inevitably resulted in considerable damage to the homes of a large number of innocent people - furnishings, doors, walls and floorboards were often smashed and torn up - the Army's reputation amongst the minority plummeted to an all-time low. In his memoir, Paddy Devlin highlights the particular resentment felt towards 'the Black Watch, a Scottish regiment, which seemed to give most of its attention to breaking religious objects and symbols of the Glasgow Celtic football club, which enjoyed huge support among Belfast Catholics'.[29] Tim Pat Coogan, however, suggests that a secondary motive for the search was to remind 'the natives' who was in charge, and develops this colonial parallel by citing an Italian film producer, trapped in the Falls, who compares the British Army operation with what he had witnessed in Algeria.[30] Subsequently, Freeland's replacement as GOC, Major General Farrar-Hockley, concluded that during the curfew there were about sixty cases of unjustifiable damage to property and looting.[31] That there was a certain inevitability about the Army taking on 'an increasingly Orange colouration' is the view of Conor Cruise O'Brien.[32] However, once they did appear to empathise more with the Protestant population, the situation deteriorated dramatically. In the wake of the Curfew, in the period between July-December 1970, recruitment to the Provisionals increased eight-fold.

In one of his most strident, most passionately partisan poems from this time, 'Credo Credo', Padraic Fiacc captures exactly that mixture of outrage and hurt defiance within the Catholic Falls at the violation that had occurred. (Bishop and Mallie note how the Falls curfew is sometimes referred to 'rather melodramatically, as the Rape of the Falls'.)[33] Within the poem Fiacc largely recycles received images derived from the past four centuries, of British military might attempting to grind down an enduringly resistant native culture.

It was our icons not our guns
You spat on. When you found our guns
You got down on your knees to them

As if our guns were the holy thing...
And even should you shoot the swarthy
-faced Mother with her ugly Jewish Child

Who bleeds with the people, she'll win
Because she loses all with the people,
Has lost every war for centuries with us.

Presented metonymically through references to 'rifle butts', 'bullets' and 'hob-nailed boots', the soldiery assert their dominance over the subject people by defiling their icons rather than by means of direct physical violence, though the latter is not ruled out. Action and allusion simultaneously link them with the iconoclasts of the Reformation, and with the Nazis - hence the stress on the Child as 'Jewish' - while the reference to the 'Machine' marks them as representative of a culture, which, though advanced in economic terms and in terms of military technology, remains crude, brutal and primitive in practice.[34] In describing how 'You got down on your knees to them/ As if our guns were the holy thing', Fiacc translates the soldiers' actions into a rite of obscene obeisance, and pits against these latter-day heretics the adherents of the Old Religion. Possessors of 'a richer dark', worshippers of the 'ancient, hag-ridden, long/ -in-the-tooth Mother',[35] the oppressed place their trust in a dubious paradox, their faith in a Pearse-like cult of failure. By deploying such words as 'swarthy' and 'ugly' to describe the Catholic mother and child, the text mirrors colonial discourse, which typically fixes both the Other and their icons in these terms; Fanon, for example, talks of how the coloniser views the native as 'the deforming element, disfiguring all that has to do with beauty and morality'.[36]

In its presentation of the Northern Catholics as an impenetrable text to outside readers Fiacc's poem bears some affinities with Heaney's 'Broagh', with its 'gh the strangers found/ difficult to manage'.[37] However, Heaney's poem constructs an opposition between Britain and Northerners of both communities, and gestures towards reconciliation by drawing attention to shared words and sounds. Yet Fiacc's response to the Falls Curfew is perhaps more typical of its time, reflecting as it does that impulse within the Nationalist community to read the contemporary narrative merely as a continuation and repetition of earlier 'history', and indeed several of Heaney's later poems in *North* come to similar, often fatalistic conclusions.[38] Their perception that the British Army was again being deployed as the coercive instrument of an illegitimate government would later receive further confirmation with the introduction of internment in August 1971.

Increasing alienation amongst the nationalist community, along with a breakdown of secret contacts between the Army and the Provisional leaders, prompted the latter's decision in February 1971 to embark on an all-out offensive against the British Army.[39] One of the worst atrocities occurring early on in this, the third phase of the Troubles, took place on Tuesday, 9 March. On that night in Mooney's Bar, in the Belfast city centre, three Provisionals, one of who had formerly served in the British Army, fell into conversation with three young Scottish soldiers, John McCaig (aged 17), his brother Joseph (aged 18) and Douglas McCaughey (aged 23). After a few drinks in another pub, the

171

Provisionals suggested to the three Scots that they might like to go to a party in Ligoniel, but instead drove them to a quiet spot on a hillside where they shot them in the back of the head as they were relieving themselves by the roadside. Horror and disgust at these murders swept the province, and the Provisional leadership felt compelled to deny their involvement. Although these assassinations had not been sanctioned and were in technical breach of the Provisionals' own 'rules of engagement', which precluded attacks on off-duty soldiers, the three killers went unpunished by the organisation, and their actions 'put down to an excess of enthusiasm.'[40] The three young Highland Fusiliers would later be commemorated within Michael Longley's 'Wounds'.[41] Like John Hewitt in two poems from an earlier stage in the conflict - 'An Ulsterman in England Remembers' (August 1969) or in 'The Scar' (January 1971)[42] - Longley attempts to find a way to address the appalling, bewildering present by invoking images of suffering from earlier history: a history which is both private and shared. The narrating voices in 'An Ulsterman in England Remembers' and 'Wounds' both begin by representing their own unhurt state:

> Here at a distance, rocked by hopes and fears
> with each convulsion of that fevered state
>   ('An Ulsterman in England Remembers')
> Here are two pictures from my father's head ('Wounds')

There is a seeming separation in time, space, experience from 'the dead lad in the entry' in the Black-and-Tan War or 'the boy about to die' at the Somme. Quickly, however, the poems establish contiguities and continuities between images from the past, images in the present, as they engage in the retrieval of 'neglected shadows' and 'secrets'. For much of Hewitt's poem the focalisation rests with his younger self, as he revisits a world observable from the relative security of 'my bedroom window'. Deserted streets, burning houses, crouching soldiers, figures furtively or nervously sheltering in doorways, 'the beat of rapid feet/ of the lone sniper', 'the briskly striding, tall young man' with 'the rifle he thought well concealed', these are the sights and sounds that marked his boyhood, mar his old age. Whereas for the sixty-two year old Hewitt, present history can 'read' as the inevitable outcome of a previous narrative which he had himself witnessed and can now 'understand' - 'I had seen/ the future in that frightened gunman's eyes' - for Longley, a poet half his age, the text is more complex, unsettled and unsettling. The closing lines of 'Wounds', like the first line, foreground the fact that the only authority the speaker holds is by proxy, the only knowledge he has of war and guns is by report. What specifically provides Longley with a means of poetic access to the present nightmare is his father's experiences in the Great War, which he bequeathed to his son shortly before his death in 1960. At seventeen - the same age as the youngest Ligoniel

172

victim - Richard Longley had queued up to enlist along with thousands of others outside Buckingham Palace in 1914, and, although not of Scottish extraction, had 'joined the London Scots by mistake and went into battle wearing an unwarranted kilt'.[43] Despite the huge differences in scale and degree between the organised, general slaughter of the Somme seen by his father and individual moments of butchery in contemporary Belfast received 'second hand', Longley successfully re-imagines these separate acts of killing and their locations, particularly by presenting recurring instances of young lives actually and metaphorically cut short.[44] A common obscenity - the obscenity that innocence has been violated, that the 'night light' has been extinguished 'for ever' - links the surreal 1916 'landscape of dead buttocks' to 1971 and 'Three teenage soldiers ... their flies undone', their bellies incongruously 'full of/ Bullets and Irish beer', and the commonplace site of the busconductor's murder, realised as it is through the precision of its domestic detail, its references to the carpet-slippers, supper dishes, and the television. The 'shivering boy' responsible could be a demoralised descendant of the 'frightened gunman' exposed in the closure of Hewitt's poem; neither is condemned. Perhaps contained within the bathos of the ending of 'Wounds', and the gross inappropriacy/ inadequacy of its apology,

> To the children, to a bewildered wife,
> I think 'Sorry Missus' was what he said

is an intimation that ultimately in such circumstances poetry itself can never find the words, or express the survivor's guilt at having survived.

The Provisionals' 1971 offensive compelled poets from the nationalist community to re-examine many of the ideological certainties they had inherited, and the confirmation they had received in the course of previous three years.[45] This is reflected in Padraic Fiacc's 'Kids at War', whose first section contains his response to a particularly reckless IRA attack on 25 May, when a suitcase filled with gelignite was hurled into the Springfield Road barracks. This injured twenty-two people and resulted in the death of a young British sergeant who saved several children's lives by throwing his body over the bomb. Fiacc's poem marks a significant shift away from the attitudes towards the Army displayed in 'Credo Credo', which had been composed perhaps only ten months previously. Though a far slighter, and certainly a far sparer poem than Longley's 'Wounds', 'Kids at War' confronts the reader with the immediate present, and with examples of appalling brutality committed in the name of 'Ireland', as

> Irish kids sneer and jeer
> At, salute with cat
> -calls the dead body

Of the young British soldier

Gave up his life to save
The Irish woman and kids
Caught in the Spring
-field Road barracks[46]

The poem's second part commemorates a second fatal act of kindness by a British soldier, shot while on lollipop duty as he went to buy ice-lollies for a group of Irish kids; amongst their number was his future killer. Like the best of Northern Irish writing, such work demonstrates a compassion which transcends competing ideologies, serves as a reminder that the taking of individual lives in the name of some exclusivist abstraction called 'Ireland' or 'Ulster' or in the interests of 'security' can never be morally justified.

What this chapter has attempted to illustrate is the importance of contextualisation in evaluating recent Northern Irish poetry. By focusing on three phases of the conflict, I have sought to make a general point about the complexity of the situation in which poets found themselves in the early years of the present Troubles, and the difficulties they faced finding adequate words and forms for a narrative resistant to language and order. As George Boyce has succinctly put it, 'the best way to read' Northern poetry, is

> as texts in contexts. That context is their duality; it is their affirmation of
> their own peculiar political and cultural identity, without which the Ulster
> person does not exist; and yet it is also their desire to do some good, to
> deny the consequences of that affirmation.[47]

Unfortunately many readers from our own and later generations, in and outside Ireland, already encounter this work detached from the contexts which pressed it into being, with a limited awareness of that larger cultural and political narrative in which the poems perform a small, but significant part. For such readers problems may be compounded if the literary or historical texts they turn to as sources of 'authority' make little or no allusion to specific political events, or have been either consciously or unconsciously 'tailored to match the prevailing political climate', which at times seems to foreground Northern Republican intransigence over other varieties.[48]

An example of this tendency can be seen in a recent radio programme, Fintan O'Toole's *The Bloody Protest*. From this one would have deduced that the last twenty-five years of conflict in Ulster was principally attributable to recidivist tendencies amongst the Northern minority, still clinging to the icons and 'irrelevant legacy'[49] of 1916. Necessarily for O'Toole's argument the years between 1966 and 1970 become a lacuna, since his aim is to forge a direct link between the Dublin and Belfast Easter Rising commemorations and the emergence of the Provisional IRA, as well as to establish a distance between Republican rhetoric of 1916/1966 and the 'maturer' Republic of today; one waits in vain for any reference to the role Stormont might have played in Northern Ireland's slip 'into chaos',[50] or mention of the interventions of the British and Irish Governments. Although I am less sure than Seamus Deane about the existence of a revisionist 'orthodoxy'[51] as such - this smacks too much of conspiracy theory, and one suspects that if it did exist its practitioners would immediately set about revising it - he is perhaps right to sound a note of caution over historical or literary analyses which may lean too heavily towards 'present-mindedness',[52] which attempt to mask their ideological positioning, and which pass judgment without taking due account of the circumstances and contexts of the time. Of course, one should be sceptical in the face of any orthodoxies, especially those which endeavour to re-write atrocities from the past as merely 'regrettable', or really the responsibility of someone else and their intransigence; such politics means never having to say you're sorry. My own view is that the detail and complexity of the painful narrative needs to be recognised, the vileness of what happened acknowledged, if understanding is ever to make it onto the agenda.

NOTES

1. Padraic Fiacc, eds. Gerald Dawe and Aodan Mac Poilin, *Ruined Pages: Selected poems*, Belfast, 1994, pp. 141-2.

2. Amongst the honourable exceptions is Marilynn Richtarik's *Acting Between the Lines: The Field Day Company and Irish Cultural Politics 1980-1984*, London, 1994, which provides an excellent detailed account of recent political history.

3. Henry Hart, *Seamus Heaney: Poet of Contrary Progressions*, Syracuse, 1993, pp. 3, 15. Andrew Murphy's *Seamus Heaney*, Plymouth, 1996, a remarkably succinct study of both the poetry and the critical debate, contains similar historical inaccuracies and gaps in the text: 'With the failure of the Civil Rights Movement, militant nationalism (and militant unionism) revived'(p. 29).

4. Hart, *Seamus Heaney*, p. 93.

5. Edward Said, *Culture and Imperialism*, London, 1993, p. 266.

6. The principal historical texts referred to in the notes included Jonathan Bardon, *A History of Ulster*, Belfast, 1993; J. Bowyer Bell, *The Irish Troubles*, Dublin, 1993; Patrick Buckland, *A History of Northern Ireland*, Dublin, 1981. Other sources include, Patrick Bishop and Eamonn Mallie,

175

The Provisional I.R.A., Aylesbury 1988; Peter Taylor, *Families at War*, London, 1989; *Ulster*, The *Sunday Times* Insight Team, London, 1972.

7.   Donald H. Akenson makes the claim that *States of Ireland* is 'the most influential book about Irish Nationalism and Irish politics written in the second half of the twentieth century'.   He is quoted in D. George Boyce's essay, 'Revisionism and the Irish Troubles', in eds. D. George Boyce and Alan O'Day, *The Making of Modern Irish History: Revisionism and the Revisionist Controversy*, London, 1996, p. 218.

8.   Cruise O'Brien, *States of Ireland*, p. 259.

9.   Ibid, p. 173.

10. Derek Mahon, *The Snow Party*, Oxford, 1975, p. 9-10.

11. These appear in *The Wearing of the Black*, ed. Padraic Fiacc, Belfast, 1974, pp. 36, 91-2, but were not reprinted for his first full collection, *The New Estate*, Belfast, 1976.

12. Roy McFadden, 'I won't dance', *New Statesman*, 1 July 1966, p. 24. The full text of the poem appeared later in *The Wearing of the Black*, p. 84.

13. James Callaghan, quoted in Desmond Hamill, *Pig in The Middle: The Army in Northern Ireland 1969-1984*, London, 1985, p. 7.

14. Bishop and Mallie, *The Provisional I.R.A.*, p. 105.

15. Paddy Devlin, *Straight Left*, Belfast, 1993, pp. 105-6.   Bishop and Mallie's account of events in West Belfast that night refers to a key incident in Leeson Street, where a World War II grenade was hurled at a police car, which then became the object of rifle-fire. 'The episode was to have important consequences', they assert, 'for it reinforced febrile R.U.C. intelligence reports that the I.R.A. were planning an uprising in Belfast, and led to a fatal police decision to mount high-velocity heavy calibre Browning machine-guns on their Shorland armoured cars to counter the threat. (p. 105)'

16. Fiacc, *Ruined Pages*, pp. 112-3. Bishop and Mallie give an account of this shooting, *The Provisional IRA*, pp. 110-1.

17. These stories can be found in Mary Beckett, *A Belfast Woman*, Swords, 1980, and Anne Devlin, *The Way Paver*, London, 1986. In 'Naming the Names', the burning-out of the home in Conway Street which she shares with her grandmother provides one of the important 'motives' for Finnuala's decision to help the Provisional I.R.A.

18. Michael Longley, 'Letter: To Derek Mahon', reprinted in *Poems 1963-1983*, Edinburgh, 1985, p. 82. Mahon later challenged the attribution of such attitudes to him in a letter to the *New Statesman*, 10 December 1971, the journal which had first published Longley's poem.

19. 'Letter: To Seamus Heaney', *Poems 1963-1983*, p. 84.

20. Ibid., p. 82.

21. Derek Mahon, *Lives*, London, 1972, p. 1. Philip Larkin's 'MCMXIV' from *The Whitsun Weddings*, London, 1964, p. 28, similarly consigns future generations of the English to irretrievable loss, with its parting refrain 'Never such innocence again'.

22. I am grateful to Dr Richard Greaves in drawing my attention to the etymology of 'innocent'. Mahon studied Classics at Trinity College, Dublin in the early 1940s.

23. Mahon, *Lives*, p. 18. Are these qualities of 'self-pity' and 'self-hate' applicable to members of both communities, or intended to distinguish one side from the other?

24. *The Collected Poems of John Hewitt*, ed. Frank Ormsby, Belfast, 1991, pp. 129-31.

25. In similar vein, Seamus Heaney in his article 'Delirium of the Brave', *The Listener*, 27 November 1969, p. 757, talks of how in 1798 - as in 1969 - 'each element of nightmare ... succeeded the dream of hope'.

26. Foreword to, 'An Ulster Reckoning', from *The Collected Poems of John Hewitt*, p. 593.

27. Some of these troops, men from the Black Watch and the Life Guards, had only just disembarked in Belfast. The number of rounds they fired that night may perhaps be indicative of their fear and panic, as the *Sunday Times* Insight Team, p. 218, suggest.

28. Bowyer Bell, *The Irish Troubles*, p. 178; the *Sunday Times* Insight Team, p. 219; Bishop and Mallie, *The Provisional I.R.A.*, p. 160.

29. Devlin, *Straight Left*, p. 129.

30. Tim Pat Coogan, *Ireland's Ordeal 1966-1995 and the Search for Peace*, London, 1995, p. 109. Bishop and Mallie, *The Provisional I.R.A.*, p. 160, Taylor, *Families at War*, pp. 35-6, and Bowyer Bell, *The Irish Troubles*, all draw attention to the verbal abuse heaped on the Catholic population by the troops.

31. The *Sunday Times* Insight Team, p. 220.

32. Cruise O'Brien, *States of Ireland*, p. 245-6.

33. Bishop and Mallie, *The Provisional I.R.A.*, p. 161. In his entry for 6 July in 'A Summer Diary', Chapter 10 of *States of Ireland*, O'Brien casts doubt on some accounts of the 'atrocious behaviour of troops', but acknowledges the widespread 'Shock and hysteria' (p. 231) which cannot be simply attributed to the success of the republican propaganda machine.

34. Brian Friel's representations of the British Army in *The Freedom of the City* and the characterisation of Captain Lancy in *Translations* similarly

conform to traditional nationalist models. Later poems by Fiacc, however, such as 'Enemy Encounter', 'Kids at War', 'Tears' (*Ruined Pages*, pp. 120, 121, 125) look differently on the ordinary British soldiers and their presence in the North, and reflect some sympathy for their position.

35. Clearly Fiacc is constructing a composite figure, uniting aspects of the Cailleac and the Virgin Mary, fusing Nationalism and Catholicism. For an informative feminist analysis of how male writers from the nationalist tradition have frequently deployed mythic representations of the 'feminine' in their work, see Elizabeth Cullingfords', '"Thinking of Her .. as .. Ireland": Yeats, Pearse and Heaney"', *Textual Practice* 4:1 (Spring 1990).

36. Frantz Fanon, *The Wretched of the Earth*, Harmondsworth, 1967, p. 32.

37. Seamus Heaney, *Wintering Out*, London, 1972, p. 27.

38. One thinks for example of 'Ocean's Love to Ireland', 'Act of Union', 'Hercules and Antaeus', and 'The Unacknowledged Legislator's Dream'.

39. Whereas the *Sunday Times* Insight Team, p. 244, suggest that Major Farrar-Hockley's decision to name five Provisional leaders at a press conference prompted the change of strategy, Bishop and Mallie, *The Provisional I.R.A.*, p. 175, emphasise that approval for the offensive had been given by the Dublin PIR Army Council a month earlier.

40. Bishop and Mallie, *The Provisional I.R.A.*, p. 178.

41. Longley, *Poems 1963-1983*, p. 86.

42. *The Collected Poems of John Hewitt*, pp. 133, 177.

43. Michael Longley, *Tuppenny Stung: Autobiographical Chapters*, Belfast, 1994, p. 18. In his latest collection, *The Ghost Orchid*, London, 1995, Longley returns several times to his father's memories of war, notably in 'The Kilt', 'Behind a Cloud' and 'The Camp Fires'.

44. It is perhaps pertinent to note that Longley's father died when the poet was barely twenty, and 'too young to appreciate his strengths and weaknesses', ibid, p. 28.

45. Seamus Heaney comments retrospectively at one point in his Nobel Prize address, *Crediting Poetry*, Oldcastle, 1995, that during the period 1968 to 1974: 'While the Christian moralist in oneself was impelled to deplore the atrocious nature of the IRA's campaign of bombing, the 'mere Irish' in oneself was appalled by the ruthlessness of the British Army on occasions like Bloody Sunday in Derry in 1972, the minority citizen in oneself, the one who had grown up conscious that his group was distrusted and discriminated against in all kinds of official and unofficial ways, this citizen's perception was at one with the poetic truth of the

situation in recognising that if life in Northern Ireland were ever really to flourish, change had to take place' (pp. 16-7).

46. Fiacc, *Ruined Pages*, p. 121.

47. D. George Boyce, in a review of Richard Kirkland's 'Literature and Culture in Northern Ireland since 1965', in *Irish Studies Review*, 2:17 (Winter 1996/7), p. 56.

48. Seamus Deane, 'Wherever Green is Read', in Ciaron Brody, ed., *Interpreting Irish History: The Debate on Historical Revisionism*, Dublin, 1994, p. 234.

49. Fintan O'Toole, *The Bloody Protest*, BBC Radio 4, 10 April 1996.

50. Ibid.

51. Seamus Deane, 'Wherever Green is Read', p. 234. 'The revisionists are now themselves more vulnerable to revision because their pseudo-scientific orthodoxy is so obviously tailored to match the prevailing political climate - especially in relation to the Northern crisis - that its claims to "objectivity", to being "value-free", have been abandoned as disguises no longer needed.'

52. For a discussion of this concept, see D. George Boyce in 'Revisionism and the Troubles', in D. George Boyce and Alan O'Day, eds., *The Making of Modern Irish History*, pp. 216-7.

Encountering Ourselves: *The Field Day Anthology of Irish Writing* as communicative space/act or, Into the Inter: The heterographia of *The Field Day Anthology*

Tom Herron

The doubled nature of my titles signifies a certain undecidability concerning the ambition and operation of *The Field Day Anthology of Irish Writing*.[1] What will become clear as the essay progresses is that while I privilege a particular way of reading the *Anthology* (announced by the second of my titles) I also want to retain the traces of an earlier way of approaching this text (announced by the first). I want to retain the unexpected, even conflictual resonances of 'encounter' and also the plurality implicit within the term 'ourselves', whilst at the same time moving towards a much more provisional and contingent approach to the anthology. In specific terms I am interested in the problematic relationship between Field Day's adoption of the 'fifth province' and the *Anthology* itself, which can be read as a materialization (albeit complex and troubled) of the imaginary realm of communicative possibilities articulated by the metaphor of the 'fifth province'. In charting the development of Field Day's relationship to the fifth province I will show how the company and its productions gradually move from a concept of communication that could be characterised as Habermasian to one that is markedly Bhabhaian. The central argument of the essay is that the *Anthology* should not be read *exclusively* as an articulation of the fifth province, but should (more productively I would argue) be seen in the less stable, less comforting light of Homi Bhabha's notion of the 'third space', in which the self-sufficiency of cultural objects is viewed with scepticism, seen as in fact an impossibility. Indeed, such a shift in emphasis encourages a reformulation of the fifth province itself: no longer should the notion be understood entirely as centre or as centripetal, but it should also be read in terms of its liminality, its inbetweenness, its centrifugal orientation.

There is little doubt that the metaphor of the fifth province has operated both strategically and teleologically within Field Day. Strategically it has informed the company's attempts to include dissensus within its productions, and teleologically it provides an imagined, desired space/time of communicative possibility that would be both on the way toward, and exemplary of, the final achievement of cultural unity. The term 'fifth province' was coined by Richard

Kearney and Mark Patrick Hederman in 1977 to describe the strategy of the Dublin-produced journal *The Crane Bag*. Referring to the mythical ancient centre of Ireland, the lost point of connection and overlap of the existing four provinces, the fifth province was, for Kearney and Hederman, a place of sanctuary, an imagined space of encounter and of dialogue. Writing in the first edition of *The Crane Bag* Kearney and Hederman foresaw the journal's function as one of 'promot[ing] the excavation of unactualised spaces within the reader, which is the work of constituting the fifth province. From such a place a new understanding and unity might emerge.'[2] In subsequent editions of *The Crane Bag* (which in its short history proved itself a remarkably mobile forum for debate not only on Irish culture, nationalism, ideologies, and so on, but also on international perspectives of relevance to the situations pertaining within Ireland),[3] Kearney expounded in more detail on the need for, and operation of, this fifth province. It was no doubt through his contact with Seamus Deane at University College Dublin that the virus spread, and from 1982 the term was adopted and adapted by various members of Field Day to articulate the company's stated desire to accommodate diverse voices, to confront Ireland's deadlocked cultural/political situation, and to carve out for itself a space hitherto disallowed by the political and cultural geographies of Ireland, North and South. In an interview with Fintan O'Toole in 1982 Brian Friel described Field Day's function as 'a kind of an attempt to create a fifth province to which artistic and cultural loyalty can be offered'.[4] In a 1984 interview with Patrick Quilligan, Friel describes how Field Day 'appropriated (from Richard Kearney) the phrase "Fifth Province", which may well be a province of the mind, through which we hope to devise another way of looking at Ireland, or another possible Ireland, and this really is the pursuit of the company'.[5] In *Ireland and the English Crisis* (1984) Tom Paulin explains that his critical position 'is founded on an idea of identity which has as yet no formal or institutional existence. It assumes the existence of a non-sectarian, republican state which comprises the whole island of Ireland. It also holds to the idea of sanctuary and to the concept of "the fifth province". This other, invisible province offers a platonic challenge to the nationalist image of the four green fields.'[6] In the 1988 *Arena* documentary 'History Boys on the Rampage' Friel expands on Field Day's adoption of the term:

> There are now only four provinces - Ulster, Munster, Leinster and Connacht - but there were five once, and that missing allotment was employed as an image for other possibilities, a location for a second centre for this troubled island. We were the people who commissioned and wrote the plays and the pamphlets and the translations that looked at Ireland from the new perspec-

tive, this fifth province, this transcendent location. And from that vantage point there are vistas that are thrilling; more than thrilling - possible.[7]

While every member (bar one) of the Field Day board acknowledged their debt to the idea of the fifth province it was, perhaps unsurprisingly, Seamus Deane who in tandem with Kearney offered the most programmatic glosses on the term. In a 1984 article entitled 'Why Ireland needs a fifth province' in *The Sunday Independent*, Deane, in conversation with Richard Kearney and Ciaran Carty, placed the fifth province in direct opposition to what he saw as a pathological colonial and neo-colonial condition: 'The aim for us [Field Day] was to ... create an equivalent centre from which the four broken and fragmented pieces of contemporary Ireland might be seen as in fact coherent.'[8] This sense of coherence is important to Deane because 'the fate we share at the moment is the fate of victimage. We feel we are victims of circumstances that have almost destroyed us but certainly fragment us and bear on us to such a degree that we can't have the lives that we feel potentially as ours.'[9]

While there are obvious differences in the various directors' imaginings of the fifth province, several characteristics or emphases are repeated. I want to concentrate here on only a few. First, there was a stress on the need for new *modes* of communication. Field Day directors restated Richard Kearney's call for communication which could 'acknowledge, and perhaps ultimately mediate between the sundered cultural identities of the island. A common sense of purpose, or at least the identification of a common problem, which is the *sine qua non* of any genuine community.'[10] The fifth province was imagined both instrumentally as a forum, or in Habermasian terms as an 'ideal speech situation' sanctioning hitherto disallowed or unactualised discourse, and also as a glimpse of future discursive possibilities. The desire to create, or at least participate in, a public forum of debate (akin to other forums such as The New Ireland Forum) can also be located within Field Day's own founding conception of itself, as an organisation committed to addressing, and indeed to creating, new audiences. Second, there was a will towards a syncretic view of Irish cultural production, leading to a sense of unified culture. Notions of wholeness, of unity, of inclusiveness embracing the whole island are common in characterisations of the fifth province.[11] The desire to create a communicative forum, allied to national inclusiveness produced a third shared characteristic: the will towards consensus within an all-Ireland context. Very little attention was paid, as Edna Longley pointed out on several occasions, to the arrangements and relationships already existing within the archipelago of the British Isles. Fourth, there was a lack of ease (to say the very least) expressed by various directors with the existing political structures in Ireland; a lack of ease which extended from questions of political and cultural discourse, to state ideologies and formations. This in its turn produced a marked sense of non-affiliation to any of the available state options (be it the Republic, the United Kingdom, or Northern Ireland). In terms of the conflicting ideologies at work within the island, while Field Day could not be aligned unproblematically to the nationalist narrative, at the same time it is true to say that it was this particular narrative, this particular ideology which figured most prominently within Field Day's considerations of the national situation; there was comparatively little interest in unionism or in Ulster nationalism. Fifth, the undoubted sense of exile (which Edna Longley characterises, referring to Friel's drama and Deane's critical writings, as 'a powerful sense of Palestinian dispossession')[12] from the existing orthodoxies and political / state formations mirrored a geo-political perspective of the entire island centred on Derry, and influenced by the city's liminal position and status. Sixth, there was a view of the fifth province as 'a theoretical location', an imagined, platonic ideal, a place of critical distance, somewhere beyond or above the existing political provinces: a desired space/time which in Paulin's words 'has as yet no formal or institutional existence',[13] but yet one sutured etymologically and mythologically onto the existing political divisions of the island. While cultural *diversity* within an all-Ireland context was emphasised, there was a comparative lack of account of *difference*. There was a certain assumption that diversity could be recuperated into some form of cultural unity. We will see such a desire re-emerge in the *Anthology*, but with a rather greater subtlety. There were also other assumptions and silences at work; most obviously concerning questions of gender difference, of sexuality, of minority discourses, of second- and third- generation Irish living outside Ireland. And most blatantly perhaps, there was precious little sustained interest in the validity or otherwise of the existing constitutional/territorial arrangements on the island. This lack of interest, compounded by Field Day's rejection of plays that interrogated notions of protestant/loyalist identity and history, was a hugely vulnerable area for the company.

Now, I do not think it is stretching the point too far to argue that the claims and aspirations held out for the fifth province within both *The Crane Bag* and Field Day (especially in the rather heady and crisis-laden rhetorics of Seamus Deane and Richard Kearney) have their analogues in the extraordinary optimism and ambition which led to the compilation of *The Field Day Anthology of Irish Writing*. This ambition lay not simply in the desire to repossess on a massive scale Irish writing in order to present it in a renovated landscape; to present Irish writing within its own context, a context other than the hegemonic English literary tradition. The major ambition, it seems to me, was the desire to lay the basis for a new discourse; for a translation, or a reshaping of existing culture and writing into an idiom that would articulate Field Day's version of Irish

183

history as one in which Walter Benjamin's vision of history as 'one single catastrophe which keeps piling wreckage upon wreckage'[14] would predominate over a postmodern, historical revisionist view of the island story as so irrevocably plural and complex as to be inassimilable to (post)colonial or nationalist interpretations. To achieve this the *Anthology* would have to be inserted provocatively within the interstices of existing political and cultural boundaries; it would have to be received as scandal, as an affront, and at the same time as an ordaining, consensual moment. So, the question I'm concerned with here and now is essentially this: how does Field Day's version of the fifth province operate in relation to the monumental, disseminatory, flawed, scandalous, still in process *Anthology*?

It is as well to remind ourselves of three or four founding statements by Deane on which the *Anthology* was based. In his 1984 pamphlet, 'Heroic Styles' (where the idea of an anthology was first raised) Deane proposed an anthology 'that could take the form of a definition ... of what writing in this country has been for the last 300-500 years'.[15] Principally, such a text would help to confront the fallaciousness of colonial stereotyping imposed upon Ireland and the Irish. A year later, in the preface to a collection of Field Day pamphlets, Deane imagined the anthology as 'revealing and confirming the existence of a continuous tradition, contributed to by all groups, sects and parties, in which the possibility of a more generous and hospitable notion of Ireland's cultural achievements will emerge as the basis for a more ecumenical and eirenic approach to the deep and apparently implacable problems which confront the island today'.[16] In a 1987 press release Deane (who was now three years into the process of editing, commissioning, fund-raising and defending the *Anthology*) saw it as 'an important act of definition which will show how the various groups, sects and races which have intermingled in Ireland have produced a literature which is unique to them and an achievement which makes it manifest what they have in common'.[17] By 1990 things had become markedly more cautious: unity and integrity would still feature but would now operate more under 'the aegis of irony'.[18] The *Anthology*, states Deane,

> is an act of repossession, resuming into the space of three massive volumes a selection of Irish literary, political, economic, philosophical, and other writings and presenting it, with a degree of ironic self-consciousness, as an integral and unitary 'tradition' or amalgam of traditions. The point is not to establish a canon as such; it is to engage in the action of establishing a system that has an enabling, a mobilizing energy, the energy of assertion and difference, while remaining aware that all such systems - like anthologies of other national literatures - are fictions that have inscribed within them principles of hierarchy and of exclusion as well as inclusion[.] ... It is not

184

merely an exercise in regaining Swift, Berkeley, Goldsmith, Burke, Shaw, Yeats, Joyce, Beckett, and so forth from the neighbouring fiction of English or British literature or literary tradition. It is a recuperation of these writers into the so-called other context, the inside reading of them in relation to other Irish writing, in order to modify and perhaps even distress other 'outside' readings that have been unaware of that context and its force.[19]

So, it is clear that the anthology would have at the very least a doubled function: first of all, it would present itself as a construction of a continuous tradition constituted out of apparent difference, which would then lay itself out as the grounds for future conciliatory possibilities. This is a clear syncretic vision. But it is syncresis with an edge: what has been added are the realms of imagination, irony and provocation.

At this point it is necessary to move on from Deane's formulations, and address the operation and effects of the anthology itself. And in doing so, we have in fact to leave behind the idea of the anthology as a discrete cultural artefact, as a self-sufficient text. The movement here is towards viewing cultural production as part of a larger network of connections, differences, antagonisms, and contradictions, so that the *Anthology* is read both in terms of its own operation and creation of effects and as part of the broader networks of differences which surround it and which constitute it simultaneously. In other words, it is necessary to allow the difference produced within the text itself (discretely, in for example Luke Gibbons's superb sections on cultural nationalism, national literature and their oppositions, and on canon formation and resistances to canonical forms in Ireland, and also in the endless interplay of texts situated in new relationships to one another), and the fundamental *différance* implicit within language, within systems of signification and meaning. The metaphor which, for me, articulates most effectively this differential condition is that of the 'third space', and it is with a consideration of this idea and how it resonates with the operation of the *Anthology* that I will close.

In his essay 'The Commitment to Theory' Homi Bhabha begins his formulation of the third space with a critique of the notion of cultural diversity which he characterises as a closed object of empirical knowledge in which is recognised only pre-given cultural contents and customs. 'Held in a time frame of relativism' cultural diversity 'gives rise to liberal notions of multiculturalism, cultural exchange or the culture of humanity.' In place of this Bhabha argues for a concept of cultural difference based upon 'the common semiotic account of the disjuncture between the subject of the proposition and the subject of enunciation which is not represented in the statement but which is the acknowledgement of its discursive embeddedness and address, its cultural positionality, its reference to a present time and a specific place'. He gives an

185

example: 'the pact of interpretation is never simply an act of communication between the I and the You designated in the statement. The production of meaning requires that these two places be mobilised in the passage through a third space, which represents both the general conditions of language and the specific implication of the utterance in a performative and institutional strategy.' One implication of this is that 'a cultural text or system of meaning cannot be sufficient unto itself [in] that the act of cultural enunciation - the *place of utterance* - is crossed by the *différance* of writing'. The third space of enunciation reveals meaning and reference as utterly ambivalent processes and ensures that the meanings and symbols of culture have no primordial unity or fixity: 'that even the same signs can be appropriated, translated, rehistoricised and read anew'. Bhabha cites Wilson Harris's notion of 'the alien territory' of cultural encounter in which contraries are situated 'in a discontinuous, intertextual temporality of cultural difference'. It is the closing section of Bhabha's essay that I wish to situate in the context of a reformulated under-standing of both fifth province and the anthology's differential status, operation and creation of effects:

> a willingness to descend into that alien territory ... may reveal that the theoretical recognition of the split-space of enunciation may open the way to conceptualizing an *inter*national culture based not on the exoticism of multiculturalism or the *diversity* of culture, but on the inscription and articulation of culture's hybridity. To that end we should remember that it is the 'inter' - the cutting edge of translation and negotiation, the *inbetween* space - that carries the burden of the meaning of culture. It makes it possible to begin envisaging national, anti-nationalist histories of the people. And by exploring this Third Space, we may elude the politics of polarity and emerge as the others of ourselves.

I quote Bhabha at such length because I want to stress the connections between his theorisation of the third space and an expanded sense of the *Anthology*'s split-site of enunciation and of its irremediably plural production of meanings and effects, which include its own conception of itself as, if not exactly an anti-nationalist, then at the very least an *ambivalently* national 'meta-narrative'. If we accept that such an ambivalence ironises every statement of tradition or narrative asserted within the anthology, then, it seems to me, that we can read it less as an authoritative attempt at cultural definition and more in its uncertain difference, and less as a melding of diverse voices and writings into consensus and more as a staging of consensuses and dissensuses. We can read it as a type of writing that is, to adapt Bakhtin's notion of heteroglossia, heterographic; operating both cetripetally and centrifugally, and referring both to an imagined centre, a legitimating origin or narrative, and at the same time to other

186

narratives, other myths of origin and continuity. Reading the anthology in this way maintains Field Day's efforts to foster a communicative praxis based on the more Habermasian features of the fifth province (*that is* universal pragmatics, ideal speech/discursive situation, and the fostering of the public sphere), but now it is more productive to complement the communicative instrumentality implicit within the notion of the fifth province with the differential, interstitial, movements of the third space. In this way the question of cultural authority (a key notion in the disputes surrounding the *Anthology*) is acknowledged and ironised. This question is, for Bhabha, intimately related to the articulation of cultural difference through the third space of enunciation. Any attempt to dominate in the name of a cultural supremacy or in the name of a referential truth will be prone to the splitting of enunciation in which any assertion of cultural authority is problematised. 'The iteration' according to Bhabha 'undermines our sense of the homogenizing effects of cultural symbols and icons, by questioning our sense of the authority of cultural synthesis in general'.[21] Even if the *Anthology* (or more correctly its general editor) was not so obviously aware of its own problematic *and* opportunistic relationship to cultural authority, to questions of performance, enunciation, and to time (the crucial deforming, deferring element within enunciation) we would still have no difficulty in reading the text through the third space as one clearly split between assertion and provisionality; between tradition and modernity; between its own 'discursive embeddedness and address' and the inescapably differential effects of time. In the 'General Introduction' Deane states that 'this anthology, like the works it presents to the reader, is at the mercy of the present moment and, also like them, derives its authority (such as it is) from that moment.'[21] Beginning to read the *Anthology* in such a way may prove to be more productive than blanket condemnations or laudations of a text which is constituted by difference, and in which even the most authoritative attempts at definition are inevitably prone to the instability of reference and meaning (in which enunciation is nonetheless never erased) generated by the third space.

NOTES

1. Seamus Deane, Andrew Carpenter and Jonathan Williams, eds., *The Field Day Anthology of Irish Writing*, Derry, 1991.
2. Richard Kearney and Mark Patrick Hederman, 'Editorial I / Endodermis', *The Crane Bag*, 1:1 (Spring 1977), p. 4.
3. Mobile in many senses, restrictive in others: women's cultural and critical production, for example, did not feature greatly in *The Crane Bag*.

4. Fintan O'Toole, 'The Man From God Knows Where: an interview with Brian Friel', *In Dublin* (28 October 1982), p. 21.
5. See Patrick Quilligan, 'Field Day's New Double Bill', *The Irish Times*, 18 September 1984, p. 10.
6. Tom Paulin, *Ireland and the English Crisis*, Newcastle Upon Tyne, 1984, p. 17.
7. 'History Boys on the Rampage', BBC2 *Arena* documentary on Field Day (December 1988).
8. Seamus Deane and Richard Kearney, 'Why Ireland needs a fifth province', *The Sunday Independent*, 22 January 1984, p. 15.
9. Ibid.
10. Richard Kearney, 'Dramatic Narratives: the Language Plays of Brian Friel', in R Kearney, ed., *Transitions: Narratives in Modern Irish Culture*, Manchester, 1988, p. 125.
11. For corroboration of this point see Shaun Richards's 'Field Day's fifth province: avenue or impasse?', in Eamonn Hughes, ed., *Culture and Politics in Northern Ireland*, Milton Keynes, 1991, p. 140.
12. Edna Longley, 'From Cathleen to Anorexia: The Breakdown of Irelands' (1990), reprinted in *The Living Stream: Literature and Revisionism in Ireland*, Newcastle Upon Tyne, 1994, p. 183.
13. Paulin, *Ireland and the English Crisis*, p. 17.
14. Walter Benjamin, 'Theses on the Philosophy of History', reprinted in Richard Kearney and Mara Rainwater, eds., *The Continental Philosophy Reader*, London, 1996, pp. 215-223. I am indebted to Richard Kirkland's superb discussion of Field Day, Gramsci, Benjamin, counter-hegemony, emergency and numerous other important questions in his chapter, '"Nothing Left but a Sense of Exhaustion": Field Day and Counter-hegemony' in his *Literature and Culture in Northern Ireland since 1965: Moments of Danger*, London, 1996, pp. 123-50.
15. Seamus Deane, 'Heroic Styles: the tradition of an idea', reprinted in *Ireland's Field Day*, London, 1985, p. 58.
16. Deane, *Ireland's Field Day*, p. viii.
17. Seamus Deane, 'Field Day Anthology of Irish Writing', press release, Derry, 1987.
18. This is Deane's description of Terry Eagleton's discussion of nationalism in his Field Day pamphlet, 'Nationalism: irony and commitment' (1988), reprinted in *Nationalism, Colonialism, and Literature*, Minneapolis, 1990, p. 4.
19. Deane, 'Introduction' to *Nationalism, Colonialism, and Literature*, p. 15.

20. All quotations from Homi K. Bhabha, 'The Commitment to Theory', in *The Location of Culture*, London, 1994, pp. 34-9.
21. Deane, *The Field Day Anthology of Irish Writing*, pp. xxi.

Notes on Contributors

Sarah Briggs is a freelance writer whose research interests centre around women's writing, involving domestic fiction, issues of national identity and sexual politics. The focus of her current research is the short fiction of Mary Lavin, upon which she has published several articles.

Julie Campbell is a lecturer in Literature and Drama at the University of Southampton whose main area of research is a comparative study of the narrative play in the prose fiction of Samuel Beckett and Vladimir Nabokov.

Sarah Ferris recently completed a doctoral thesis on John Hewitt's myth and its place in contemporary literary debate on Northern Irish Writing. She is currently researching for a study of Roy McFadden and working on Thomas Carnduff's papers and correspondence.

Colin Graham teaches at the University of Huddersfield. He is the author of a number of works on post-colonial theory and Irish culture including *Ideologies of Epic: Nation, Empire and Victorian Epic Poetry* (Manchester University Press, 1998).

Richard Greaves teaches at Liverpool Hope University College. He is currently working on a major study of W.B. Yeats.

Tessa Hadley is a lecturer in English at Bath Spa University College, where she has just completed a PhD on Henry James.

Tom Herron is a lecturer in the School of English at the University of Aberdeen. He is currently working on a book on *The Field Day Anthology of Irish Writing* and a critical study of the thought and influence of the Irish poet, novelist and academic, Seamus Deane.

190

Siobhán Holland is a lecturer in Literature at Staffordshire University. She has published a variety of articles on the role of voices attributed to women in contemporary Irish fiction and is also examining the uses of the fantastic by contemporary Irish authors.

William Hughes is a lecturer in the School of English at Bath Spa University College. He is working on the cultural background to the works of several nineteenth-century writers including Bram Stoker and Le Fenu with a particular interest in Victorian medical discourses. He has published a number of articles on Stoker and is currently writing *Beyond Dracula: Bram Stoker: Fiction and its Cultural Context* (Macmillan, forthcoming).

Willy Maley is Reader in English Literature at the University of Glasgow. He has published widely on Renaissance literature, and on aspects of early modern and modern Scottish and Irish culture. He is editor, with Andrew Hadfield and Brendan Bradshaw, of *Representing Ireland: Literature and the Origins of Conflict, 1534-1660* (Cambridge University Press, 1993). His current research interests include early modern and modern national identities, postcolonialism, and contemporary Irish and Scottish fiction.

Alan Marshall is a lecturer in the School of Historical and Cultural Studies at Bath Spa University College. He is the author of *Intelligence and Espionage in the Reign of Charles II* (Cambridge University Press, 1994), *Court Politics, 1660-1702* (Manchester University Press, 1999) and *The Strange Death of Edmund Godfrey* (Sutton, 1999).

Michael Parker is a senior lecturer in English at Liverpool Hope University College. He is the author of *Seamus Heaney: The Making of a Poet* (Macmillan, 1993) and is currently working on *The Writers and the Troubles: Northern Irish Literature* 1968-1998 (Macmillan, forthcoming).

Stephen Regan is a lecturer in English at the Open University. He is the editor of *The Eagleton Reader* (Blackwell, 1998) and *Philip Larkin* in the New Casebook series (Macmillan, 1997).

Neil Sammells is Dean of the Faculty of Humanities at Bath Spa University College. He has published a book on Tom Stoppard and has co-edited two collections on Irish Writing and Censorship in Britain. He is co-editor of *Irish Studies Review* and General Editor of the interdisciplinary writing series

Crosscurrents published by Longman. He is currently writing a monograph on Oscar Wilde, about whom he has published widely.

Barry Sloan is a lecturer in English at New College, Southampton, and has written various articles on Irish writing and is the author of *The Pioneer of Anglo-Irish Fiction* (1986) and *Heirs to Adamnations? Writers and Protestantism in the North of Ireland* (Irish Academic Press, forthcoming).

Gerry Smyth has written various works on Irish fictions including *The Novel and the Nation: Studies in the New Irish Fiction* (Pluto Press, 1997) and *Decolonisation and Criticism The Constructions of Irish Literature* (Pluto Press, 1998).

Gerwin Stobl is a lecturer in the School of History at the University of Wales, Cardiff. He is working on Shakespeare and Germany in the modern period.

Index